Dead Queens

The Cemeteries of New York City's Largest Borough

Richard Panchyk

—with Lizz Panchyk—

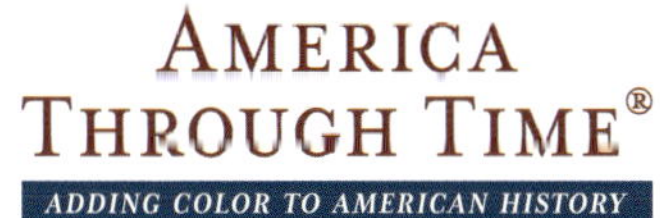

Acknowledgments

Thanks to Alan Sutton for his continued support in my local history adventures. Thanks to Kena Longabaugh for her editing and coordination. Thanks to Lizz for all her help with the book and her company on many cemetery visits. Also, thanks to Matt for accompanying me to a couple of Queens cemeteries as well.

America Through Time is an imprint of Fonthill Media LLC
www.through-time.com
office@through-time.com

Published by Arcadia Publishing by arrangement with Fonthill Media LLC
For all general information, please contact Arcadia Publishing:
Telephone: 843-853-2070
Fax: 843-853-0044
E-mail: sales@arcadiapublishing.com
For customer service and orders:
Toll-Free 1-888-313-2665

www.arcadiapublishing.com

First published 2021

ISBN 978-1-63499-330-2

Typeset in Trade Gothic
Printed and bound in England

Photo credits: All photos and images courtesy of Richard Panchyk except page 53 bottom, 55 bottom, 56 bottom courtesy of Lizz Panchyk, and pages 21-22, 24 top, 36, 106, 107 courtesy of the Library of Congress

CONTENTS

Acknowledgments 2
Preface 4
Introduction 6
1 All Faiths Cemetery 8
2 Calvary Cemetery 14
3 Cedar Grove Cemetery 21
4 Cypress Hills Cemetery 24
5 Flushing Cemetery 29
6 Fresh Pond Crematory and Columbarium 34
7 Friends Meeting House Cemetery 36
8 Grace Church Cemetery 39
9 Johnson Family Cemetery 43
10 Lawrence Cemetery 46
11 Maple Grove Cemetery 48
12 Montefiore Cemetery 53
13 Moore Burial Grounds—Elmhurst 58
14 Moore-Jackson Cemetery 61
15 Mount Carmel Cemetery 64
16 Mount Hebron Cemetery 67
17 Mount Olivet Cemetery 72
18 Mount St. Mary Cemetery 77
19 Mount Zion Cemetery 81
20 The Olde Towne Burial Ground of Flushing 86
21 Old Springfield Cemetery 89
22 Prospect Cemetery 92
23 Pullis Family Cemetery 96
24 Queens Vietnam Veterans Memorial 98
25 Reformed Church of Newtown Cemetery 100
26 Remsen Cemetery 104
27 Riker Family Cemetery 106
28 St. James Church Cemetery 108
29 St. John Cemetery 112
30 St. Michael's Cemetery 116
31 Zion Episcopal Churchyard 121
Appendix: Cemetery Businesses 125

Preface

As a bright-eyed toddler, I frolicked happily in the Moore Homestead Playground in Elmhurst, at Broadway and 54th Street in the heart of this vibrant and diverse community. I lived in a big pre-war apartment building just a couple of blocks away, and mom would put me in the stroller and take me to the playground as often as possible to get some sunshine and fresh air. Little did I know until recently, that the site where I played as a two-year-old—formerly the location of a seventeenth-century house belonging to one of the oldest and most well-known families in Queens (we've all heard of Clement Clarke Moore and his poem *A Visit from St. Nicholas*)—was also where the old Moore family burial ground was located.

Elmhurst (*aka* Newtown, its official name until 1898) is one of the oldest communities in the borough and is probably the only place in the entire city where there are two churchyards directly across the street from each other, just a few blocks west of the Moore Homestead site. One of them belongs to the St. James Church, where I was baptized and whose history dates back to 1735, and the other belongs to the Reformed Church of Newtown, whose beautiful nineteenth-century church I always admired. A few blocks away, on the site where my favorite childhood eatery, the Georgia Diner, was located, previously stood a Presbyterian cemetery before its graves were relocated.

It seems that long before I was conscious of it, Queens cemeteries were an integral part of my early life.

But I'm probably not alone among you readers. If you have spent any time in any part of Queens, you've encountered a cemetery or two (or ten). The reason for that is simple: There are more dead people in Queens than living people. Queens has a great many cemeteries, including the massive 365-acre Calvary Cemetery, which is among the largest cemeteries in the entire country. There is an entire swath of Queens from Woodside through Maspeth and Middle Village where it seems like one cemetery leads to another to another and yet another, a vast continuum of graves dating back to the mid-nineteenth century.

In a previous book, *Hidden History of Queens* (History Press, 2018), I devoted one chapter to talking about some of the borough's cemeteries. There was so much more I wanted to cover, and I knew then that I needed to devote an entire book to the subject, so here we are! In this book, I'll take an in-depth look at everything from little known private burial grounds to massive cemeteries, from war memorials to funeral homes, from gravestones to florists.

In short, this book is all about every possible aspect of Dead Queens.

Richard Panchyk

Because my dad grew up in Queens, I've become quite familiar with the area. My grandmother still lives there, and her house, just down the street from my dad's old school, holds many memories for me. What I didn't know about Queens when I was younger is how much history actually occurred there. That changed when I helped my dad research his books *Hidden History of Queens* and *Abandoned Queens* in the last few years. I was hooked. After going to fifteen of the places in this book with him, I've gained even more knowledge about its history.

Whether large cemeteries with winding pathways, or small churchyard cemeteries, we've visited all types. One memorable cemetery visit was on a brutal winter day in December 2019, to Mount Zion Jewish Cemetery in Maspeth. I found it extremely interesting because it was so densely packed with gravestones, as far as the eye could see. Fast forward to May 2020, which was one of our first times wearing face masks out in public during the pandemic. At this early stage, masks weren't being made in bulk, as they were a month or so later; the ones we wore were homemade versions that were not the most comfortable. Being that it was finally a warm day, it was especially stifling to wear these thick masks that were made from clothing fabric. I left my jacket in the car as we wandered around Maple Grove, the sun beaming down on us after days of cloudy skies. This also happened to be where my great grandfather is buried, and it was the first time I got to visit his grave. I left a dandelion next to his name on the bronze plaque, the delicate yellow matching the shade of my shirt.

The larger cemeteries I visited had some of the most beautiful statues and memorials I'd ever seen. St. John Cemetery in Middle Village, the last cemetery I visited for this book, was full of these memorials that stood tall, some even tall enough to embrace the trees. These magnificent works of art made for a very beautiful place. One of the most intriguing moments of these trips was seeing the gravestone of Louis Armstrong. The grave was showered with beads, rocks, and candles, among other mementos. I didn't know beforehand that this was where he was buried, so it was especially fascinating to see.

Each cemetery I saw had its own unique personality, one differing greatly from the next, which was compelling to me. After visiting many of these locations, one thing's for sure: Queens has a lot of area to cover. The sizeable number of cemeteries that blanket it reminds us of all those who came before us.

Lizz Panchyk

INTRODUCTION

If there's one county in the United States that deserves its own book about cemeteries, it's Queens County in New York. With a stunning array of cemeteries of all faiths and sizes from the seventeenth century to the twentieth century, Queens' burial grounds reflect the diversity and indeed the very story of New York City itself.

The earliest cemeteries in Queens were churchyards, town burying grounds, and private family cemeteries. These were the main types of cemeteries until the nineteenth century. But things would soon change. By the mid-nineteenth century, New York City (which then consisted solely of Manhattan) was growing rapidly. The population had increased from 185,000 in 1830 to 327,0000 in 1840 and 590,000 in 1850. Such a dramatic increase in the live population also meant the flip side—an increase in the dead population. Problem was, there was only so much space in the city and its existing cemeteries simply did not have enough capacity to handle all the dead. The streets north of 14th Street had been laid out on paper in 1811 according to the Randel Plan, and by 1850 the physical grid was rapidly being filled in with tenements, rowhouses, and businesses. There was a large open space laid out in the plan, but that was intended for what was to become Central Park, not a cemetery. Most of Manhattan's dead would have to be buried elsewhere—someplace close enough to be convenient but sprawling enough and unpopulated enough to handle the many thousands of burials. The answer was just across the East River—Queens.

In 1847, the New York State Legislature had passed the Rural Cemeteries Act, which allowed commercial for-profit cemeteries (unaffiliated with churches) to operate throughout the state, which paved the way for the use of Queens as cemetery land. Back then, Queens County extended beyond present-day Queens and through what is now Nassau County. Even then, in 1850 the entire population of Queens was only about 37,000, so there was plenty of open land. Parts of Queens were certainly remote and distant, so cemeteries made the most sense closer to Manhattan. And within a few years, that is exactly what happened. Broad swaths of land in western Queens were purchased and set aside for use as cemeteries, forever changing the landscape of what was to become one of the five boroughs of New York City at century's end (and even without the Nassau portion is still five times as large as Manhattan).

The headstones in these cemeteries reflect the changing ethnic composition of the city over time, with the earliest being those of Dutch and English descent, followed by Irish, German, Italian, and other European countries, and then into the twentieth century, Asian, African, and South American as well.

The placement of these large cemeteries dictated the layout of roads and residential neighborhoods by creating boundaries and barriers between different parts of Queens. If you look at an aerial view of Queens, there are lots of patches of green, representing a combination of parks and cemeteries.

This book covers thirty-three Queens cemeteries. This is by no means all the cemeteries in Queens, but it's certainly most of them. The cemeteries appear in alphabetical order, with a brief description and history followed by selected photographs.

1

All Faiths Cemetery

67-29 Metropolitan Ave, Middle Village, NY 11379

This sprawling cemetery (540,000 burials over 225 acres) lies in the heart of Middle Village. I have distinct memories of passing the cemetery on numerous occasions as a kid, when we were driving to the Times Square Stores (TSS) department store that used to lie directly adjacent. Back then it was an odd thing for me that a cemetery could be so large. It seemed to young me that the entire Middle Village was nothing but cemeteries and TSS. Though its original name was the Lutheran Cemetery, All Faiths was founded with the idea that plots would be offered at prices affordable to people of all faiths. In researching this book, I made a trip to the cemetery to try to find the grave of my great-great grandfather and his family. I located the approximate site, but there seemed to be no marker, which is quite possible because some could only afford the price of a plot, not a headstone as well. The cemetery is one of the most interesting in Queens because of its location adjacent to Christ the King High School and its sections of vastly different nature. According to a friend of mine who attended Christ the King, the cemetery was a part of the school experience; students would cut through the cemetery on their way to and from school, and sometimes hang out there after school was out. Some of the cemetery sections close to the railroad tracks are overgrown, while other sections look almost like open country fields with few gravestones.

LUTHERAN CEMETERY.

Middle Village, L. I., July 31st 1901

Received Three Dollars, from

Mr. Ehlenberger Undertaker,

For the Burial of Charlotte Neuman

full in Grave No. 265380 on Public Lot 15 Map 3/a Row 35

Grave, 7 Aged, 1 Years, 4 Months, and 10 Days.

Which Grave shall forever belong to the family (except in case of disinterment the Grave shall revert); with privilege of two reinterments therein, for which they shall only pay the regular price for the reopening and closing of the same. The Grave to be held, however, subject to all By-Laws, Rules and Regulations of said Cemetery.

N. B.—No Wooden Monument, Rail or other Structure shall be erected on said Lot, nor Mineral Knobs used to ornament the same.

D. Stoemius Jr

SUPERINTENDENT.

A receipt from 1901 for three dollars for the burial of Charlotte Neuman in Public Lot 15 at the Lutheran Cemetery (later called All Faiths).

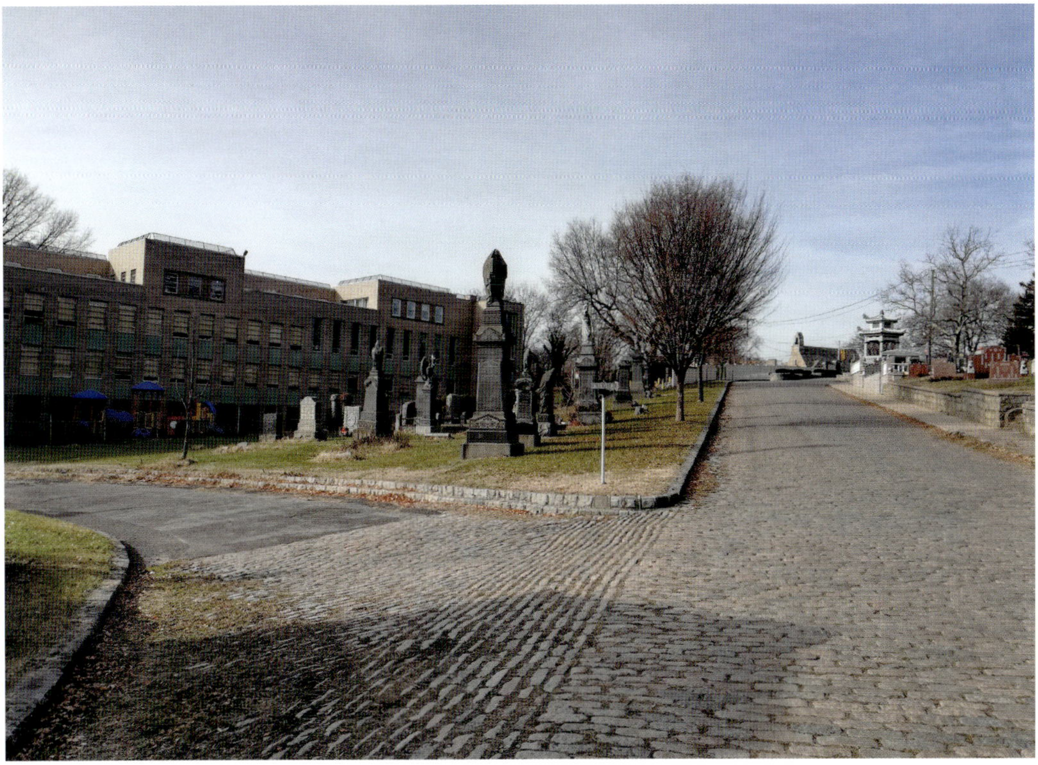

These photos show the proximity of All Faiths to Christ the King High School, a Catholic school.

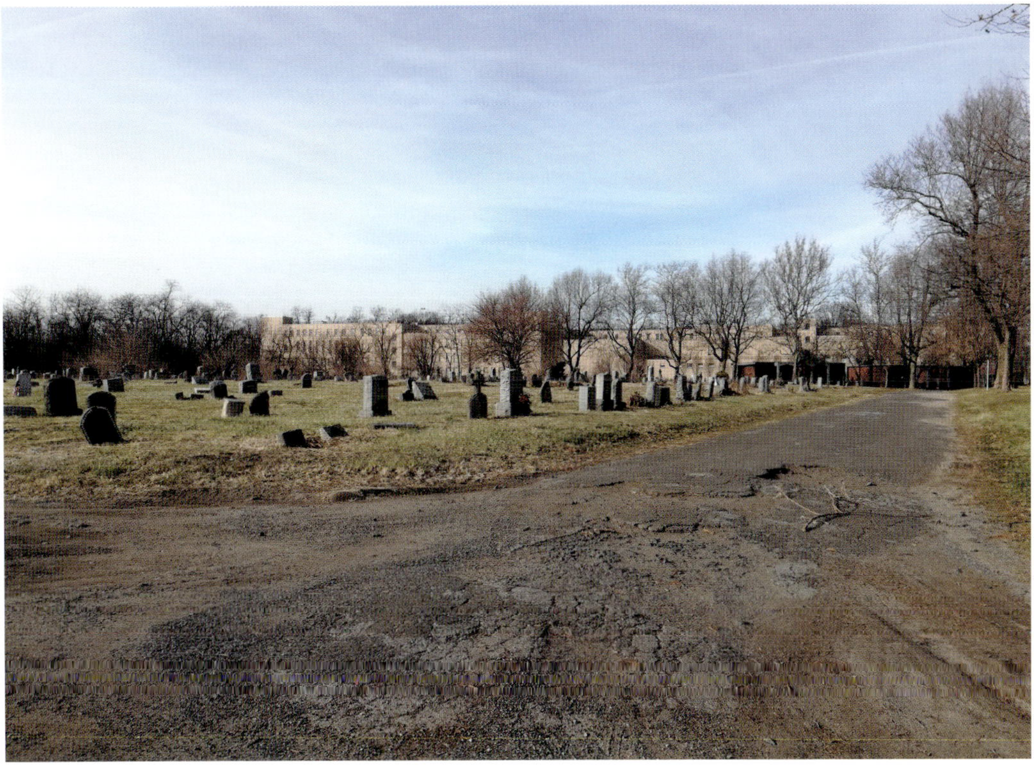

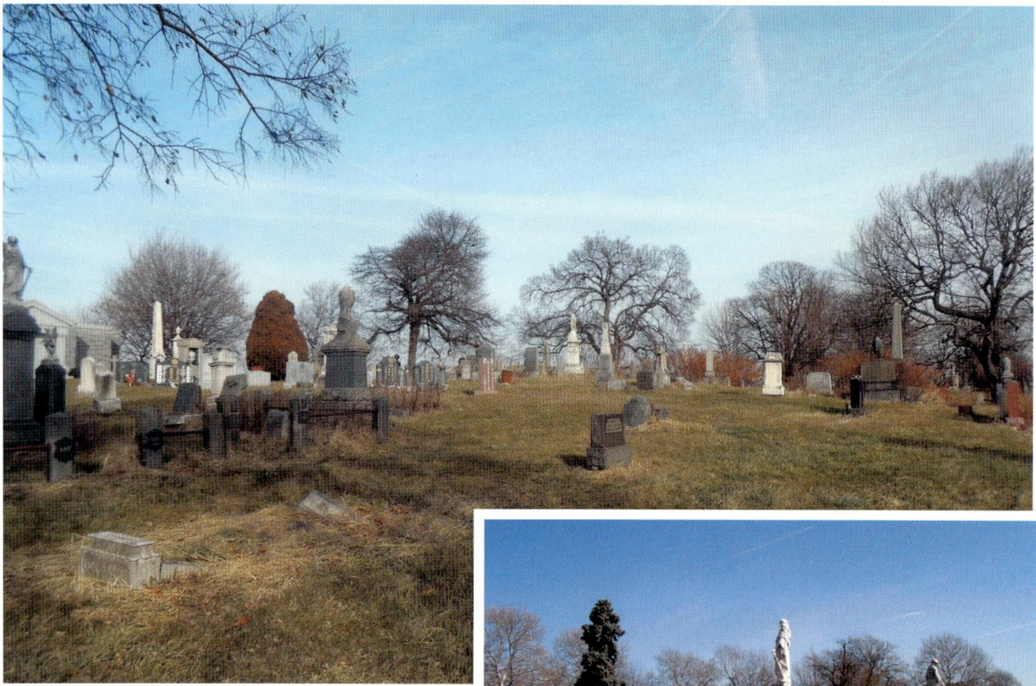

Lack of headstones does not mean no interments; some people were simply buried without one if their family could not afford a stone.

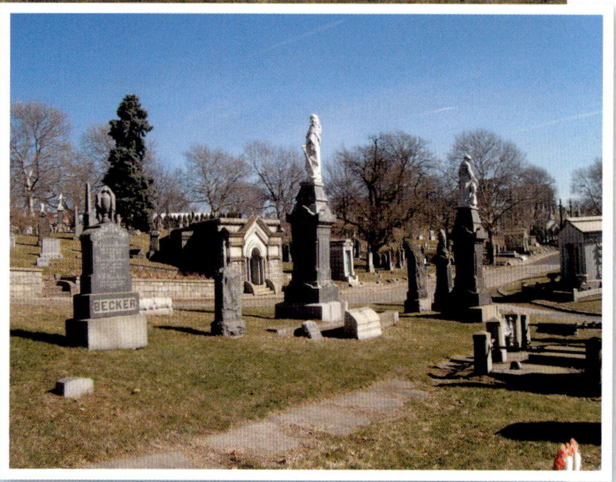

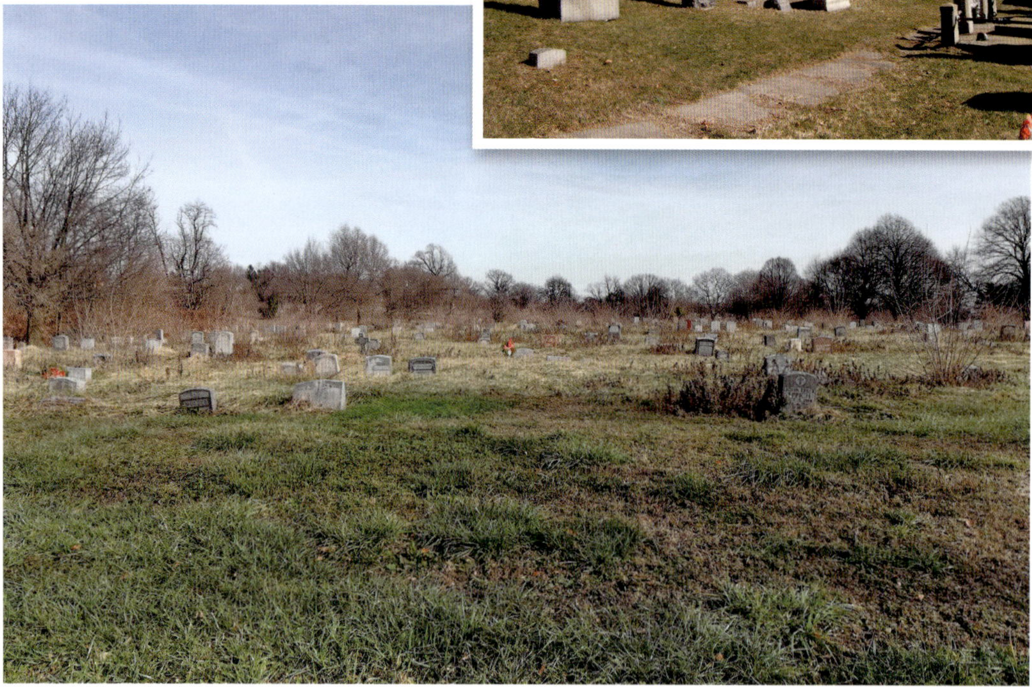

Some parts of All Faiths feel quite rural and remote, such as this section adjacent to the railroad tracks in the southwest corner. *Inset:* All Faiths is so large it would take many hours to explore all the different sections.

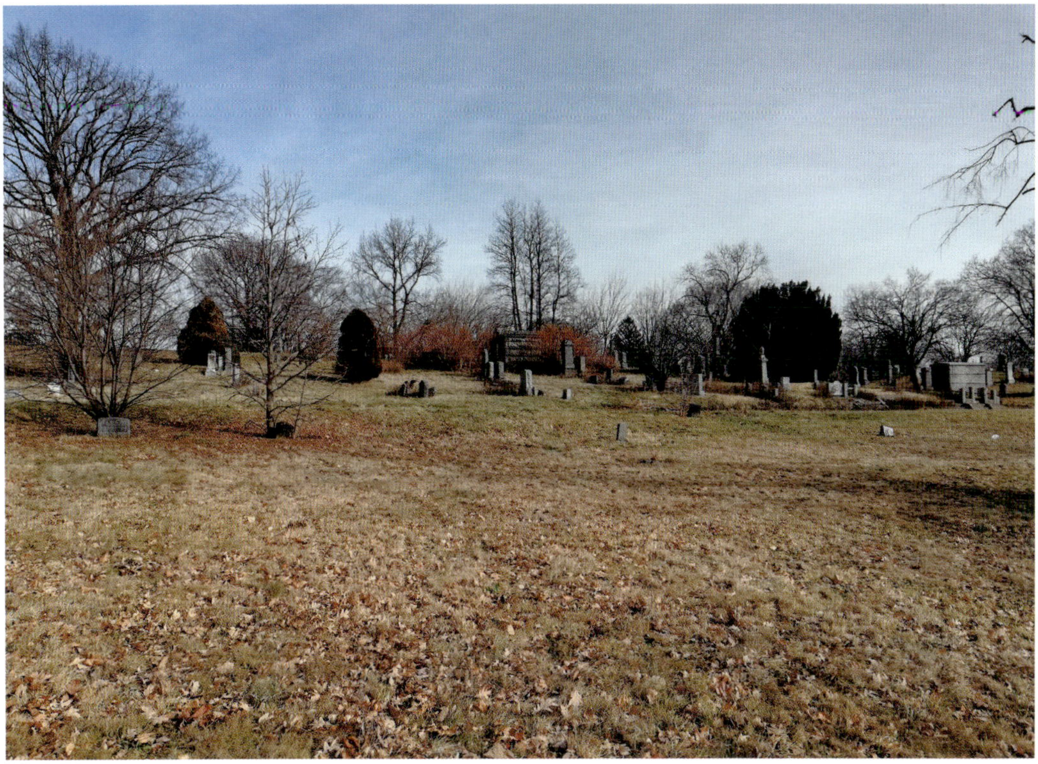

Sparse gravestones made it difficult for me to locate rows and figure out the burial site of my great-great grandfather.

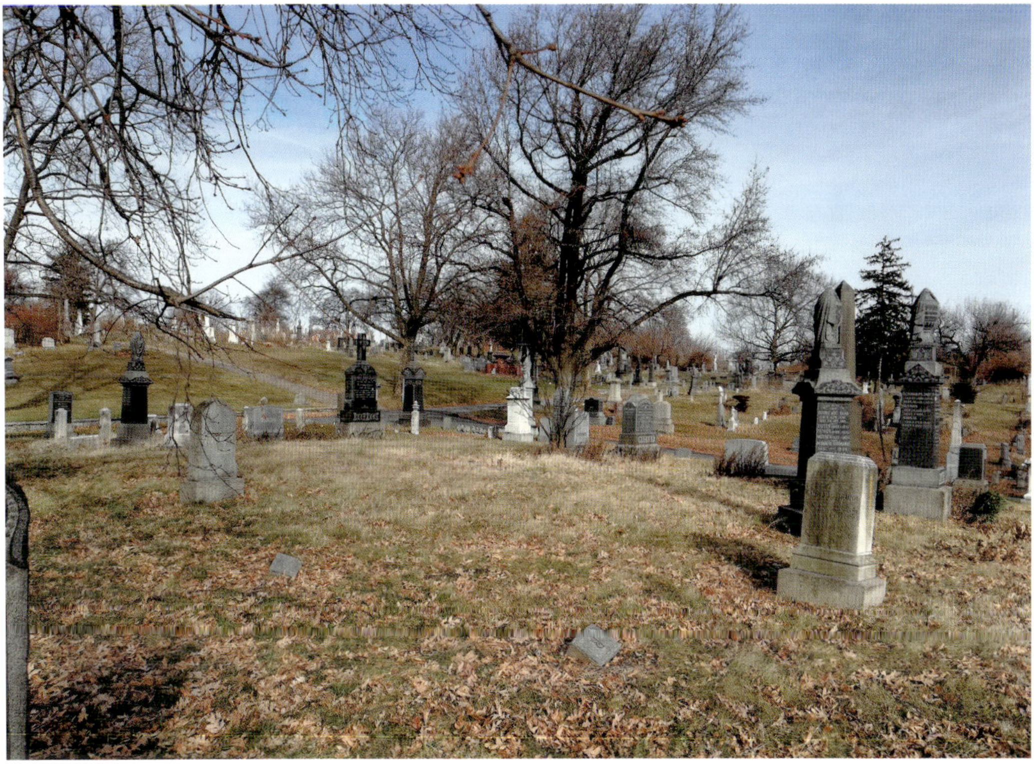

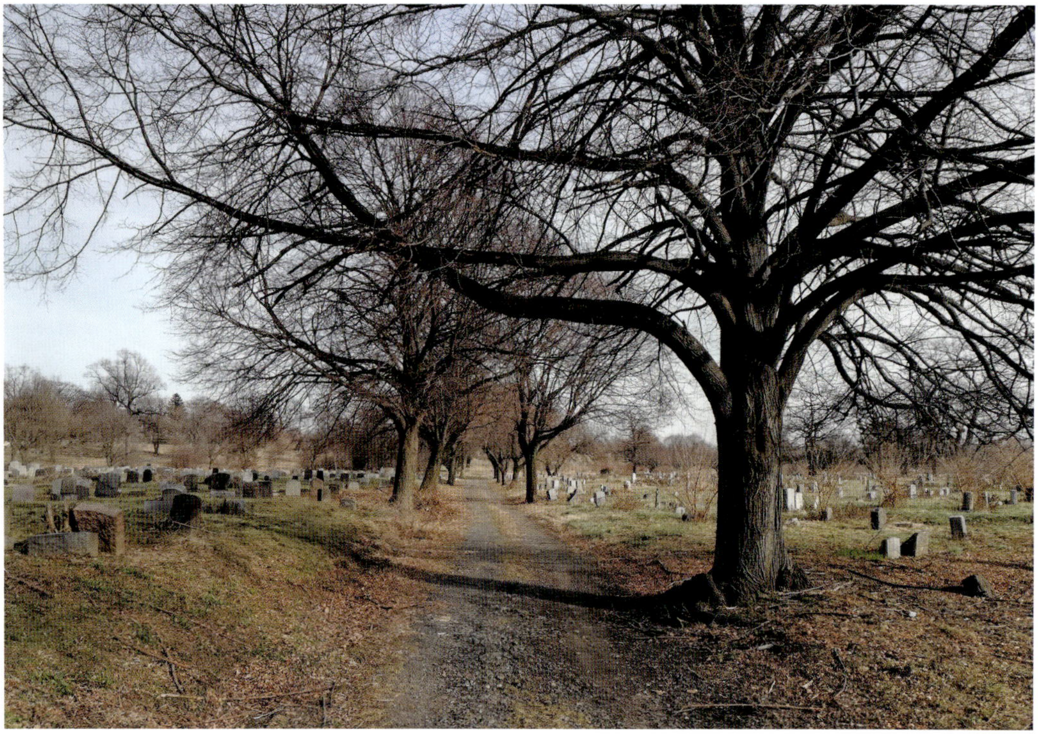

Cemetery in the middle of Queens or family burial ground along a quaint country road in Vermont?

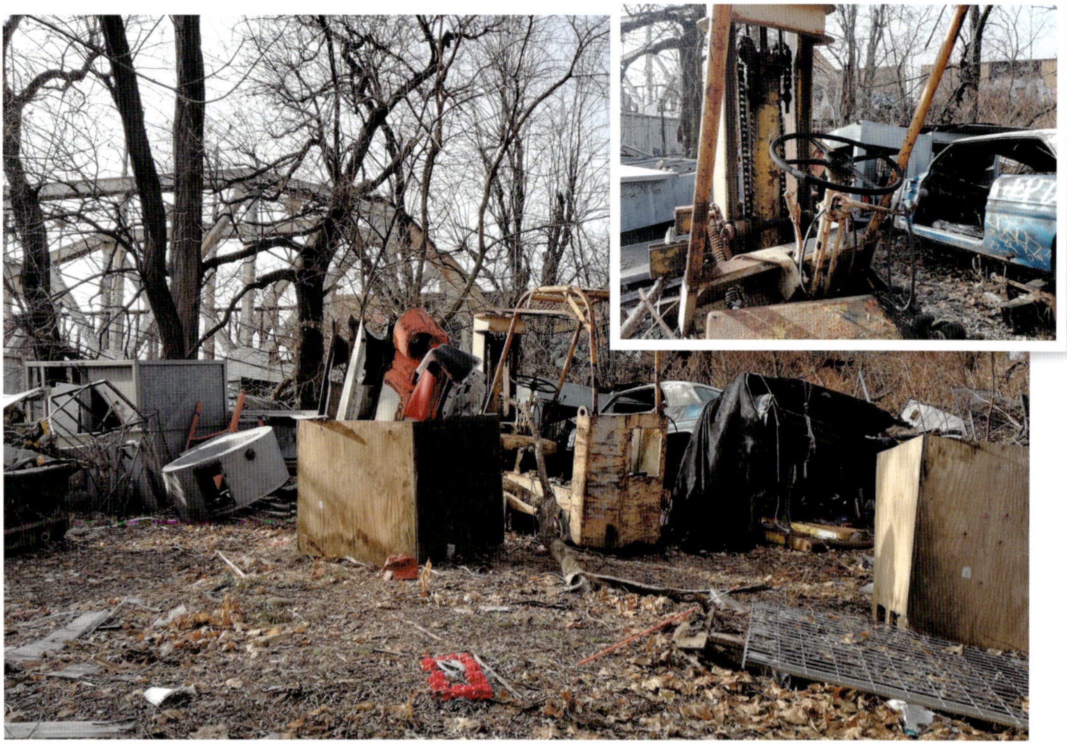

Some abandoned junk lies near the railroad tracks just outside of the cemetery perimeter in the southwest corner.

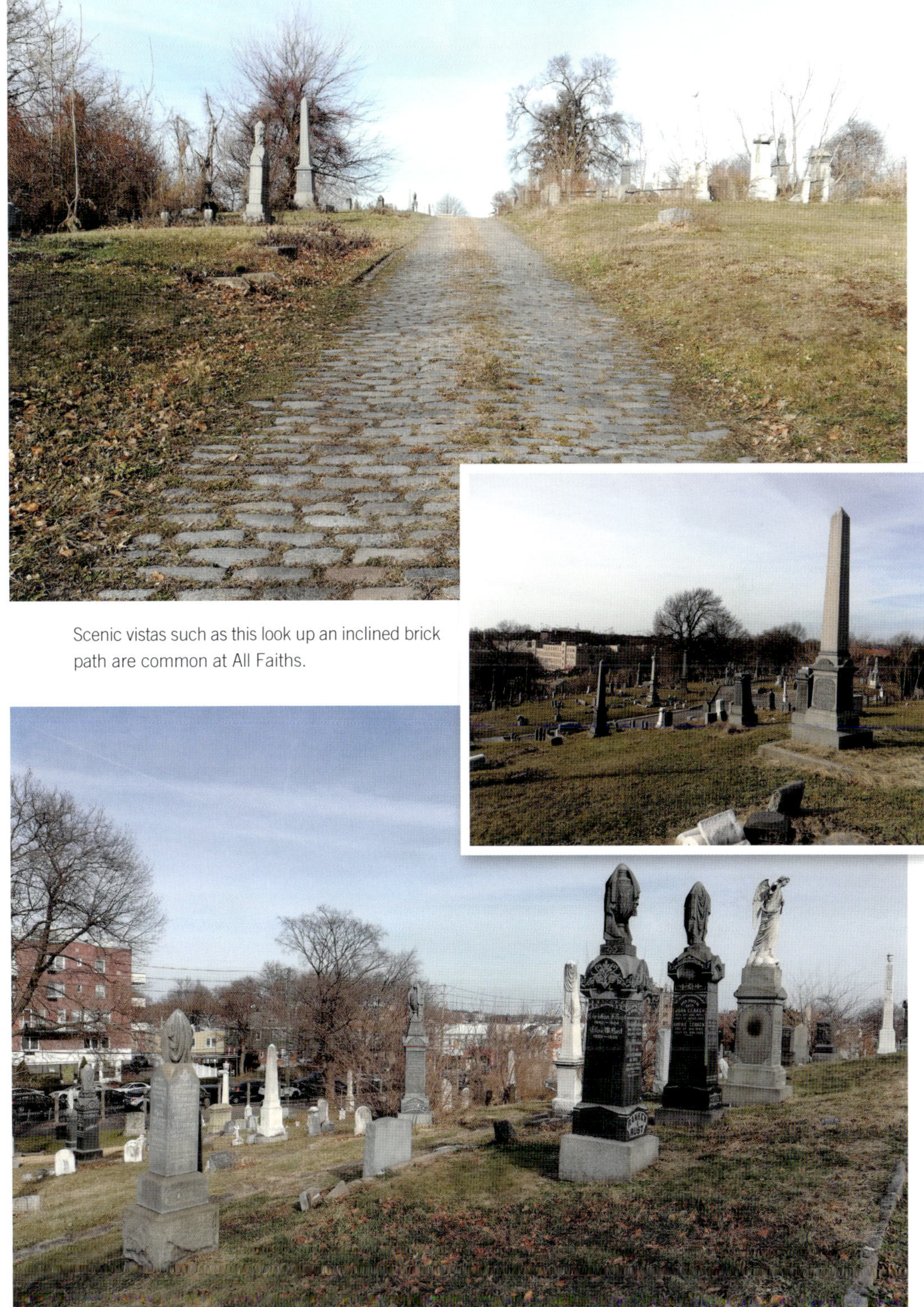

Scenic vistas such as this look up an inclined brick path are common at All Faiths.

The cemetery fronts Metropolitan Avenue for more than half a mile, from Mount Olivet Crescent to 73rd Place. *Inset:* Like many Queens cemeteries, All Faiths has hills. Christ the King High School is in the background.

2

CALVARY CEMETERY

49-02 LAUREL HILL BOULEVARD, WOODSIDE, NY 11377

Calvary Cemetery is a behemoth in a borough of large cemeteries, the most massive of all of them. With 365 acres, there are over 1.75 million graves in Calvary, making it one of the largest cemeteries in the entire country. The cemetery is so large that it is split into four sub-cemeteries, Calvary I-IV, with a total of seventy-one numbered sections. Founded in 1848, Calvary was the first major area cemetery to be established outside of Manhattan. The oldest part of the cemetery, First Calvary, is located the furthest west, just east of Greenpoint Avenue in Long Island City/Sunnyside and Second, Third, and Fourth are east of First and the intersection of the LIE and BQE, just south of Queens Boulevard. An important scene from one of the most famous movies of all time, *The Godfather*, was filmed at First Calvary. The funeral procession of Vito Corleone can be seen entering the cemetery gates on Greenpoint Avenue and proceeding through the cemetery to the "burial site." Aside from that famous fictional 1955 Calvary burial, there have been many notable actual burials here, including NYC Mayor Robert Wagner, U.S. Senator Robert F. Wagner (father of Robert Wagner), and Alfred E. Smith, governor of New York and presidential candidate in 1928.

Above: The main entrance to First Calvary, famous for its appearance in *The Godfather*.

Middle: A plaque at the entrance to First Calvary celebrates the employees of the cemetery who served in World War II.

Below: A view from near the entrance to First Calvary. The spire of nearby St. Raphael's Church (on Greenpoint Avenue) can be seen in the distance.

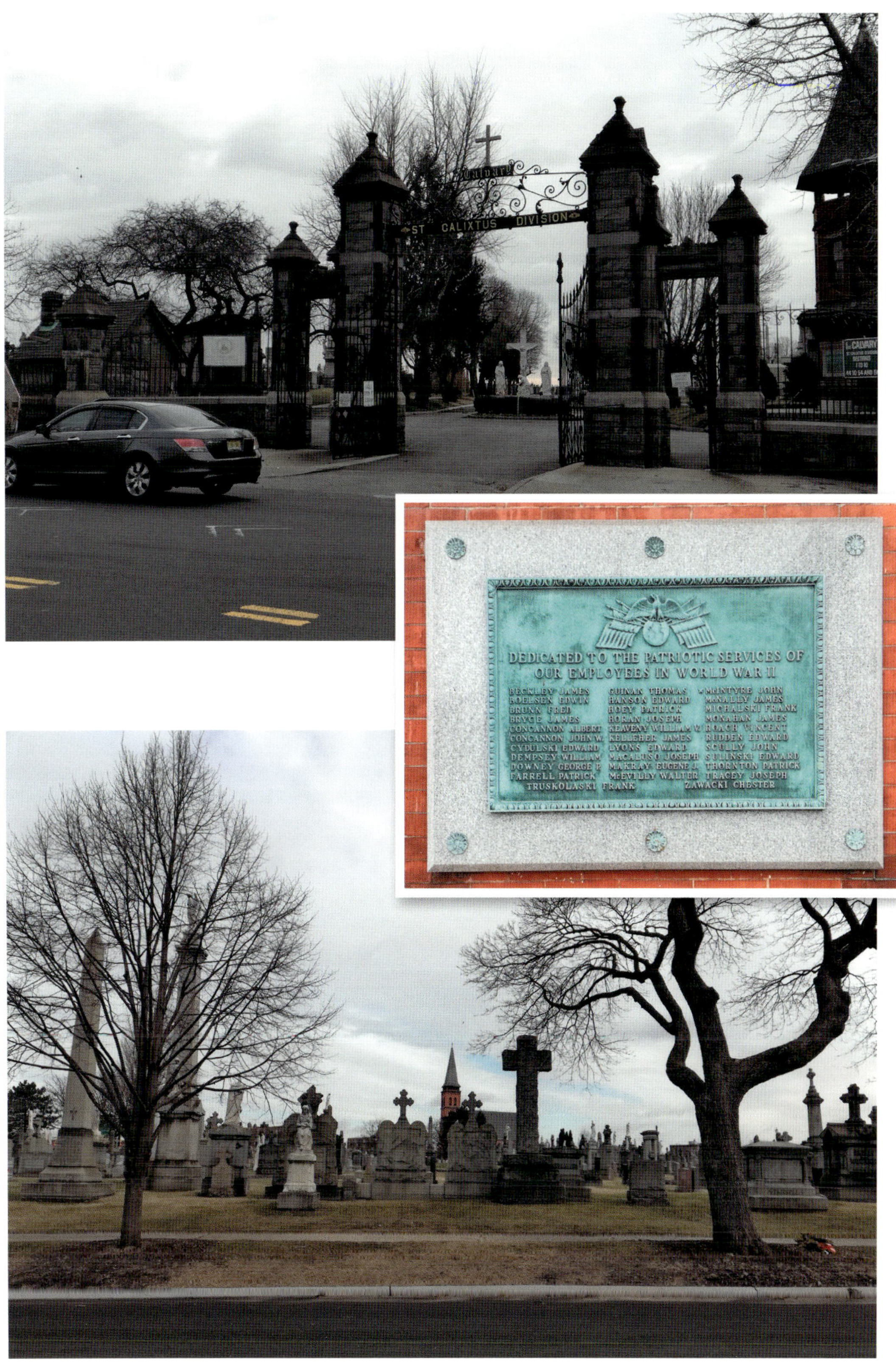
Calvary
ST CALIXTUS DIVISION
DEDICATED TO THE PATRIOTIC SERVICES OF
OUR EMPLOYEES IN WORLD WAR II
BECKLEY JAMES
BOELSEN EDWIN
BRUNN FRED
BRYCE JAMES
CONCANNON ALBERT
CONCANNON JOHN W.
CYDULSKI EDWARD
DEMPSEY WILLIAM
DOWNEY GEORGE P.
FARRELL PATRICK
GUINAN THOMAS
HANSON EDWARD
HOEY PATRICK
HORAN JOSEPH
KEAVENY WILLIAM V.
KELLEHER JAMES
LYONS EDWARD
MACALUSO JOSEPH
MAKRAY EUGENE J.
McEVILLY WALTER
McINTYRE JOHN
McNALLY JAMES
MICHALSKI FRANK
MONAHAN JAMES
ROACH VINCENT
RUDDEN EDWARD
SCULLY JOHN
SULINSKI EDWARD
THORNTON PATRICK
TRACEY JOSEPH
TRUSKOLASKI FRANK
ZAWACKI CHESTER

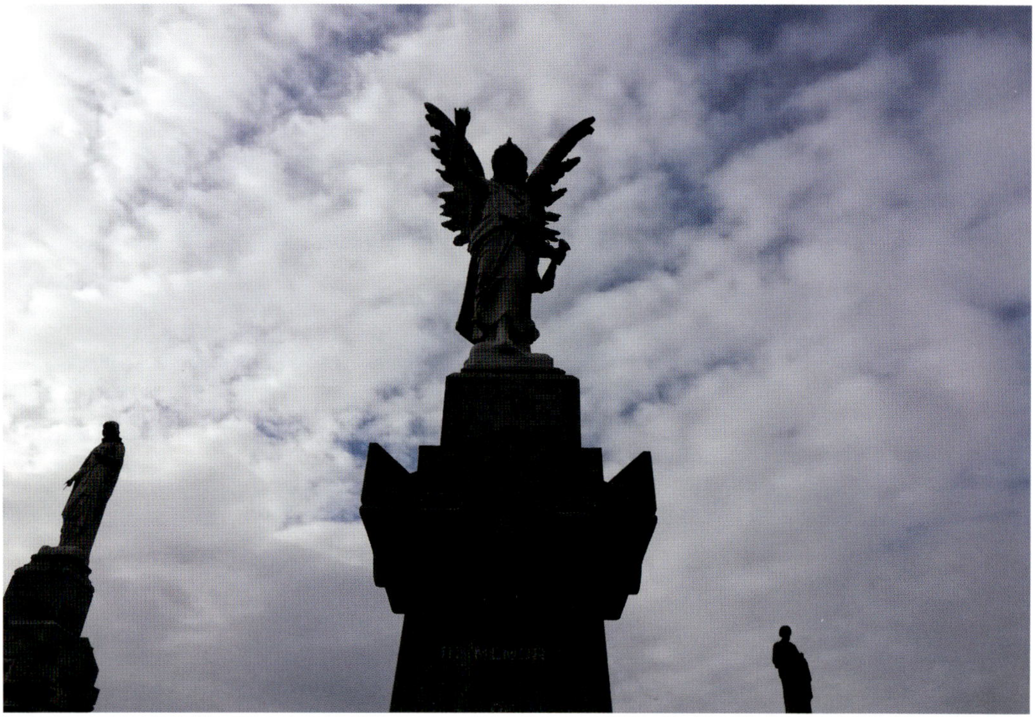

Some of the statuary in First Calvary, such as this angel, is truly spectacular.

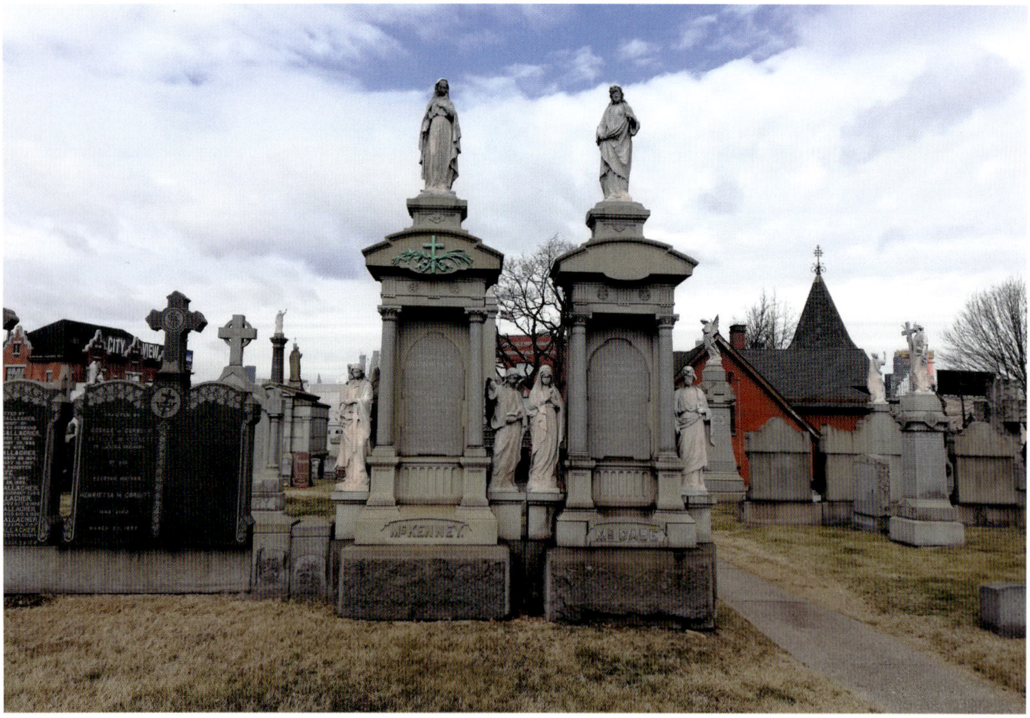

Impressive twin monuments for the McKenny and McCabe families in First Calvary.

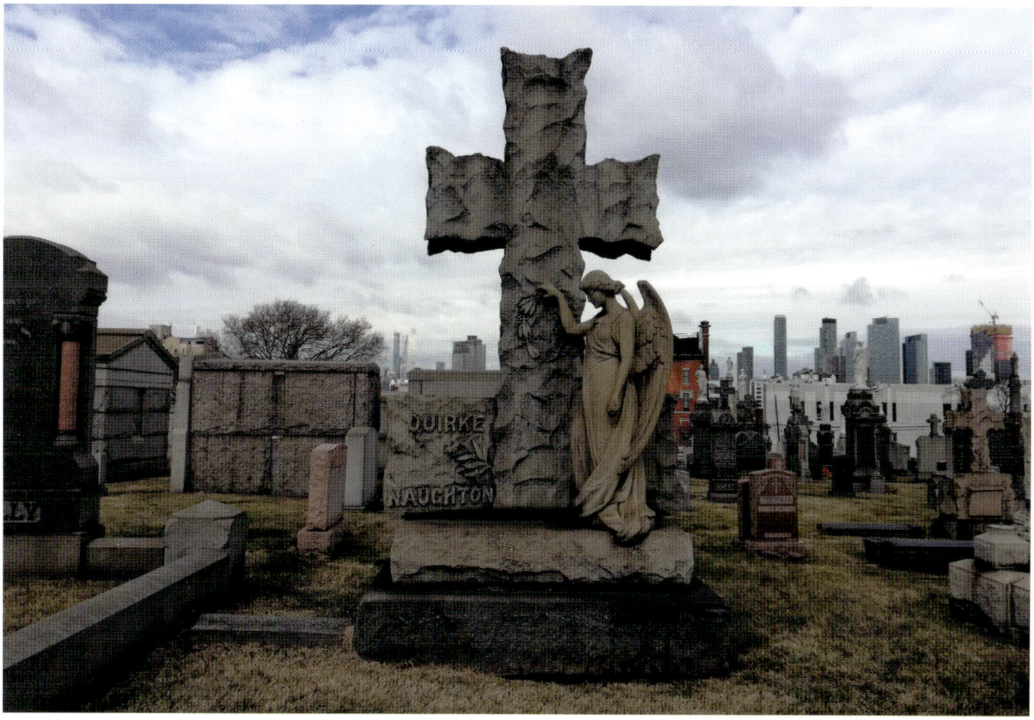

Some monuments are truly works of art in their unique and melancholy beauty.

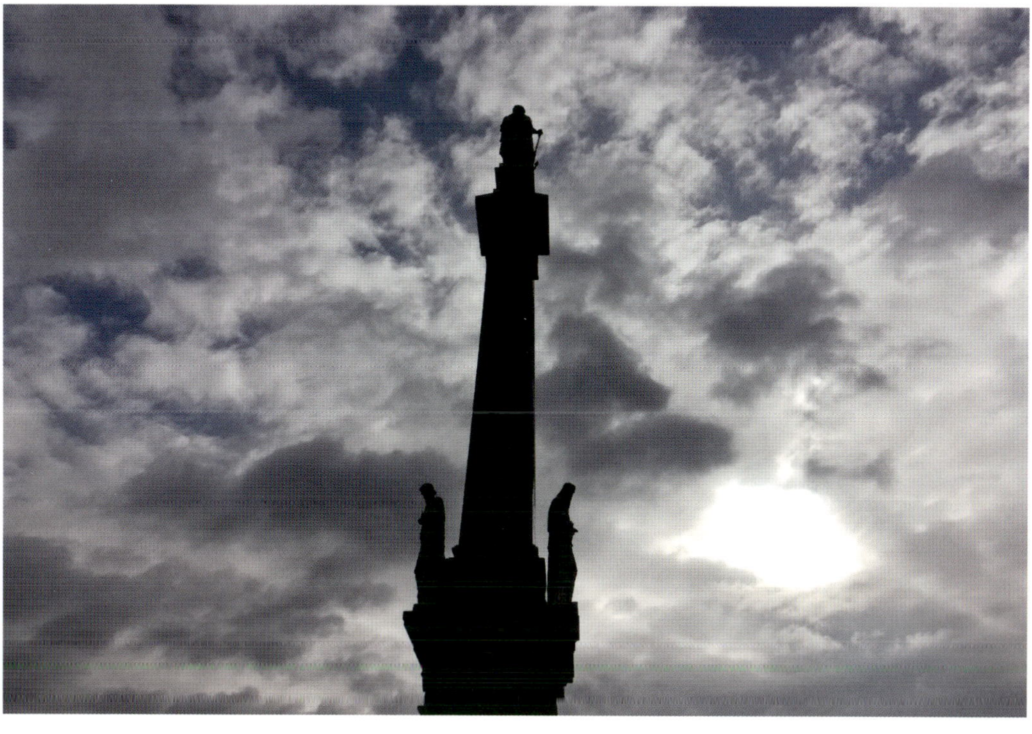

There's really no limit to how big or tall a monument can be other than the sheer mechanics of its stability—and the money it costs to create something of this size.

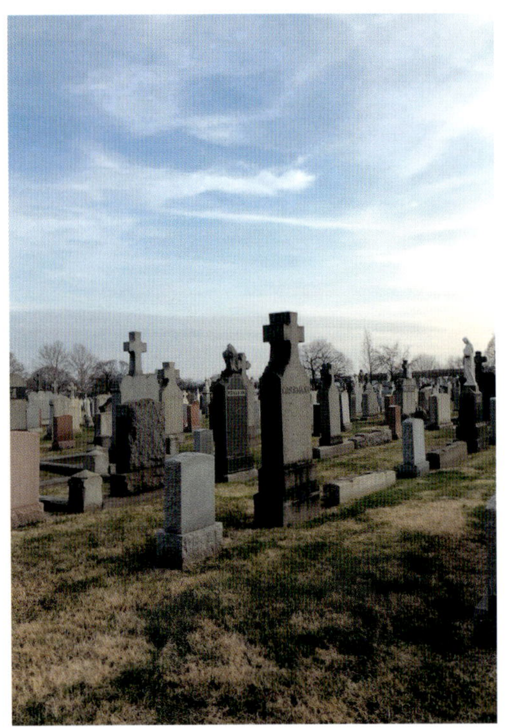

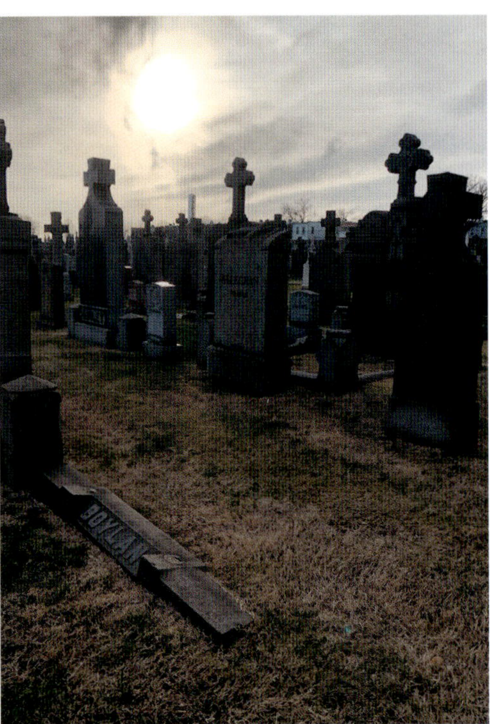

Two views in First Calvary, looking opposite directions from the same row on a winter afternoon.

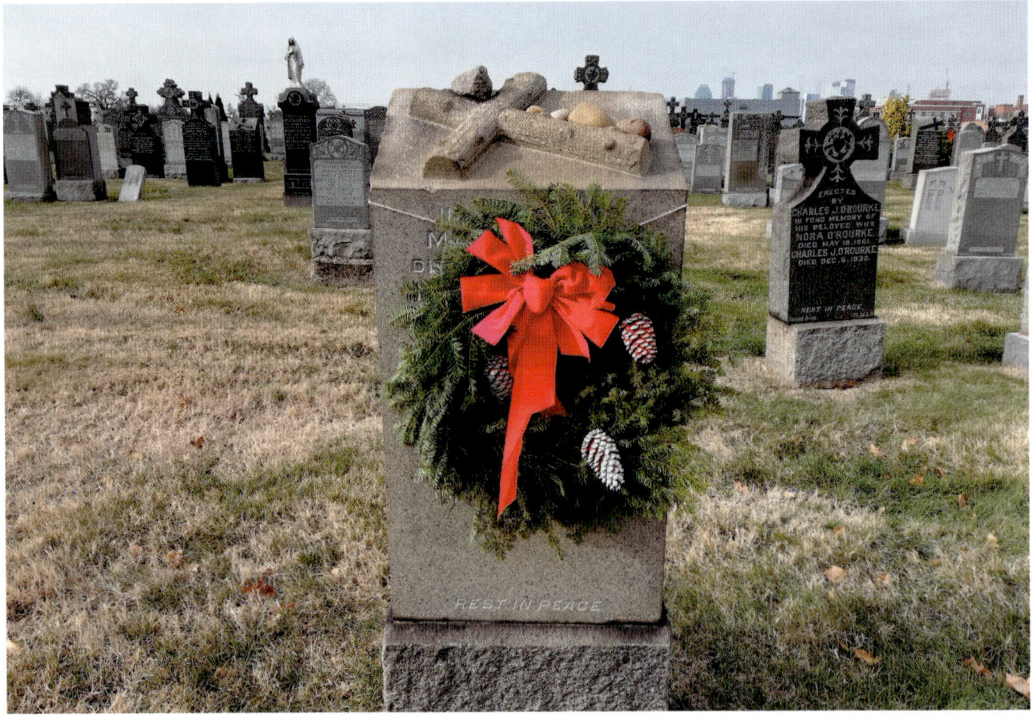

A wreath adorns a tombstone in Third Calvary on the day after Christmas.

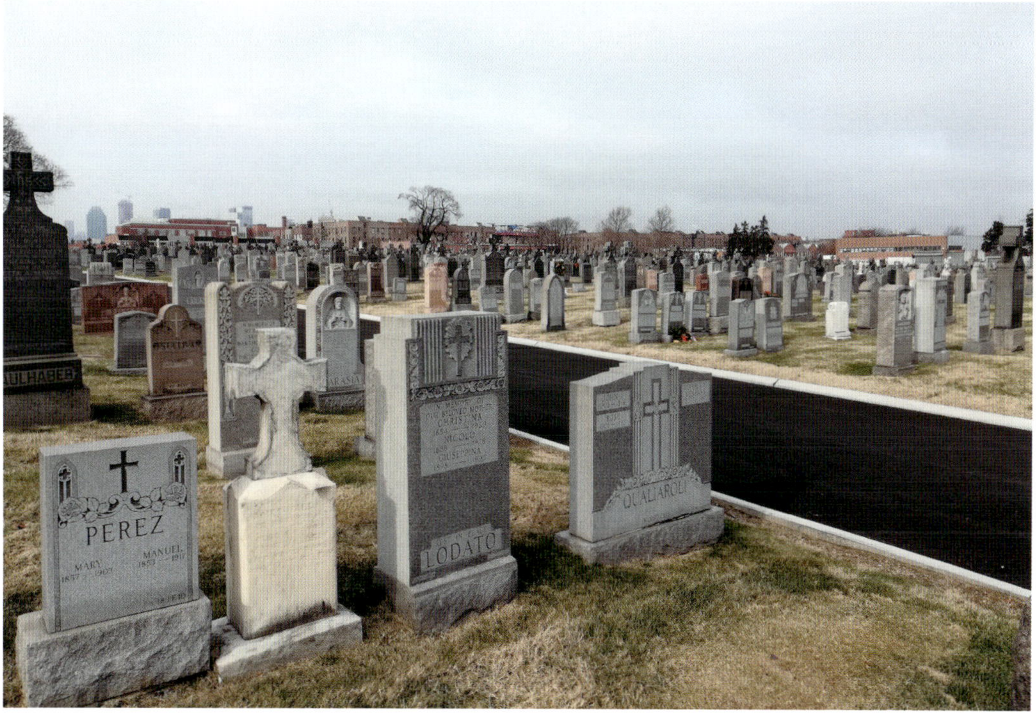

The infrastructure in Third Calvary is new and smooth in this photo from 2019. Cemetery roads are almost never this perfect.

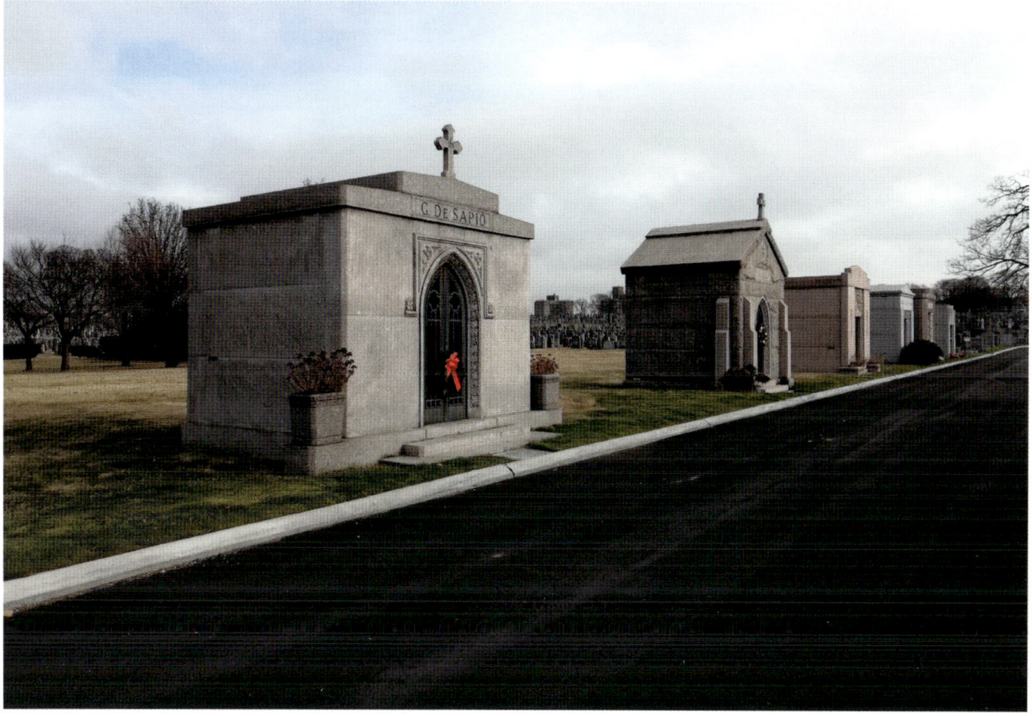

A row of mausoleums along one of the main roads in Third Calvary.

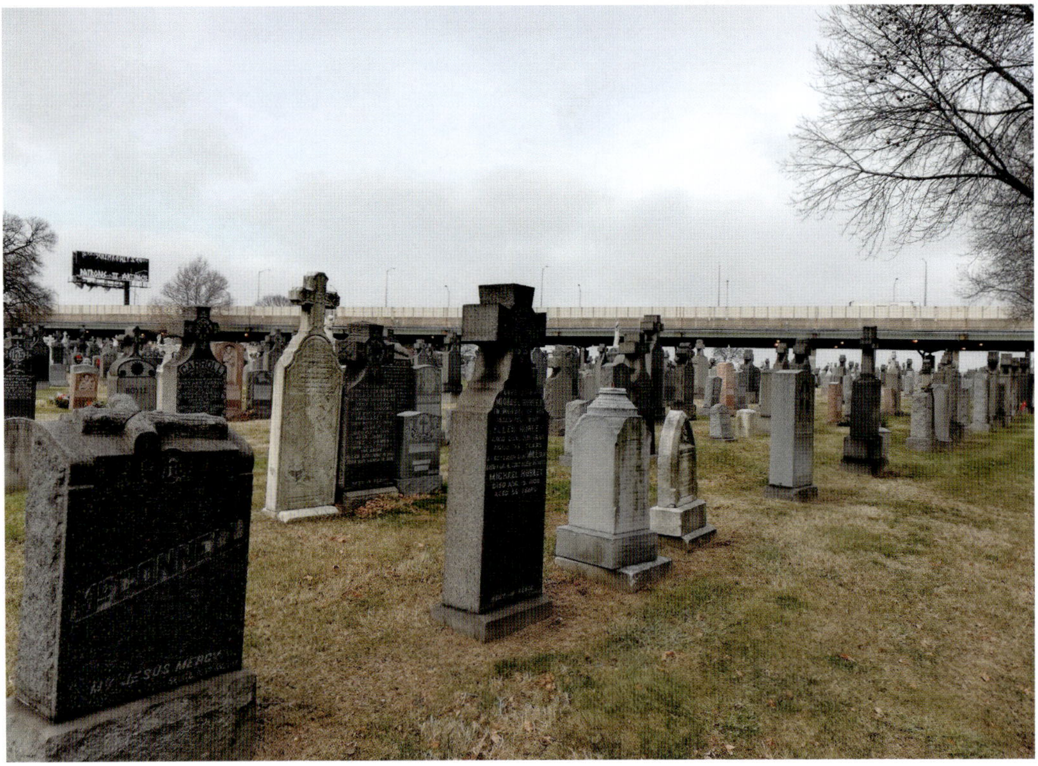

Two views of the Long Island Expressway as seen looking south from near the entrance to Second Calvary.

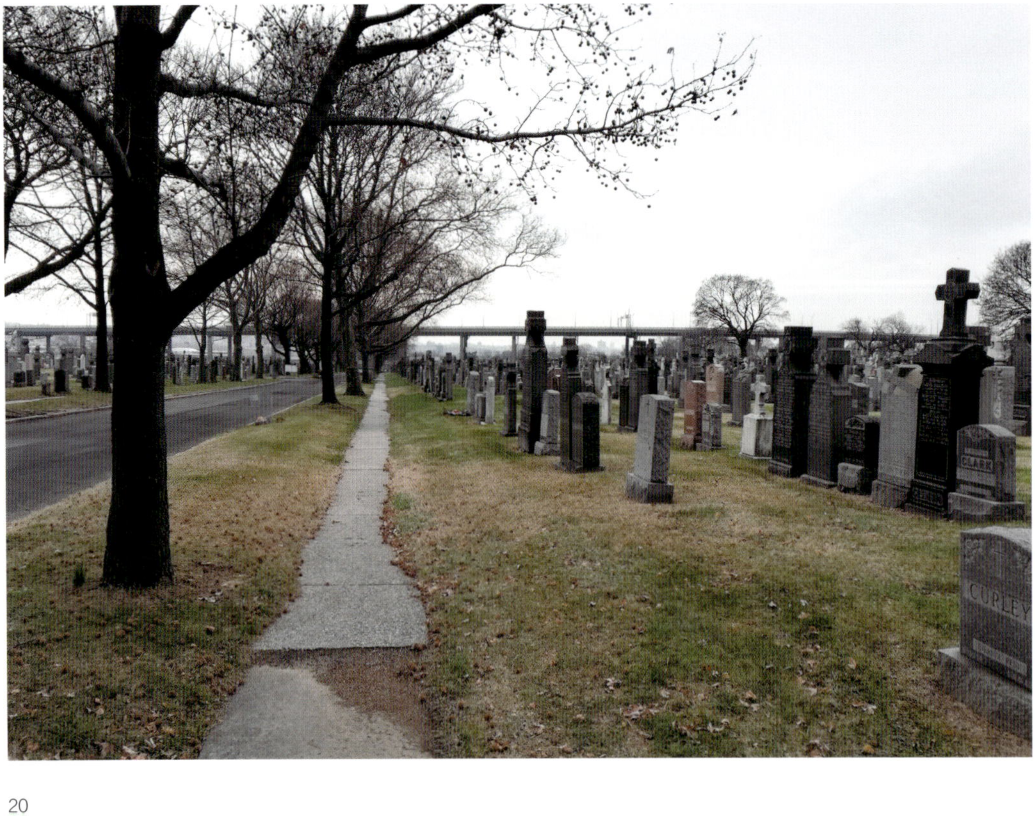

3

Cedar Grove Cemetery

130-04 Horace Harding Expressway, Flushing, NY 11367

A non-sectarian cemetery in Flushing, Cedar Grove was opened in 1893 and has 36,000 interments (according to the cemetery website; the Find a Grave website shows nearly 40,000). It is located just east of the Van Wyck Expressway (and the southern portion of Flushing Meadows Corona Park), just south of the Long Island Expressway, and just west of Main Street and the Queens College campus. It is actually tucked inside of a niche in the much larger Mount Hebron Cemetery. The Cedar Grove website touts the cemetery as a "melting pot of nationalities and religions" and a scan through some of the names of those buried there proves that point. In just the A's alone there is Abajian, Abarno, Abdul-Salaam, Abelsted, Abramowitz, Acemyan, Ackerstrom, Adlington, Ahahamian, and Ahlstrom.

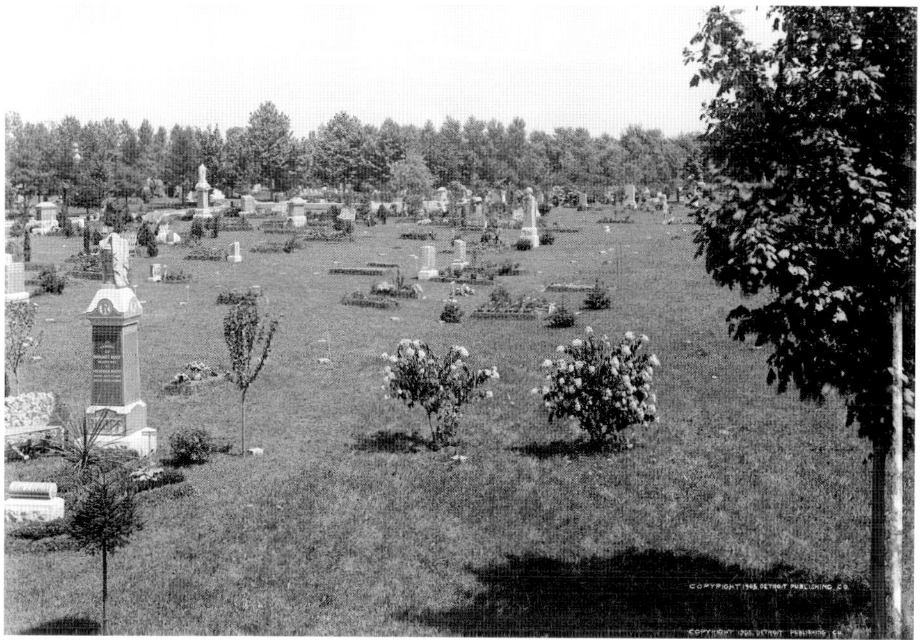

This photograph of the cemetery was taken by the Detroit Publishing Company in 1905. There are not too many century-old professional images of cemeteries in existence.

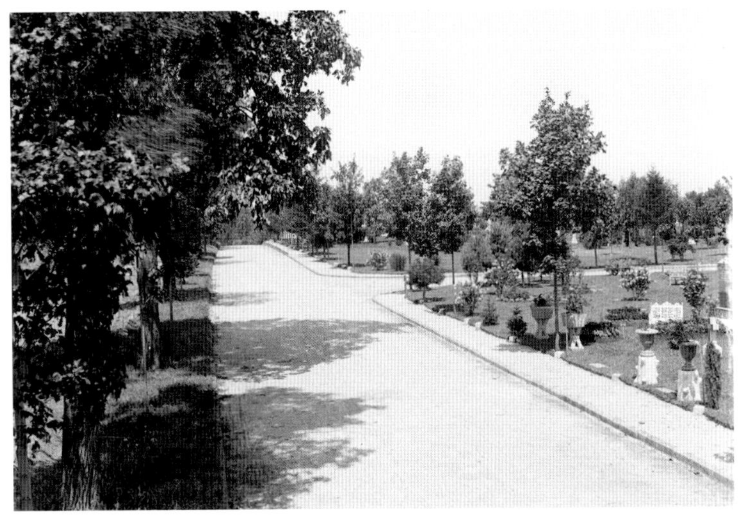

The cemetery was just twelve years old when these images were captured. The roadway infrastructure looks brand new.

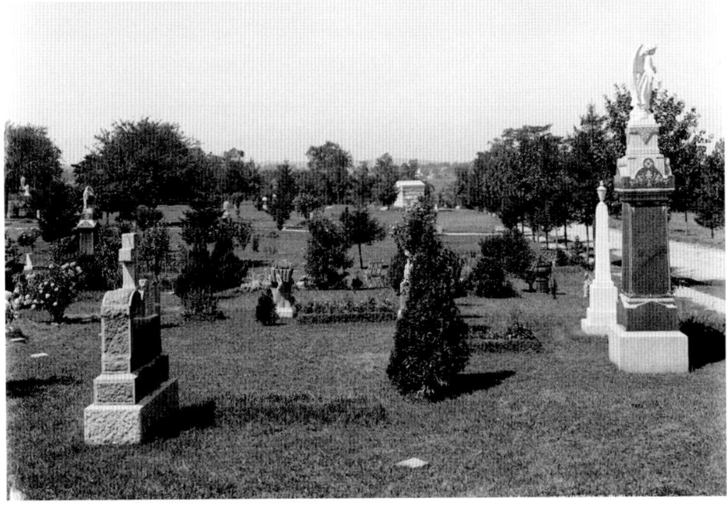

The late-Victorian style is very evident in the adornment on the tombstones that can be seen in these images.

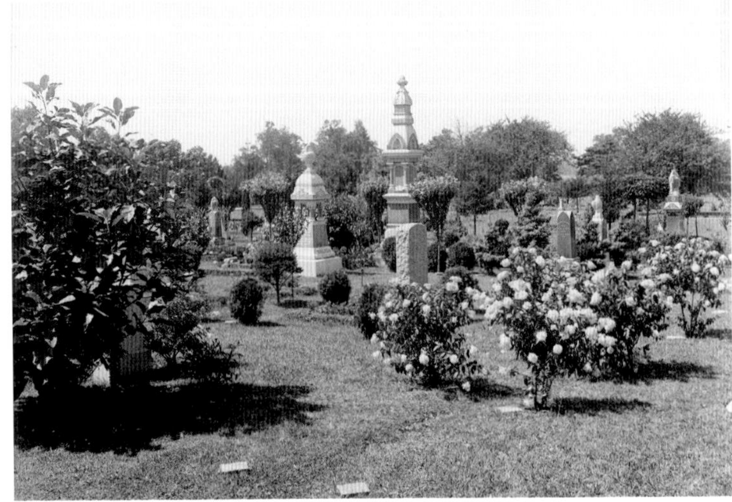

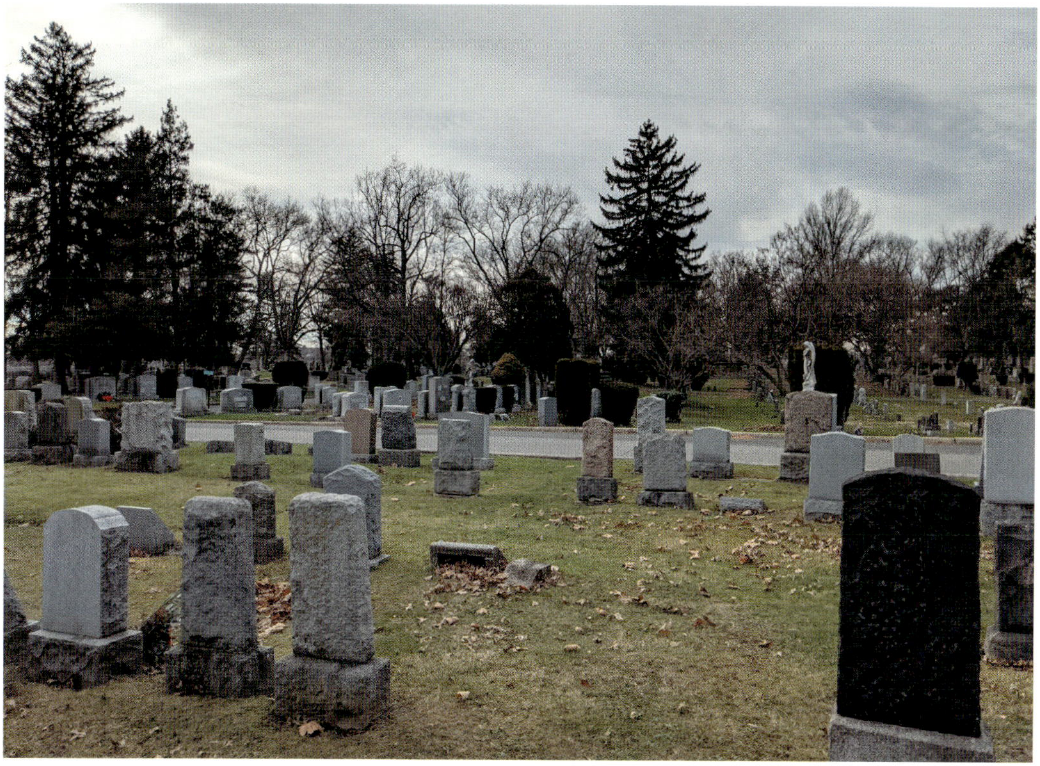

The eastern edge of Cedar Grove Cemetery abuts dead end streets off Main Street in Flushing.

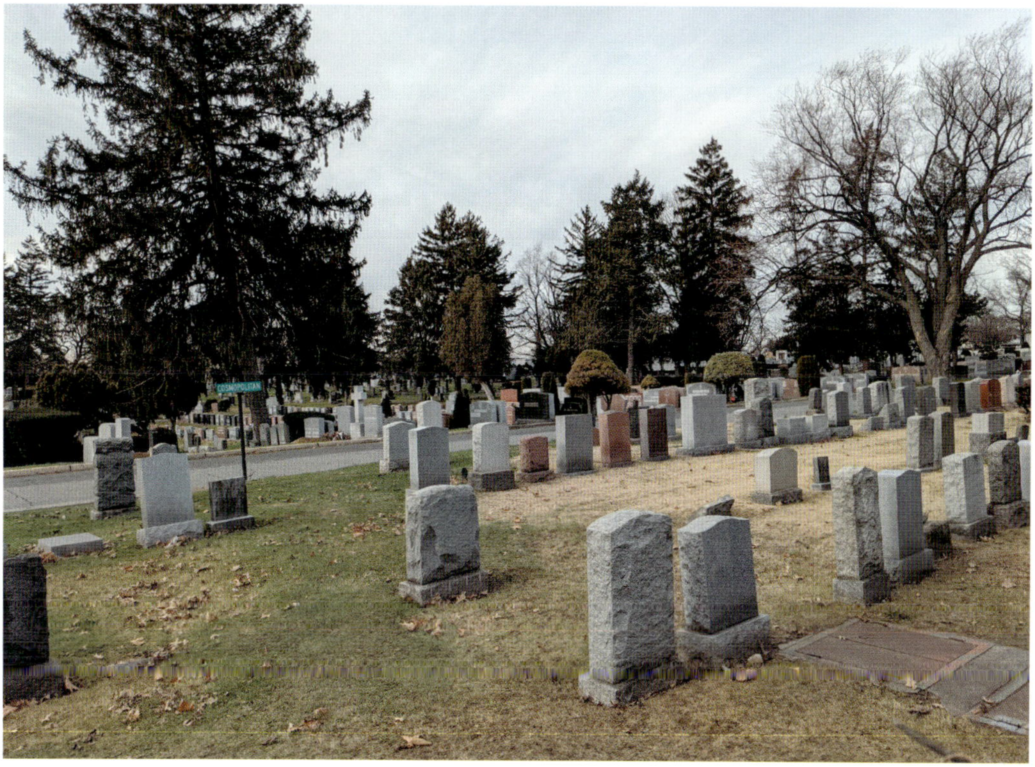

4

Cypress Hills Cemetery

833 Jamaica Ave, Brooklyn, NY 11208

At 225 acres, this cemetery is not only quite large, but also unique in that it straddles both Queens and Brooklyn. Much of the cemetery falls in Brooklyn, with only the northern portion (roughly parallel to Park Drive South) falling in Queens. Founded in 1848 and opened in 1851, the Queens portion of the cemetery in Glendale/Woodhaven includes the three-story Memorial Abbey mausoleum, built in 1936. It also features hills from which spectacular views of the surrounding areas and beyond are to be had. Famous baseball player Jackie Robinson's grave is located in Cypress Hills. About 35,000 dead were relocated from overcrowded Manhattan churchyards to Cypress Hills in the mid-nineteenth century. The main entrance to the cemetery is in Brooklyn, on Jamaica Avenue. Directly adjacent to the Queens part of the cemetery is the western end of neighboring Forest Park. Other cemeteries lie to the north of Cypress Hills.

Above: Cypress Hills Cemetevry in a 1961 aerial view.

Below: The grand old entrance to the cemetery on Jamaica Avenue in Brooklyn is one of the finest looking cemetery entrances in Queens.

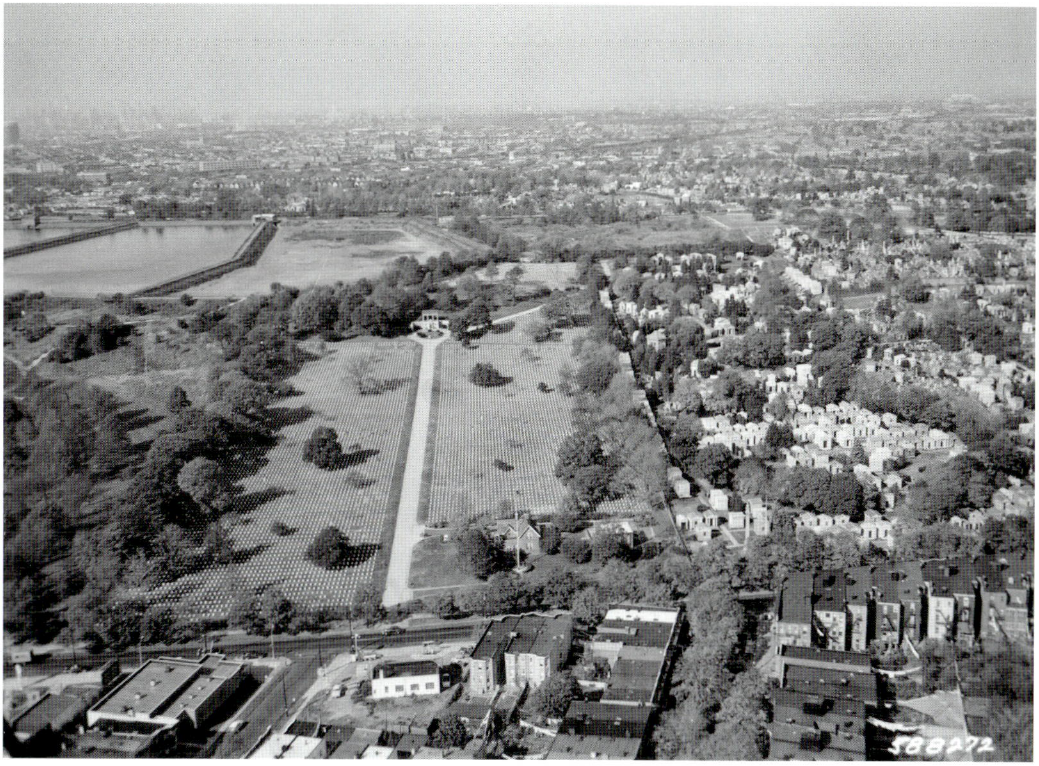
588272

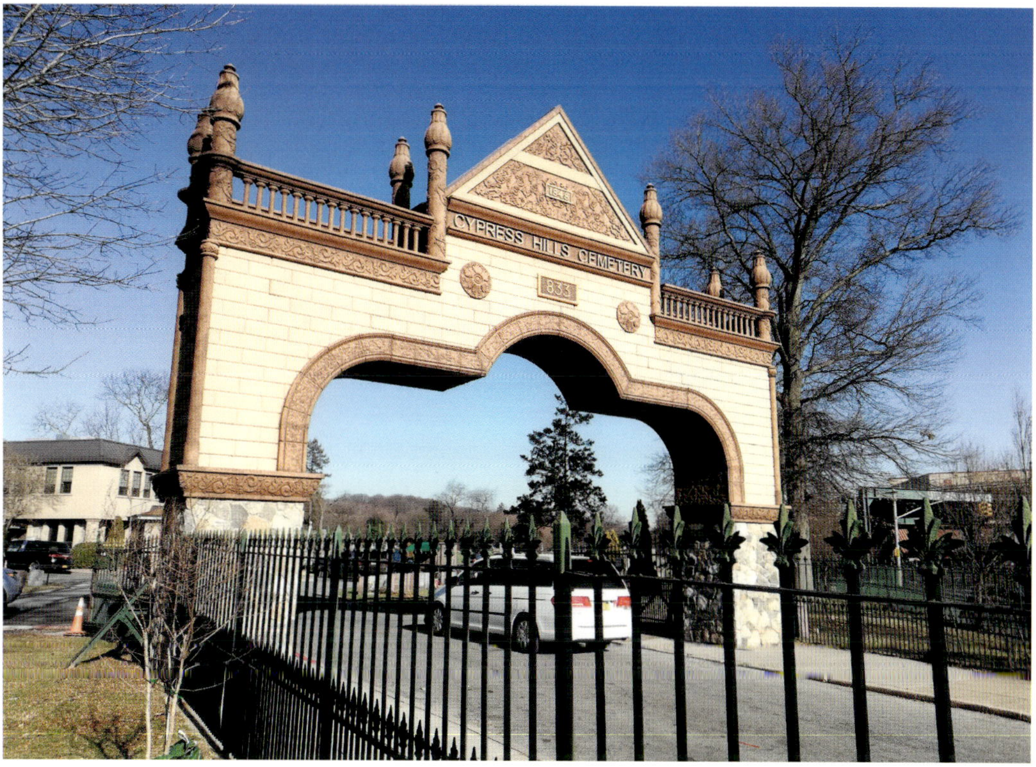
CYPRESS HILLS CEMETERY

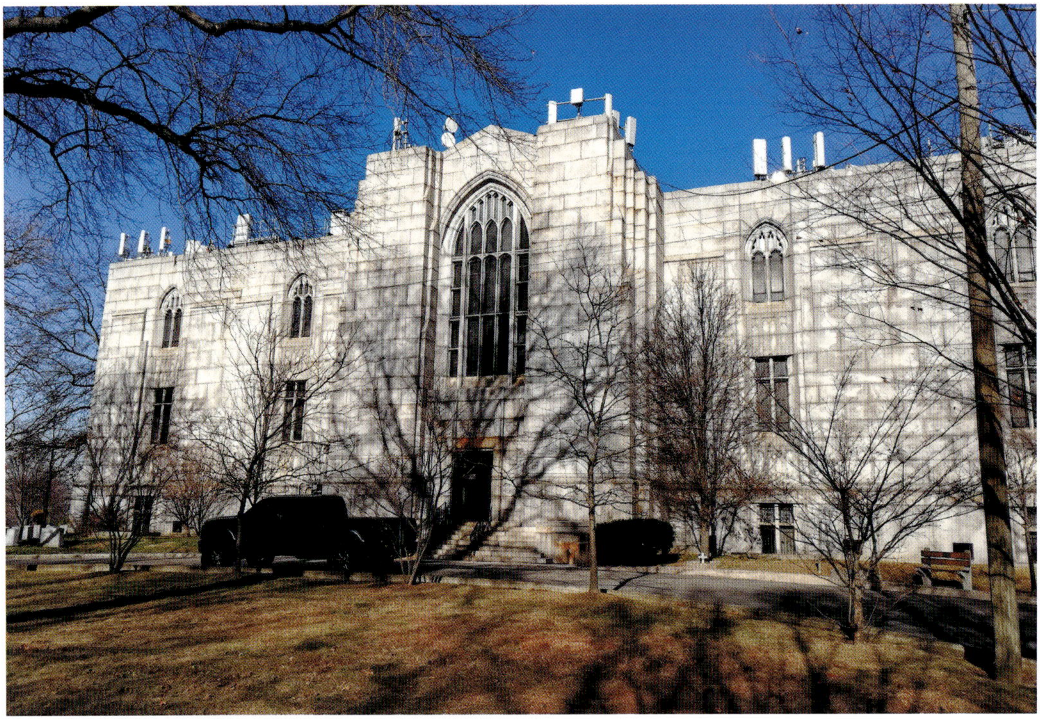

The imposing Memorial Abbey mausoleum was built in 1936.

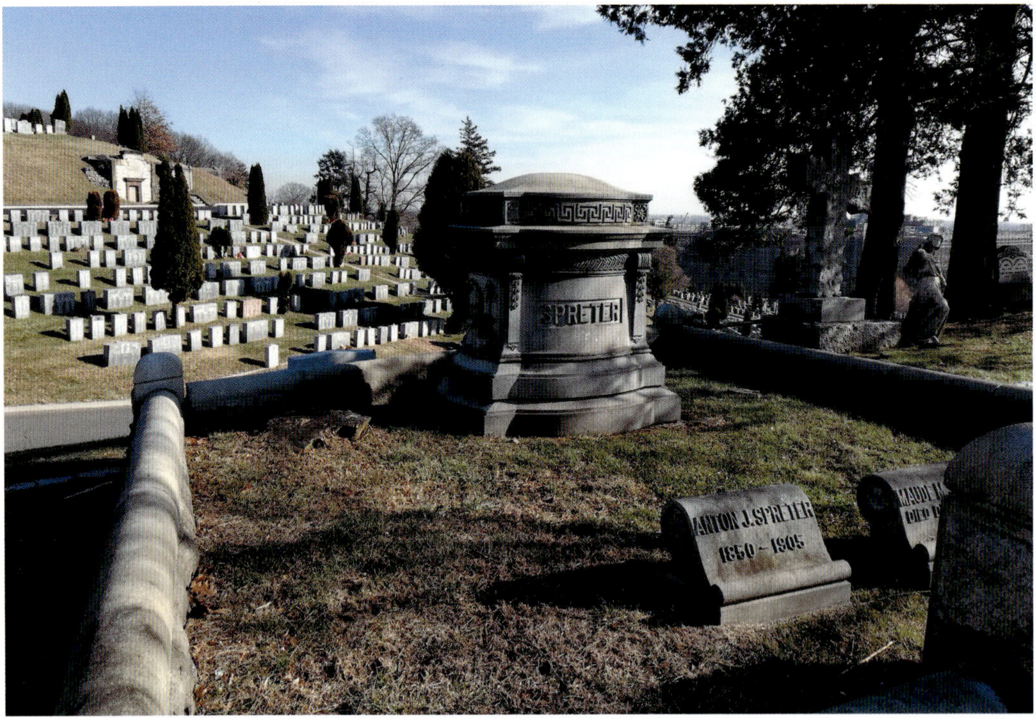

In the foreground, the interesting Spreter family monument. In the background you can see a mausoleum or crypt built into a hill at Cypress Hills.

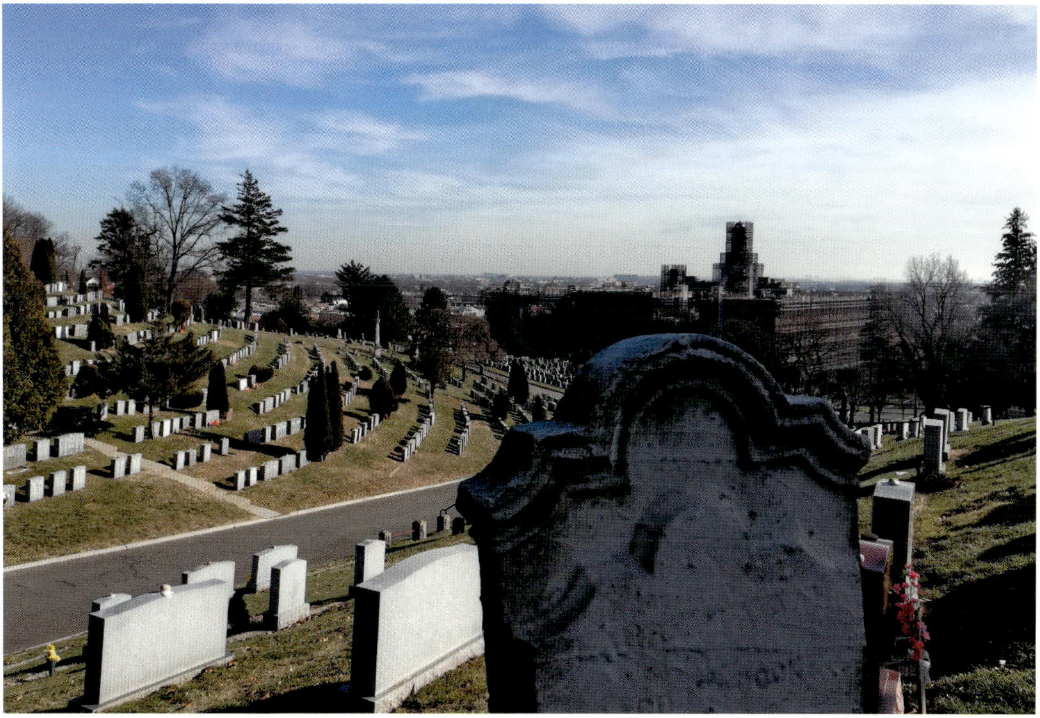

From the higher ground of the cemetery, the visibility is many miles.

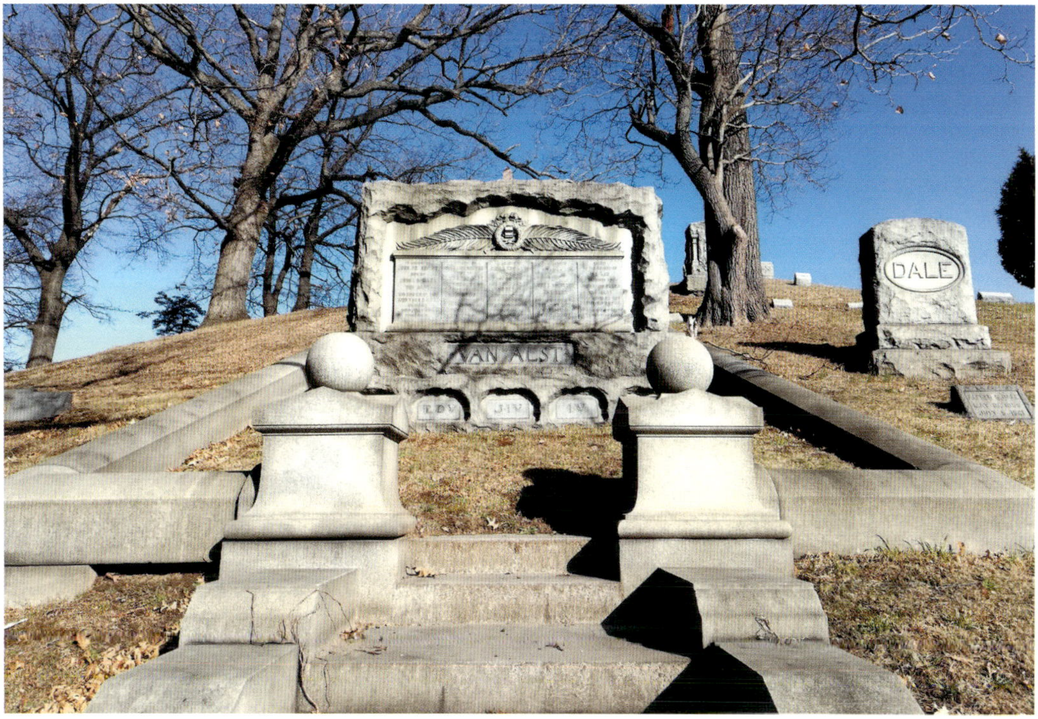

Hills in cemeteries allow for some innovative monument design and layout. Van Alst is an old Queens family; there is a playground by that name in Astoria.

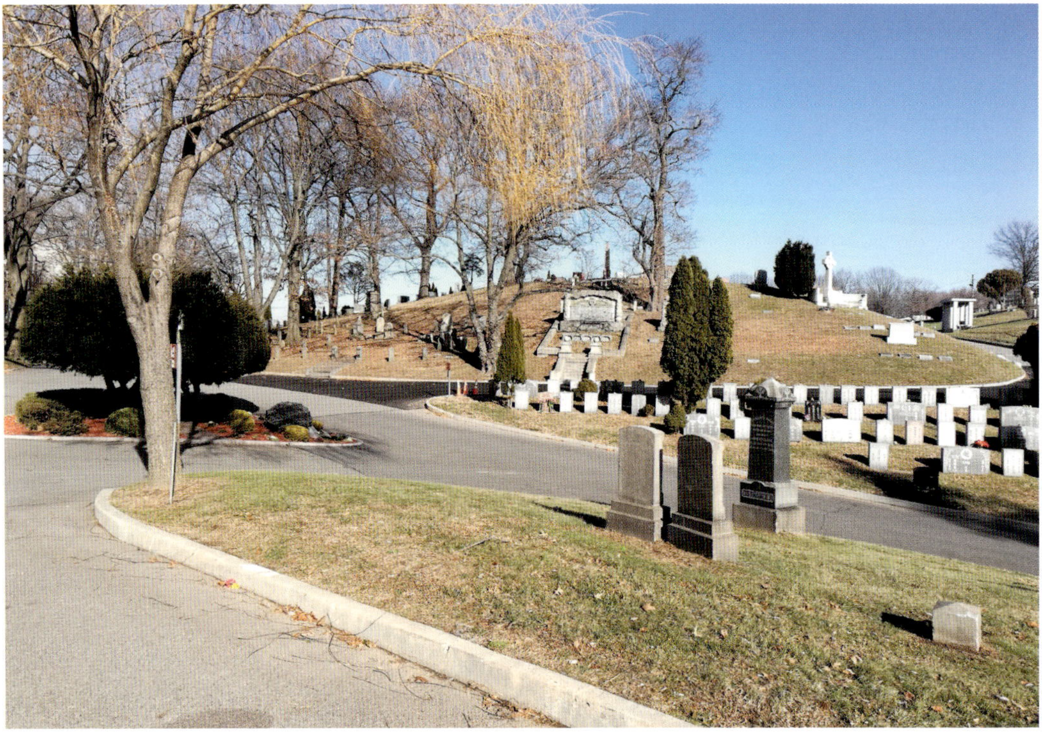

Most cemeteries have at least some evergreens to provide greenery during winter months.

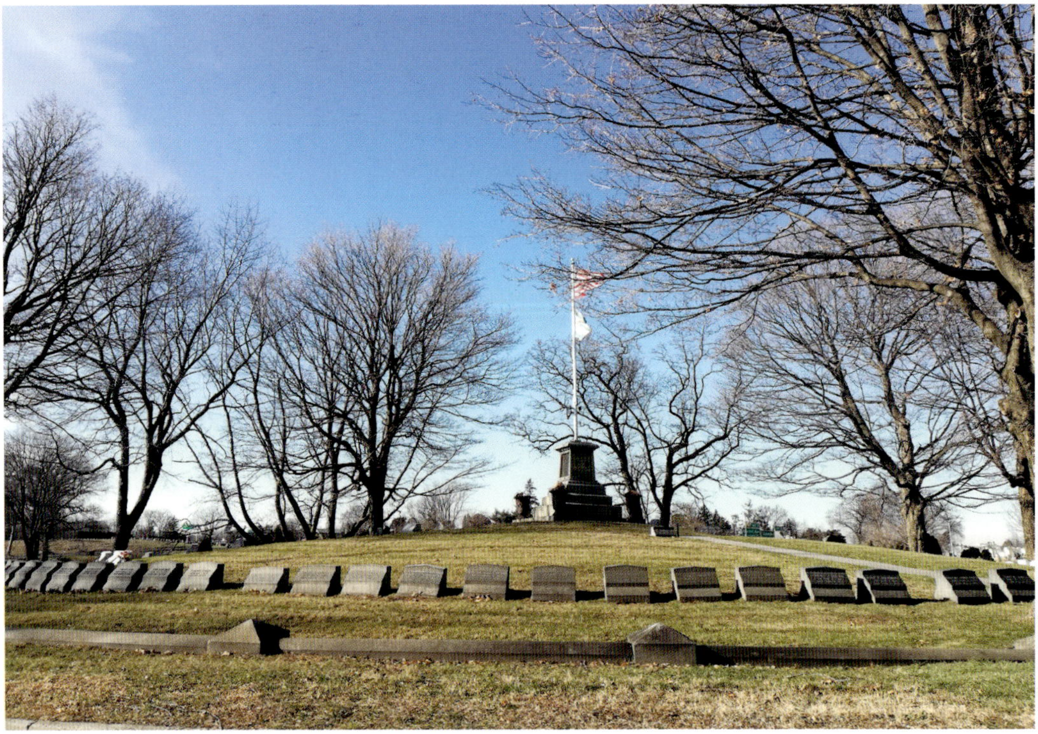

Cypress Hills has numerous interesting gravestone layouts and features.

5

Flushing Cemetery

163-06 46th Ave, Flushing, NY 11358

The 75-acre flower-filled Flushing Cemetery has an undeniable park-like setting, and it is actually just a stone's throw from the sprawling Kissena Park to its south (which had its origins as an eighteenth-century plant nursery). When I visited the cemetery in the month of May, the numerous pink azalea bushes (which are clearly large and quite vintage) were in stunning full bloom. With its entrance at the junction of 46th Avenue and Pidgeon Meadow Road, the cemetery was established in 1853 at a time when many of the first cemeteries in Queens were founded. The two most famous burials among the 41,000 or so here are both musicians: the singer Louis Armstrong, who lived his final years in nearby East Elmhurst, and the jazz trumpet player Dizzy Gillespie.

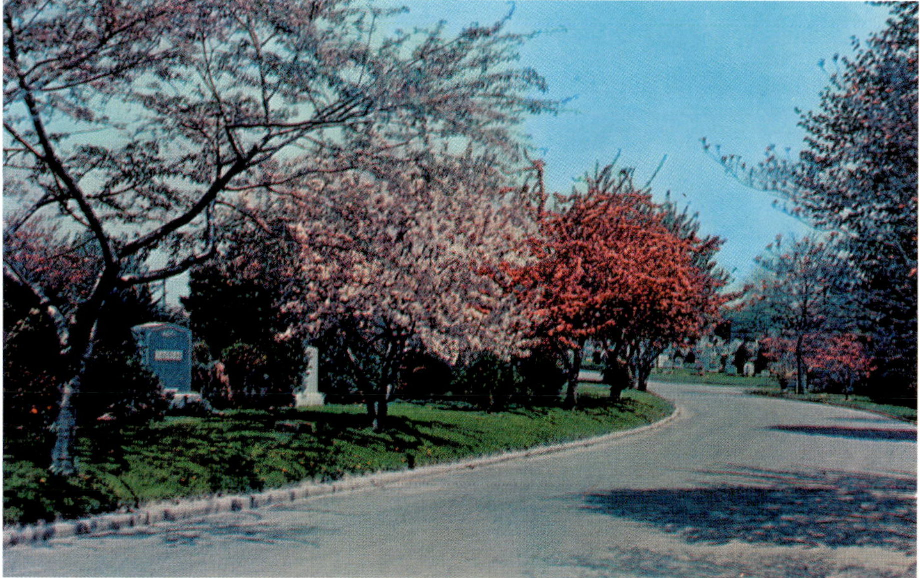

A vintage postcard for the Flushing Cemetery proclaims it as "A Wonderland of a Million Blooms."

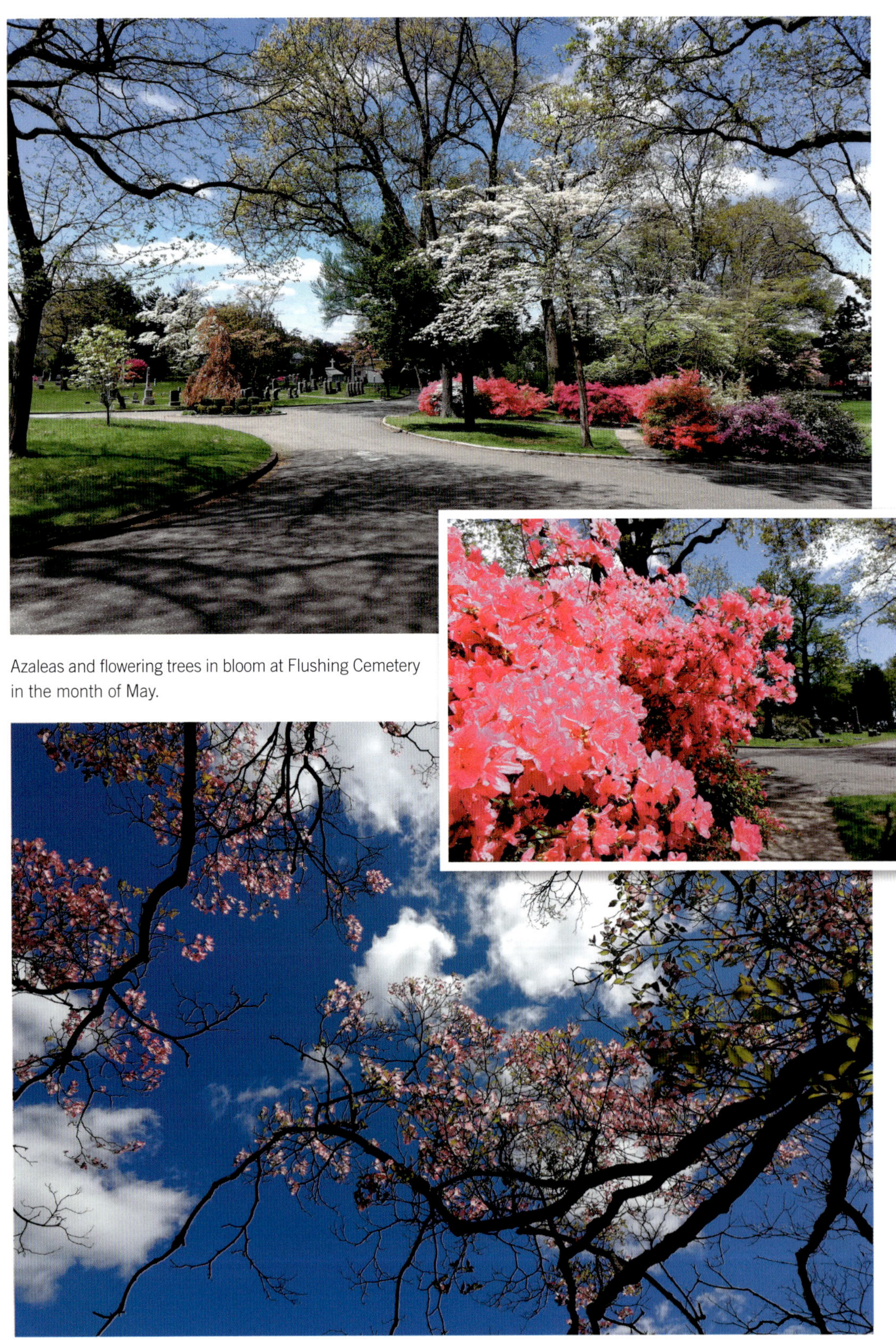

Azaleas and flowering trees in bloom at Flushing Cemetery in the month of May.

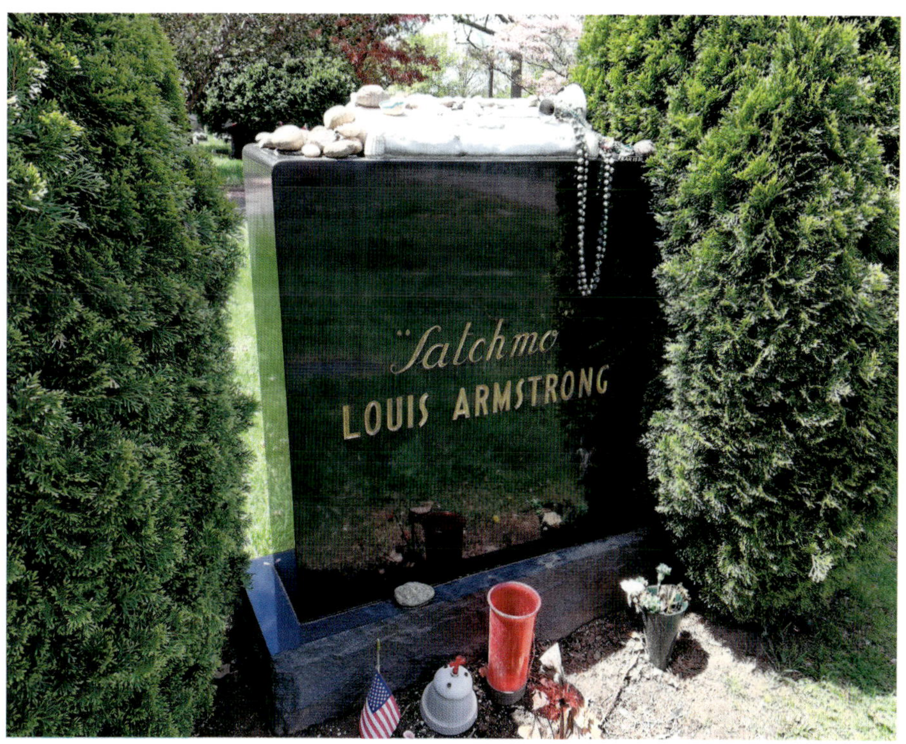

The grave of musician Louis Armstrong gets many visitors.

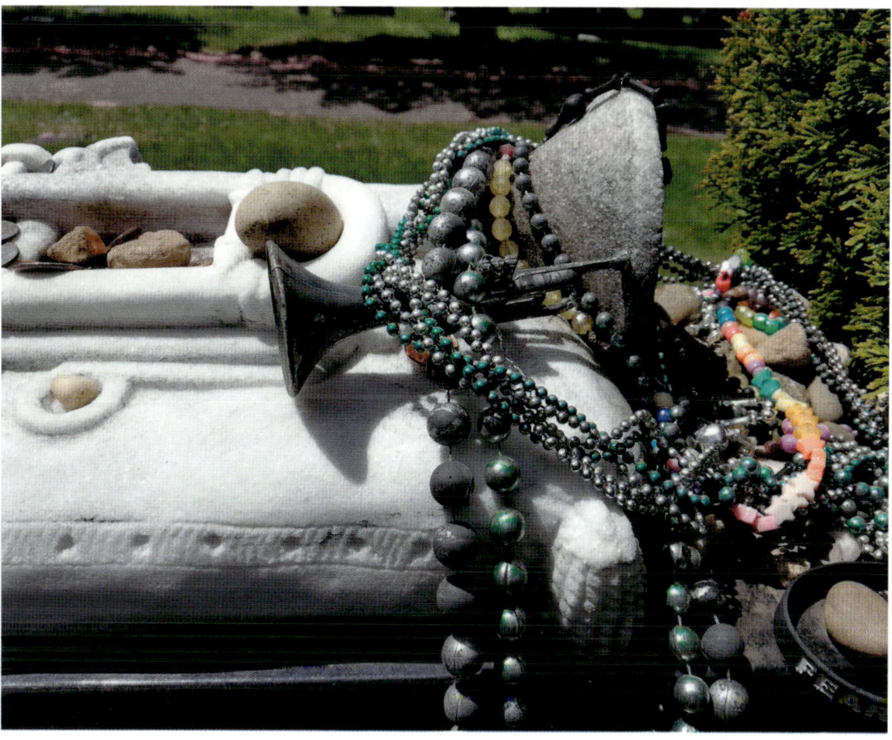

Adornments added by fans on Louis Armstrong's monument.

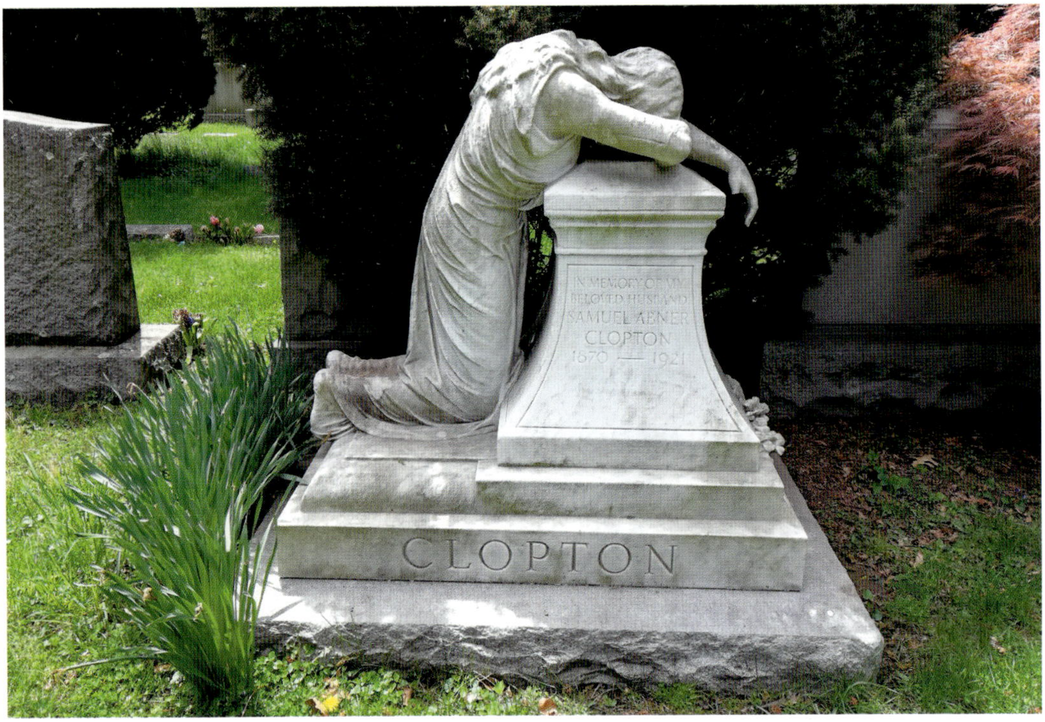

The sheer desolation depicted in some cemetery monuments is touching.

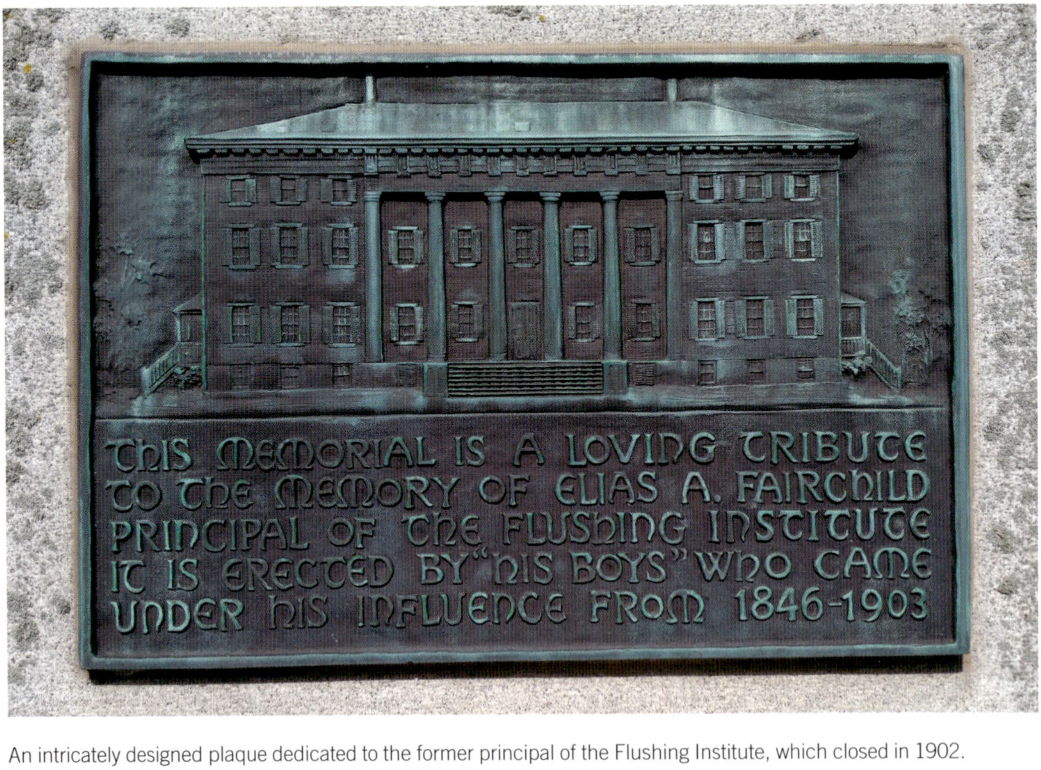

An intricately designed plaque dedicated to the former principal of the Flushing Institute, which closed in 1902. The building depicted was constructed in 1827 and demolished in 1922.

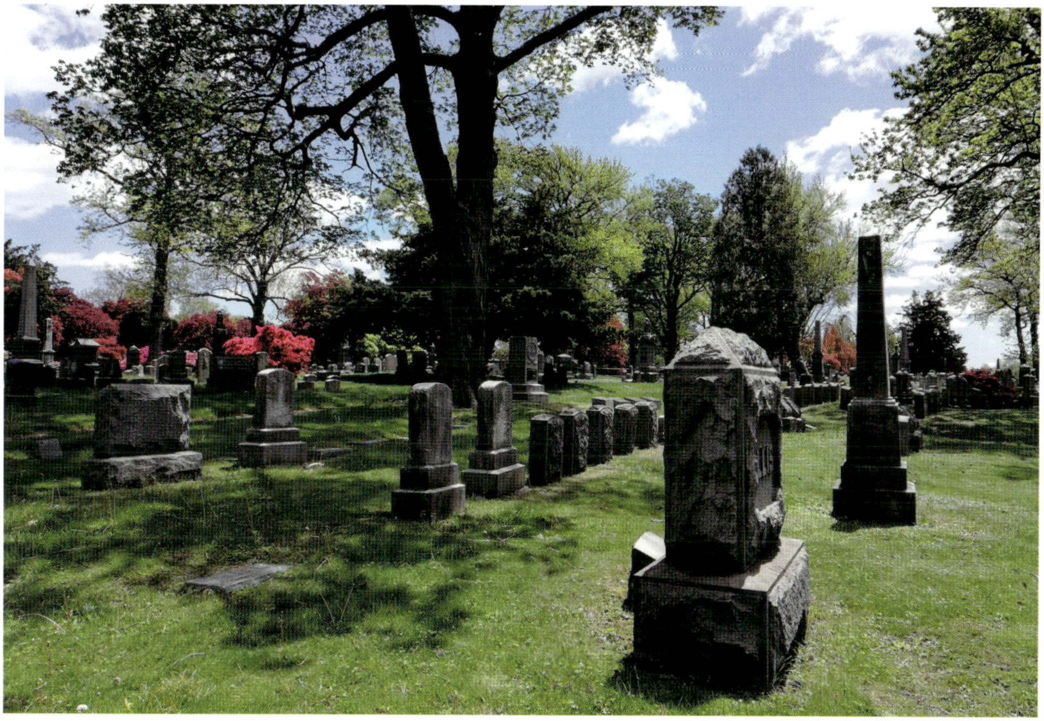

Walking through the cemetery in springtime is a pleasant scene of colorful rebirth.

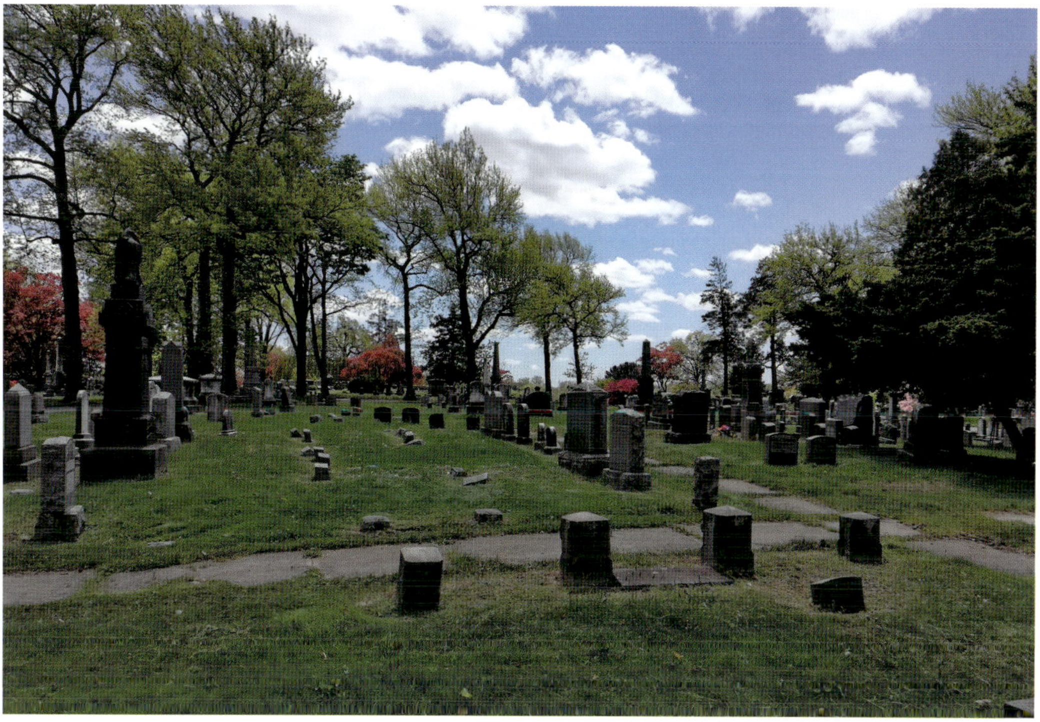

Footpaths lead from the roads deeper into the cemetery.

6

Fresh Pond Crematory and Columbarium

61-40 Mt. Olivet Crescent, Middle Village, NY 11379

Founded in 1884, the Fresh Pond Crematory and Columbarium is located across the street from the All Faiths Cemetery in Middle Village. Per the Fresh Pond website, a columbarium is "a public storage of cinerary urns holding cremated remains. It consists of many niches, or recessed compartments designed to hold urns." Though you may take the cremated remains of your family member with you, the website explains the benefits of purchasing a memorial niche for your urn in their columbarium (and the legal and religious ramifications of scattering ashes; the Catholic Church permits cremation but not scattering of ashes). There are over 40,000 remains within the columbarium, with plenty of space for more. The most famous person memorialized at Fresh Pond is Ring Lardner, Sr., author and screenwriter and father of Ring Lardner, Jr.

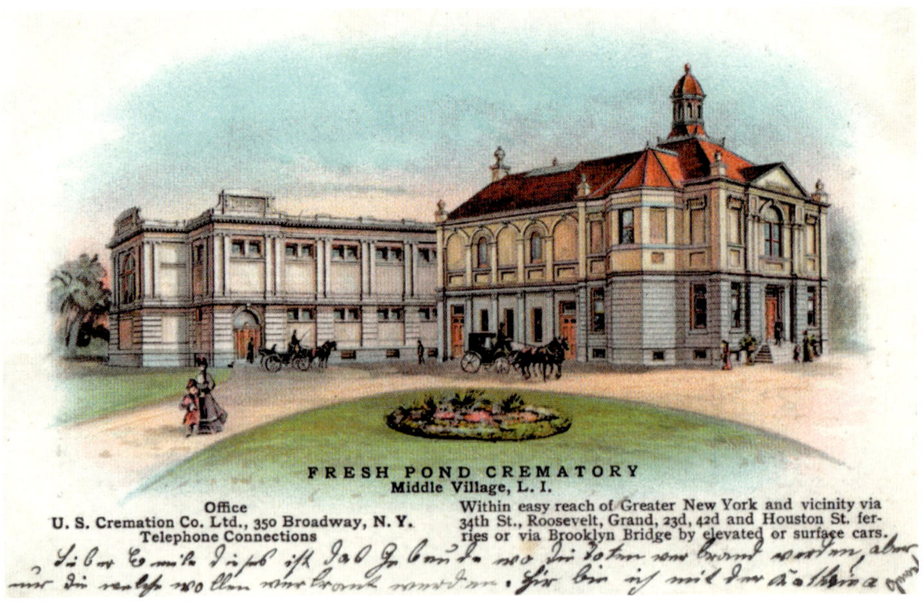

A *circa*-1900 postcard of the Fresh Pond Crematory with writing in German on the bottom. The card was addressed to an Emile Loeffler in St. Ludwig, Germany.

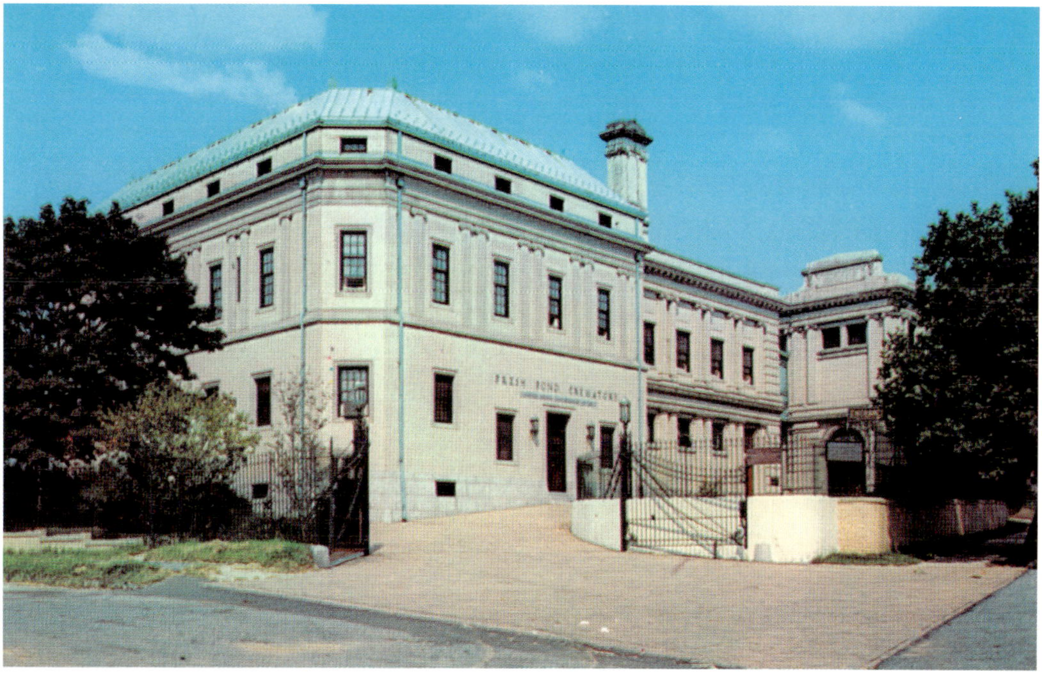

A *circa*-1960s image of the crematory.

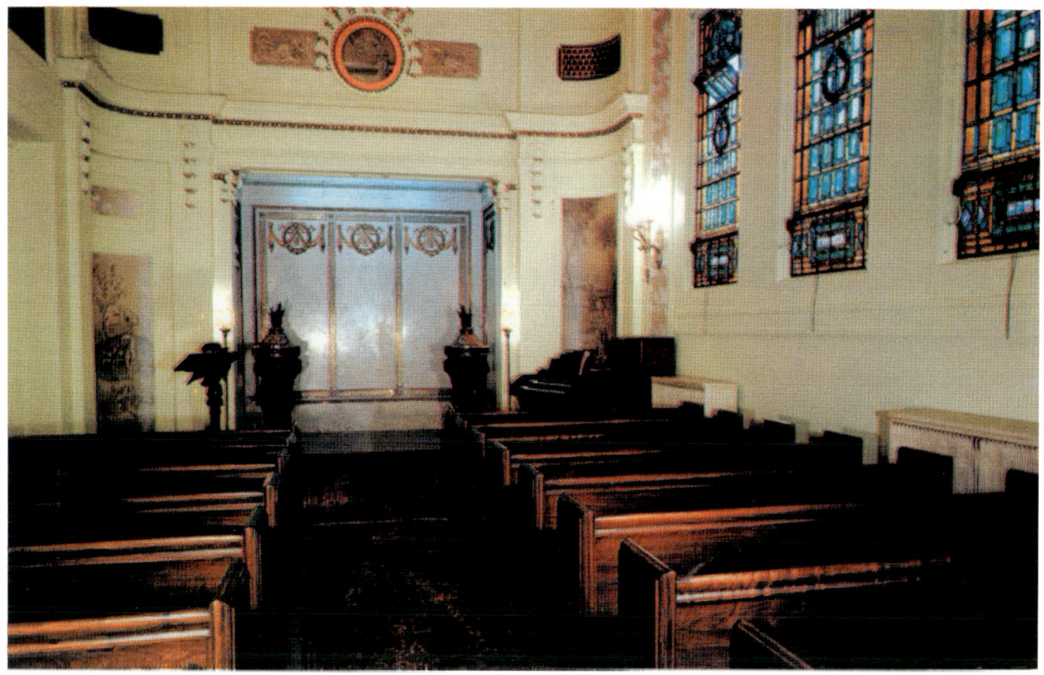

A *circa*-1960s image of the chapel inside the crematory.

7

Friends Meeting House Cemetery

137-16 Northern Blvd, Flushing, NY 11354

In the heart of historic downtown Flushing, the Friends Meetinghouse on Northern Boulevard is a throwback to seventeenth-century Queens. Like some other local Quaker meetinghouses, this one has a burial ground on the property. In this case, the burial ground came first, in the 1670s, followed by the house in 1694. The graveyard closed to new burials at the end of the nineteenth century. The prominent early Queens citizen John Bowne is believed to be buried with at least sixteen other Bowne family members here, as are other early Queens Quakers such as members of the Titus and Willets families.

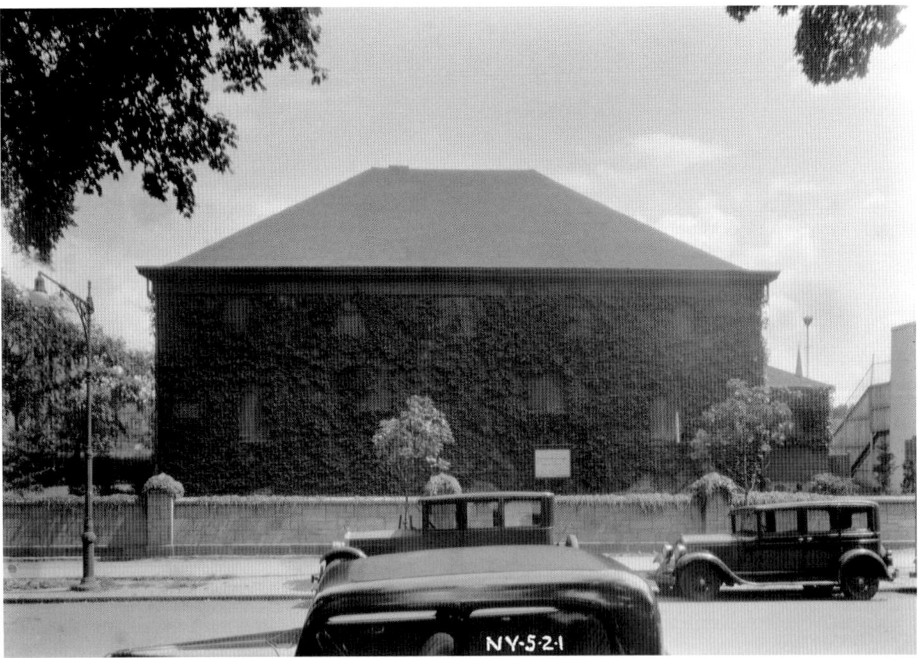

The ivy-covered Friends Meetinghouse in a 1936 photo.

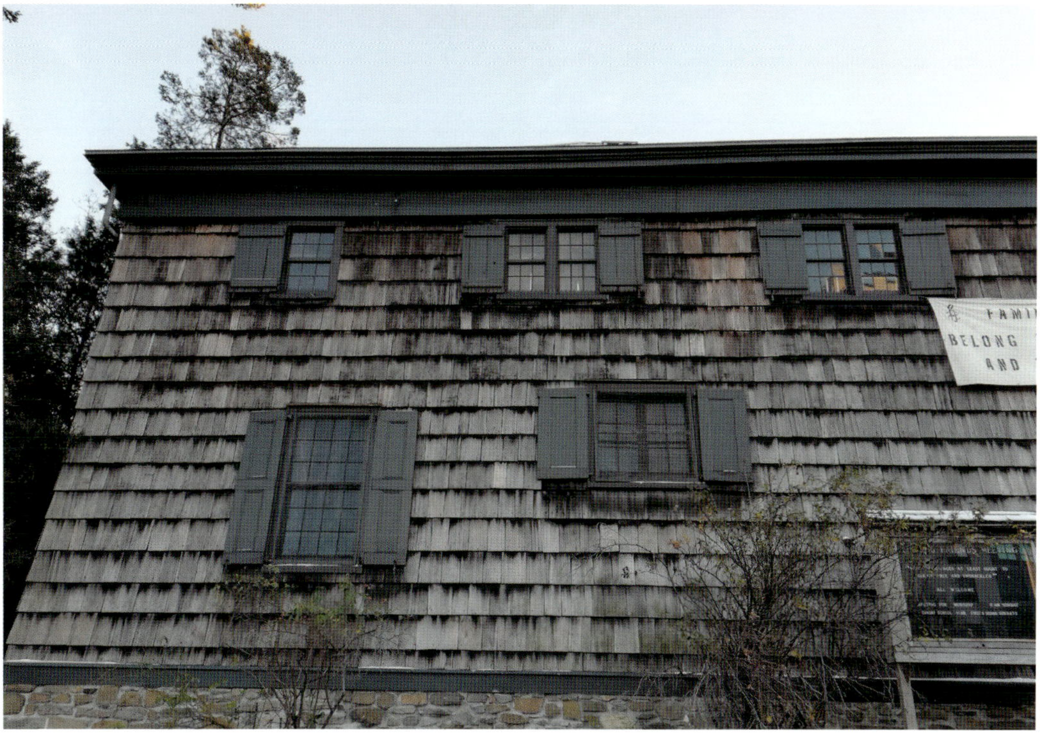

Fast forward to 2019 and the building looks much cleaner.

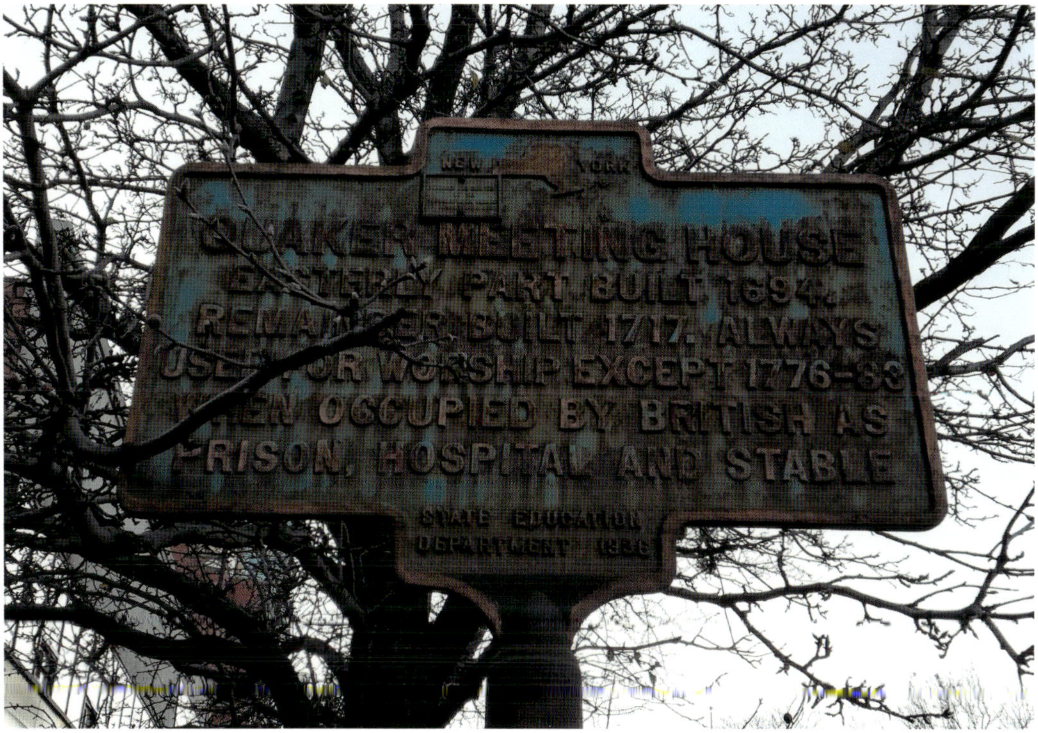

A 1936 historic marker in front of the old building.

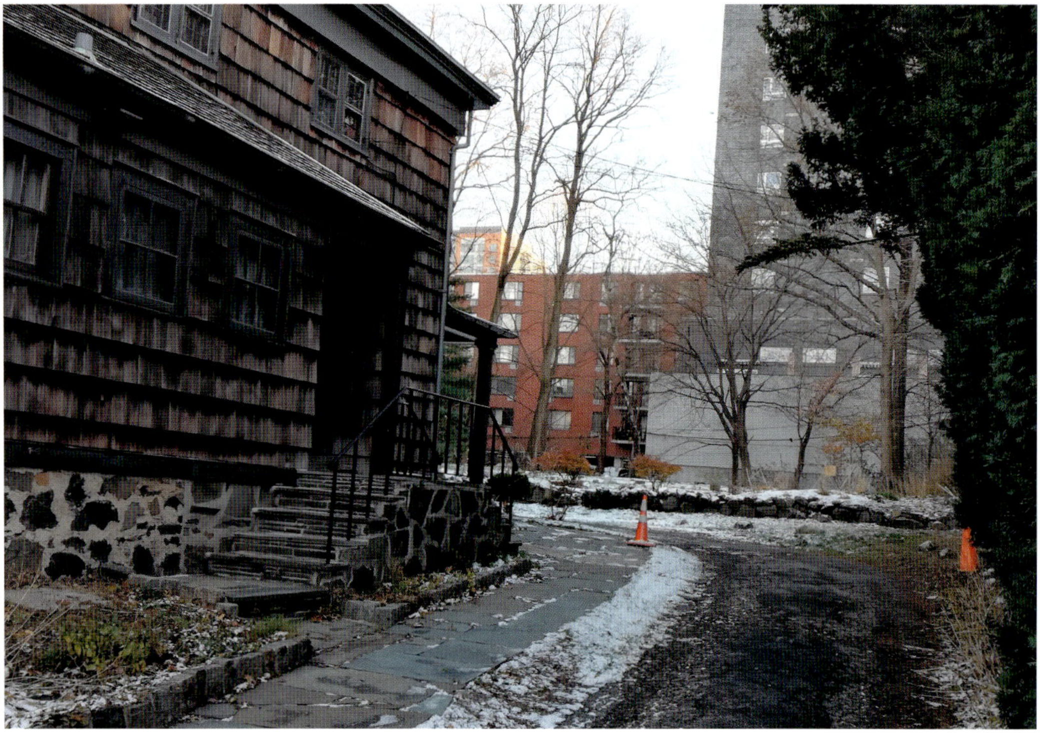

The old cemetery lies behind the building, barely visible from the sidewalk.

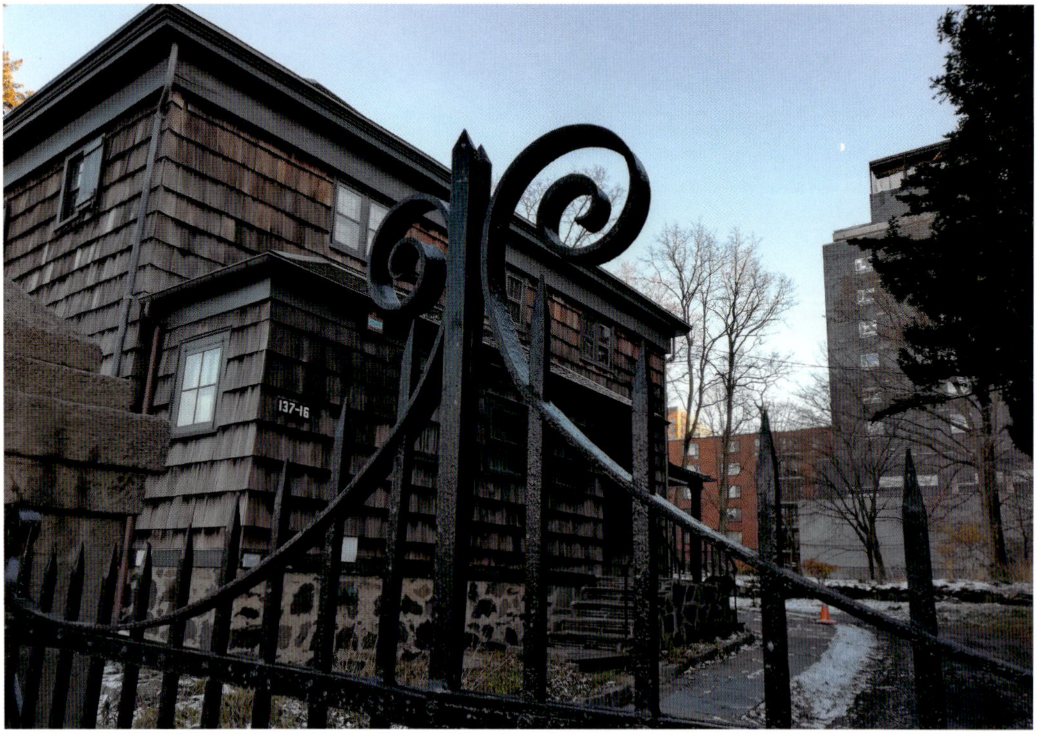

An old iron fence fronts the property.

8

Grace Church Cemetery

155-15 Jamaica Ave, Jamaica, NY 11434

One of the oldest cemeteries in Queens (or all of New York City for that matter) is tucked away in the heart of downtown Jamaica, next to the 1862 Gothic-style Grace Episcopal Church on Jamaica Avenue (not the original building on the site). It is also one of the few remaining churchyard cemeteries in Queens. Rufus King, signer of the Constitution and Jamaica resident (he lived across the street and his home still stands today as a museum) is buried at the Grace Cemetery, as is his son, John Alsop King, governor of New York from 1857-1859. Other important New Yorkers are here, too, such as Cadwallader Colden, mayor of New York City from 1818-1821. The gravestones date from the early eighteenth century to the twentieth century, with the older ones toward the front of the church. Many are faded and hard to read, but there are several fine examples of eighteenth-century stones (among the finest existing in New York City), with a variety of cherub heads. Some stones have poems, including this one on a stone from 1738:

> External bliss shall innocence enjoy, & endless pleasures which can never cloy, while here entombed a virtuous youth doth rest, in certain hoped of being completely blessed.

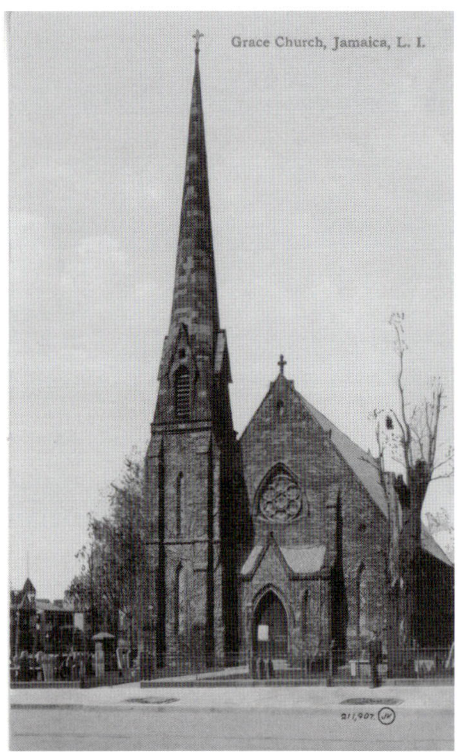

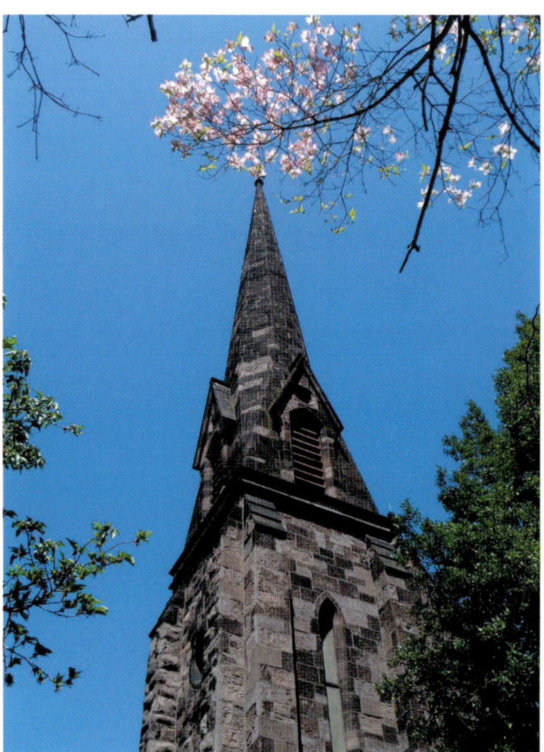

Above left: An early twentieth-century photo postcard of Grace Church and cemetery.
Above right: The church steeple today is an impressive throwback in the heart of downtown Jamaica.

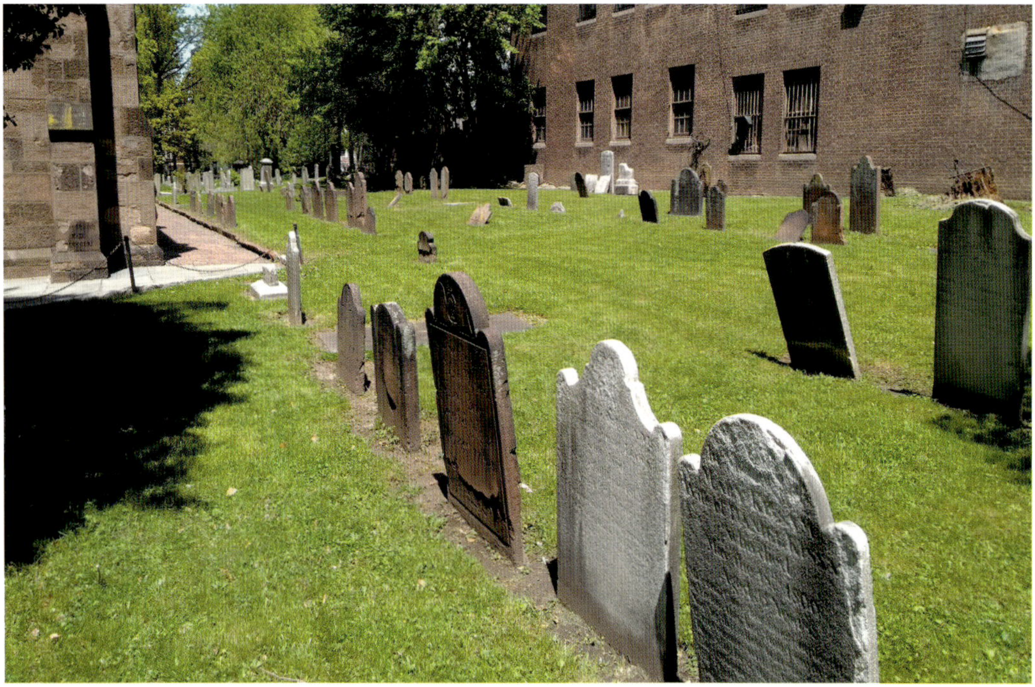

An impressive array of ancient gravestones surrounds the church.

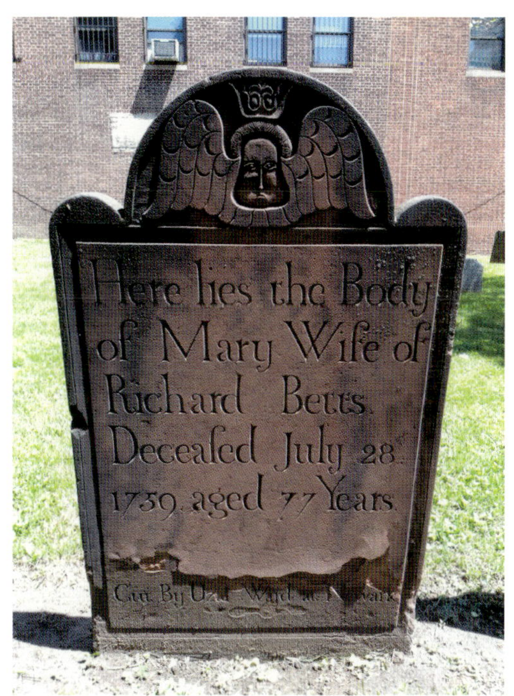

Impressively large, crisp lettering on this 1759 gravestone for Mary Betts.

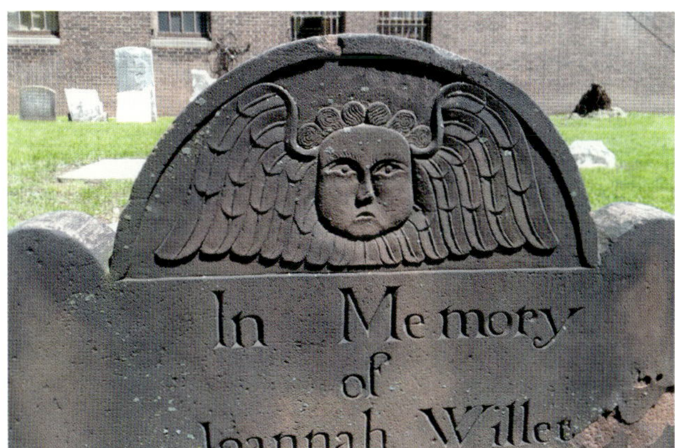

The winged cherub was a popular eighteenth-century gravestone detail.

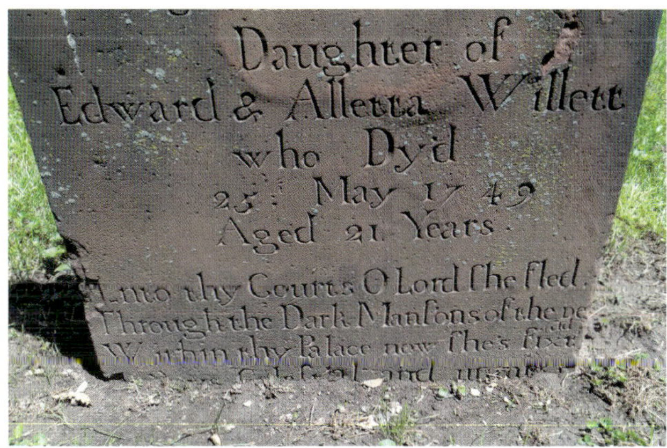

A partly legible poem carved into a 1749 gravestone.

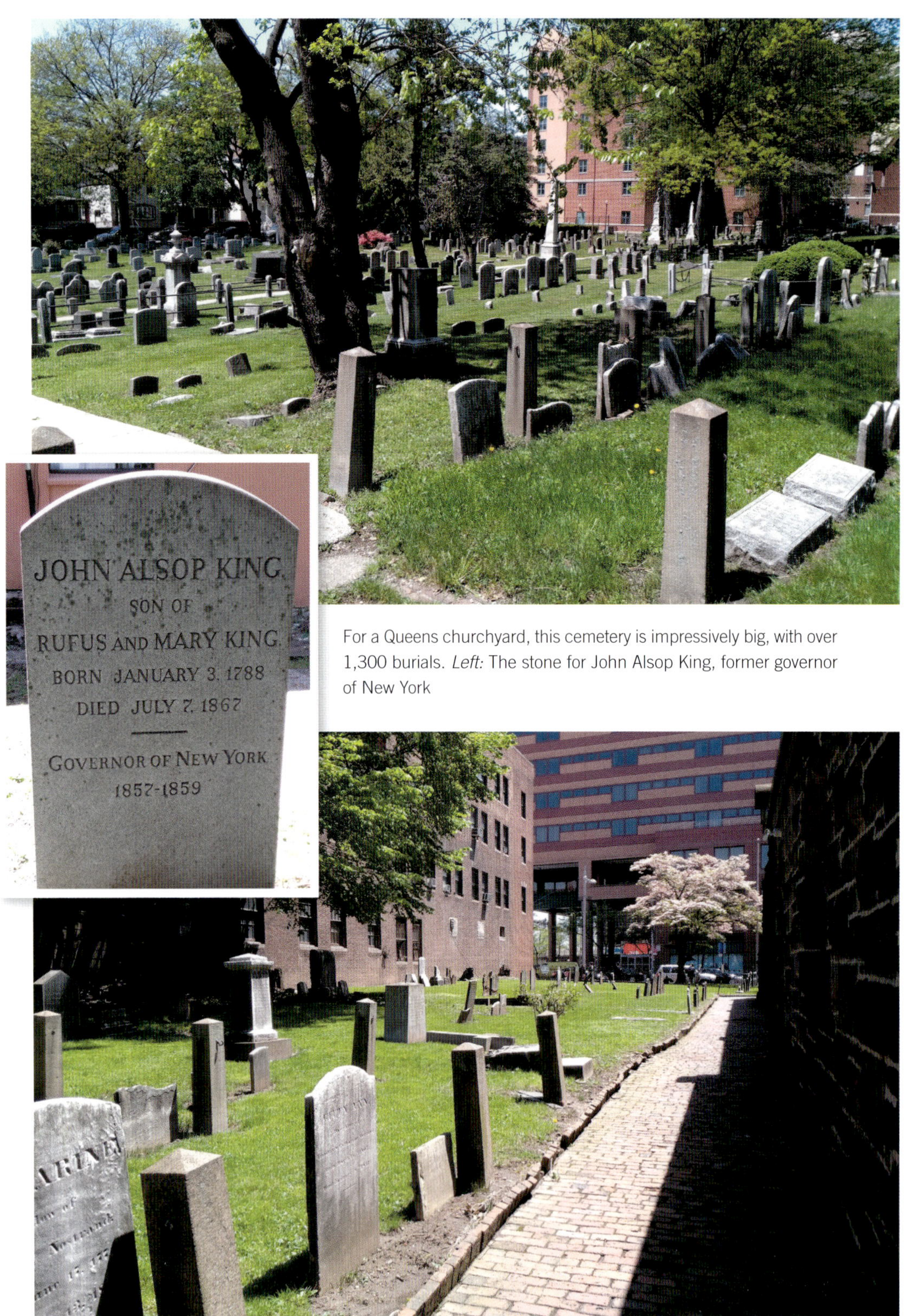

For a Queens churchyard, this cemetery is impressively big, with over 1,300 burials. *Left:* The stone for John Alsop King, former governor of New York

Gravestones sit very close to the old brick path around the church.

9

Johnson Family Cemetery

Adjacent to 226-15 Kingsbury Avenue, Oakland Gardens, NY 11364

The remains of the former Long Island Motor Parkway meander through Alley Pond Park and Cunningham Park. When the parkway, the country's first modern highway (which extended from Queens through Nassau and Suffolk counties), closed in 1938, New York City acquired the right of way in Queens and reused a miles-long section as a bicycle path, pretty much intact. Aside from some fairly bucolic scenery, the abandoned highway offers a glimpse of what was once an old quarter-acre family cemetery. Climbing up the embankment to the fencing, you can see the scrub area where there are several unmarked burials of members of a nineteenth-century African American family. The property is adjacent to Alley Pond Park, and though owned by New York City, not part of it.

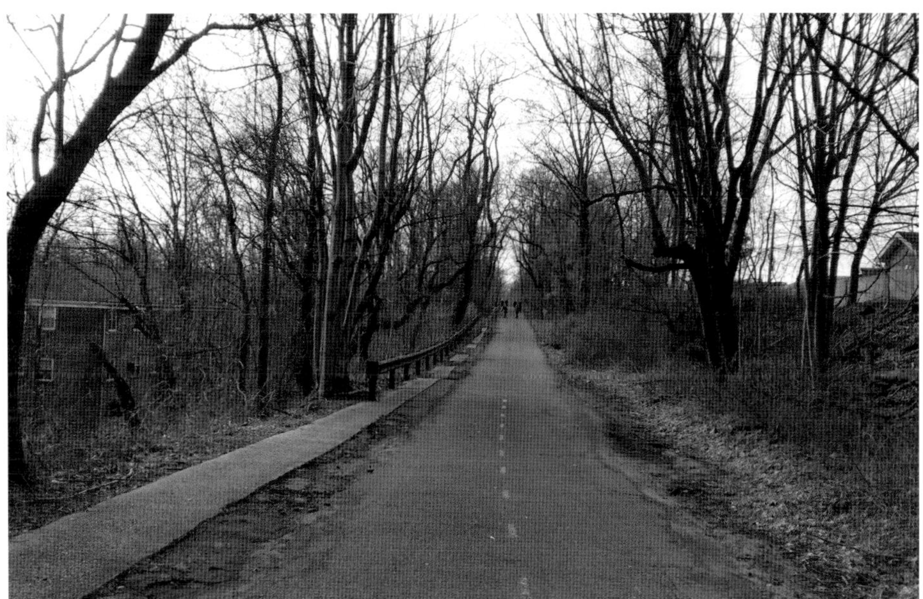

The former Long Island Motor Parkway has been preserved in Alley Pond Park. Directly adjacent to it lies an old unmarked family cemetery.

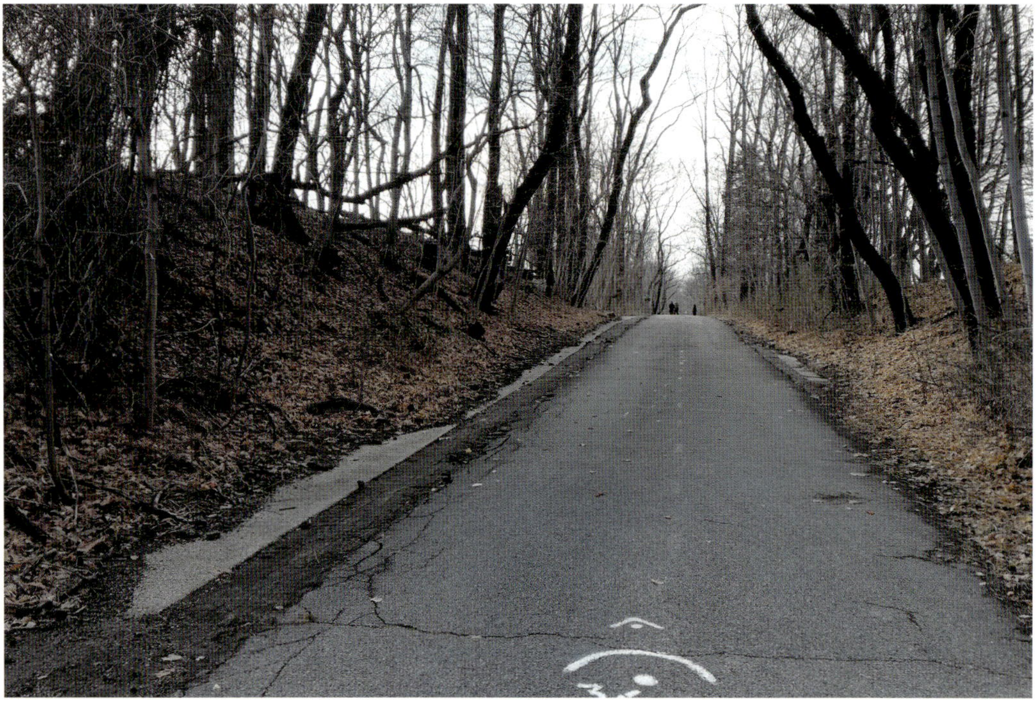

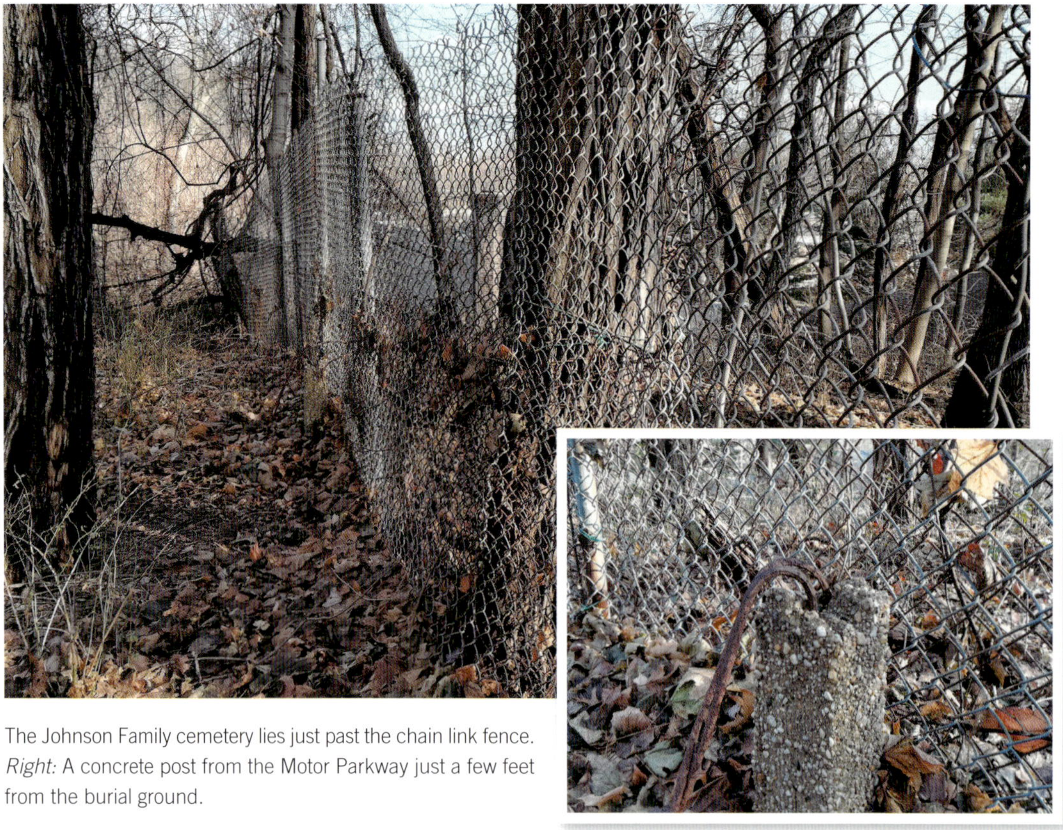

The Johnson Family cemetery lies just past the chain link fence. *Right:* A concrete post from the Motor Parkway just a few feet from the burial ground.

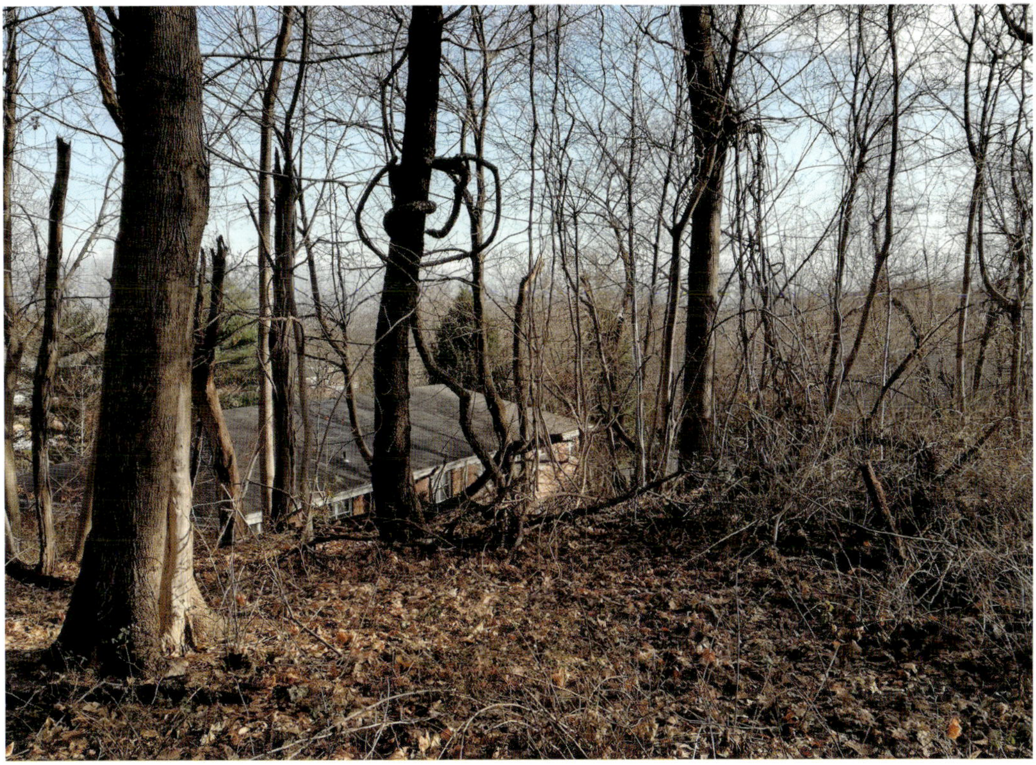

Two views of the burial ground, which is on high ground adjacent to an apartment complex. No grave markers remain.

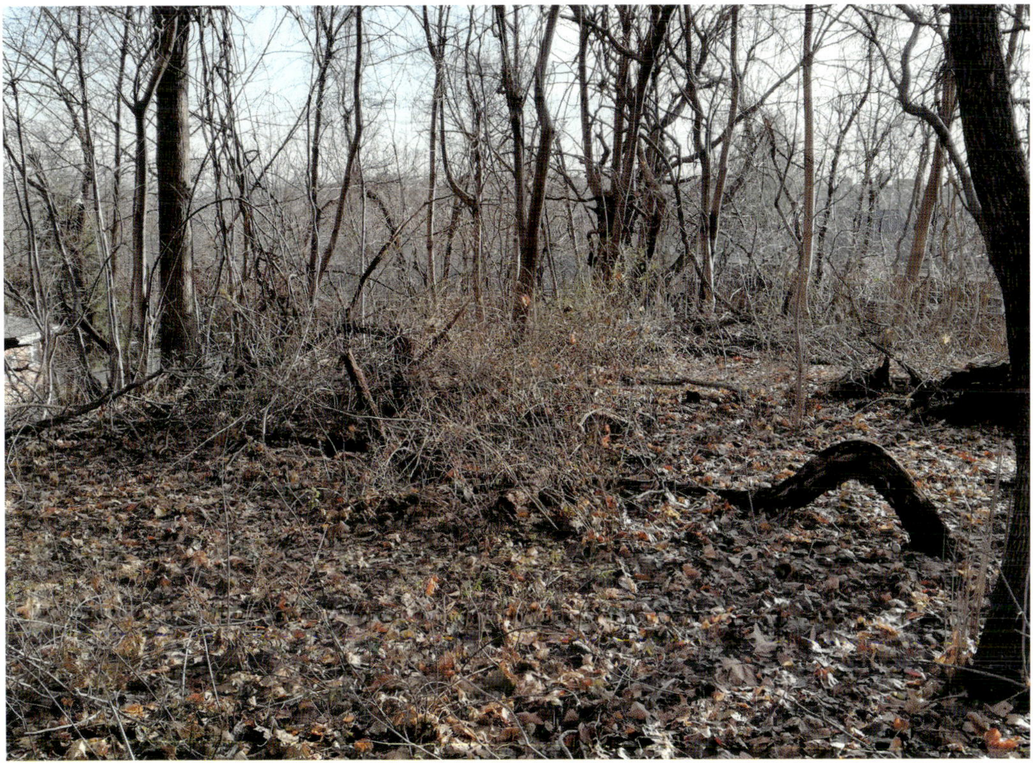

10

Lawrence Cemetery

20th Road, Astoria, NY 11105

One of the oldest cemeteries in New York City is tucked away in the northern reaches of Astoria, between 35th and 36th Streets on 20th Road, which itself is a vestige—a curving thoroughfare that breaks out of the grid around it. The road is a remnant of the old Bowery Bay Road from colonial times, as is the cemetery. Set aside in 1654 by Major Thomas Lawrence, who had recently emigrated from England, the private walled cemetery has about 100 burials, all of them members of the Lawrence family, starting in 1703 with Thomas Lawrence himself. Lawrence family members who actually are buried here include Abraham Lawrence Riker, Justice of the New York State Supreme Court; Isaac Lawrence, president of the United States Bank; Major Jonathan Lawrence, Revolutionary War veteran who helped General Washington obtain additional forces for the Army and a member of the New York Provincial Congress; and Brigadier General Albert Gallatin Lawrence, a Civil War hero. The Lawrences intermarried with other famous Queens families and the names on the stones reflect that heritage: Riker, Suydam, Rapelye. The half-acre cemetery was designated as a NYC Landmark in 1966.

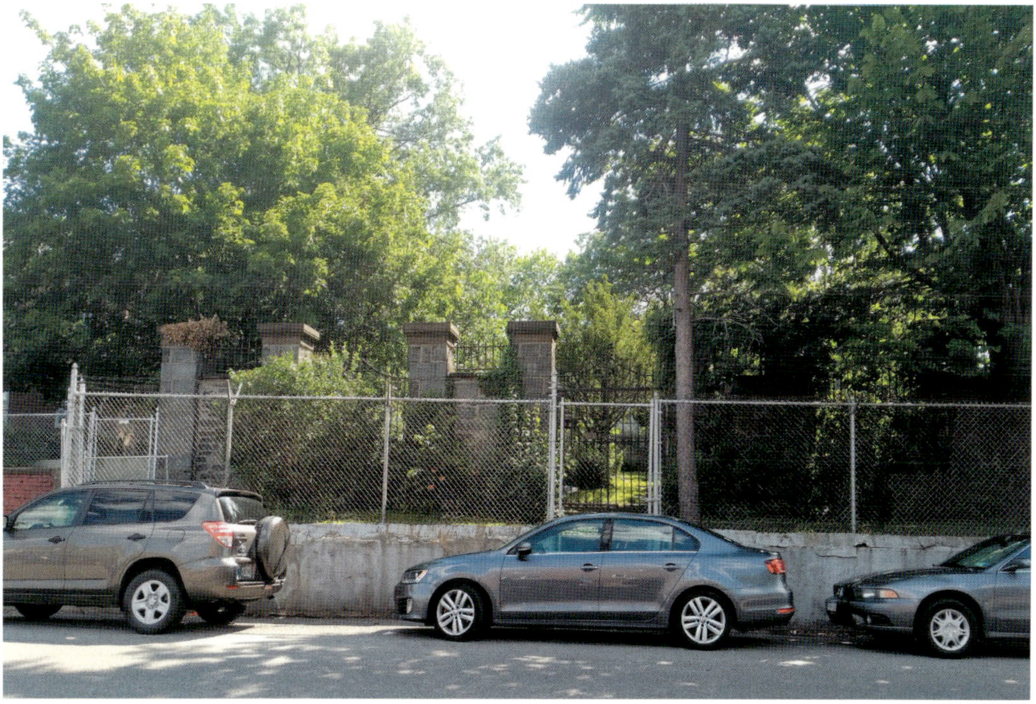

The Lawrence Cemetery is on private property in Astoria, behind a high chain link fence.

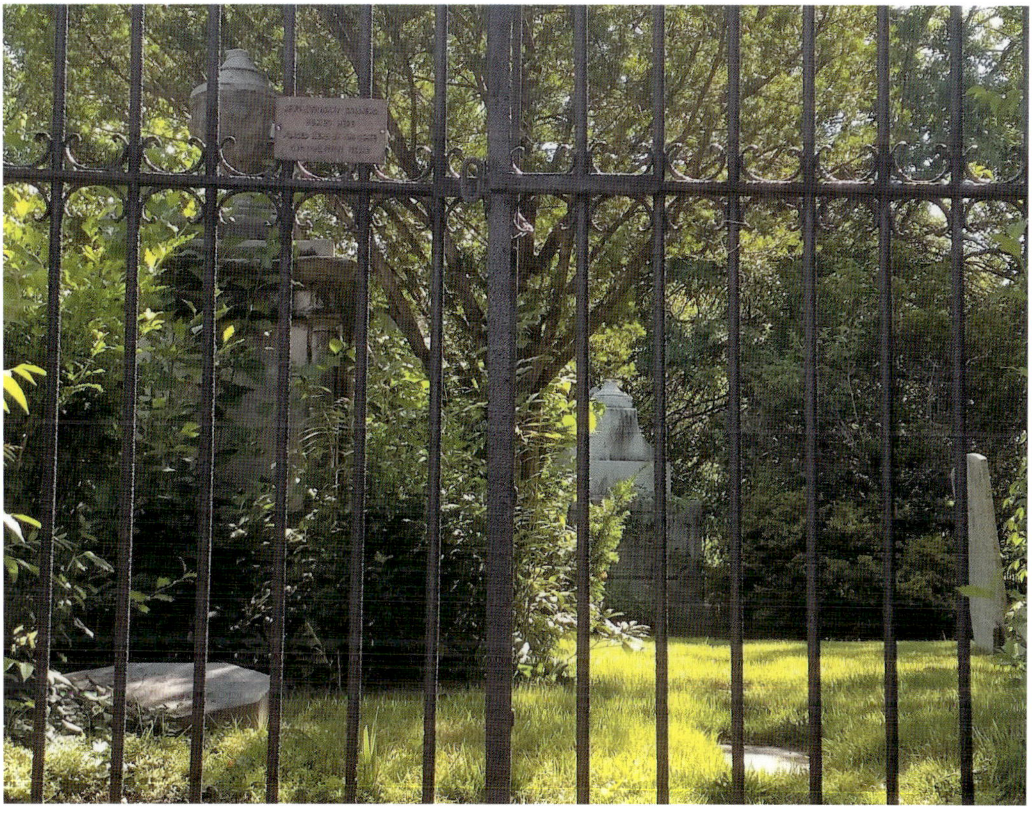

11

Maple Grove Cemetery

127-15 Kew Gardens Rd, Kew Gardens, NY 11415

With entrances located off Queens Boulevard and Kew Gardens Road in Kew Gardens, Maple Grove is a beautiful place. It's also probably the first cemetery I ever visited, to pay my respects at my grandfather's grave. The location, under the shade of a big old tree not far from the entrance, always struck me as an ideal place. The 65-acre cemetery was founded in 1875 and offers, according to their website, "a tranquil rural setting with gentle hills, majestic shade trees and a vibrant lake." That is actually an amazing thing about some of the cemeteries in Queens—they transport the visitor away from the bustle of the borough and into a separate peaceful world. Maple Grove is very beautiful, and surrounded on three sides by a residential neighborhood. The non-sectarian cemetery has a diverse array of famous burials ranging from some local political and business names like Archer and Sutphin, to Elisabeth Riis (wife of Jacob Riis), Civil War heroes, Sam Lloyd (America's Puzzle King), and a pair of noted Russian pianists.

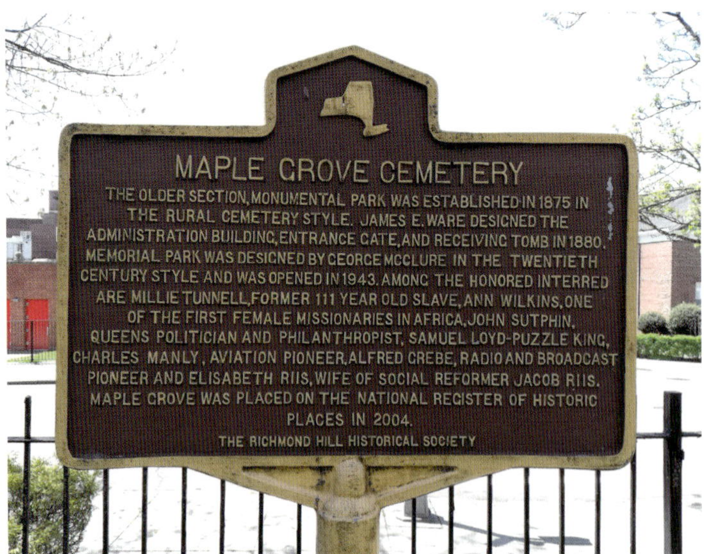

A sign placed at the entrance to Maple Grove by the Richmond Hill Historical Society explains some of the historical highlights.

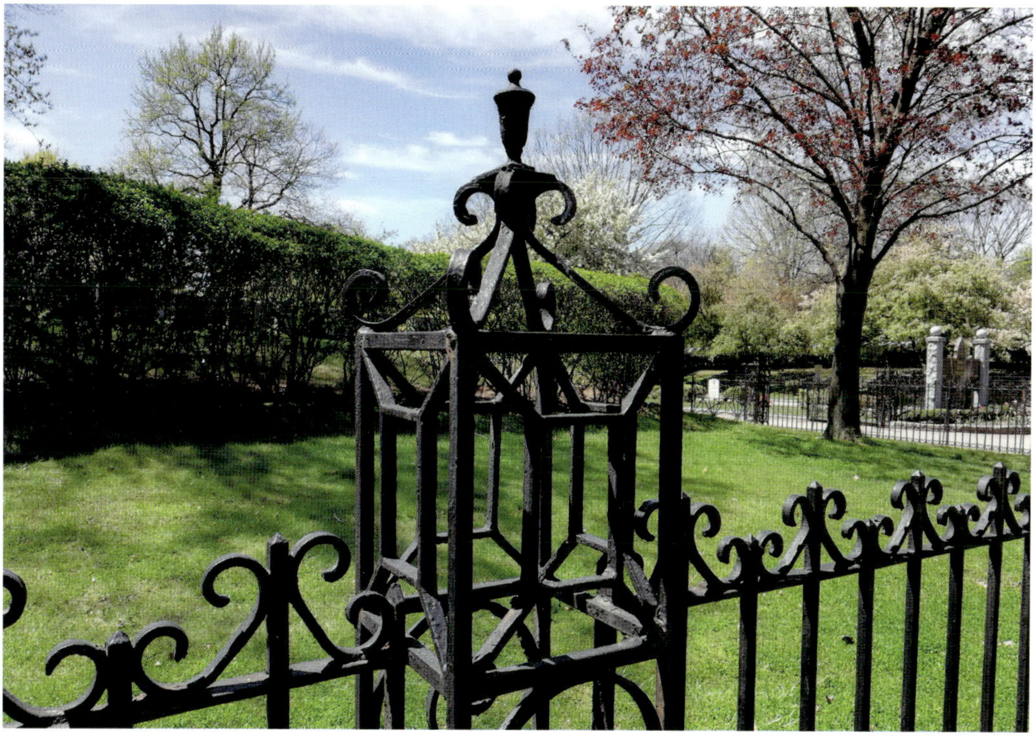

Ornate vintage iron fencing along Queens Boulevard.

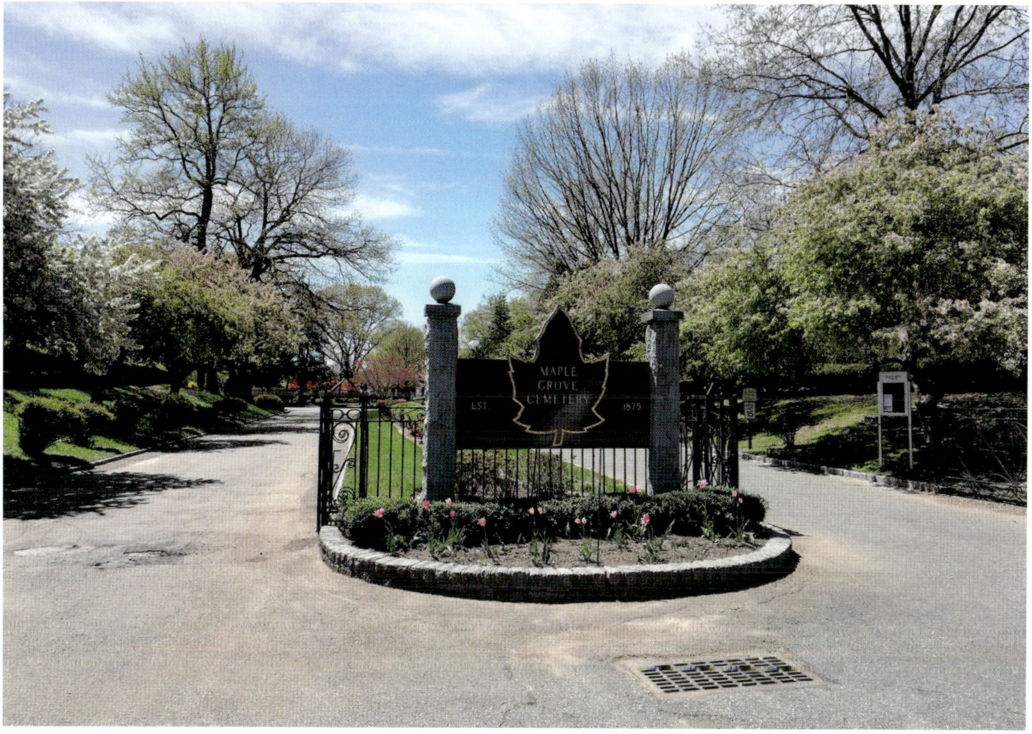

The main entrance to Maple Grove, on Queens Boulevard.

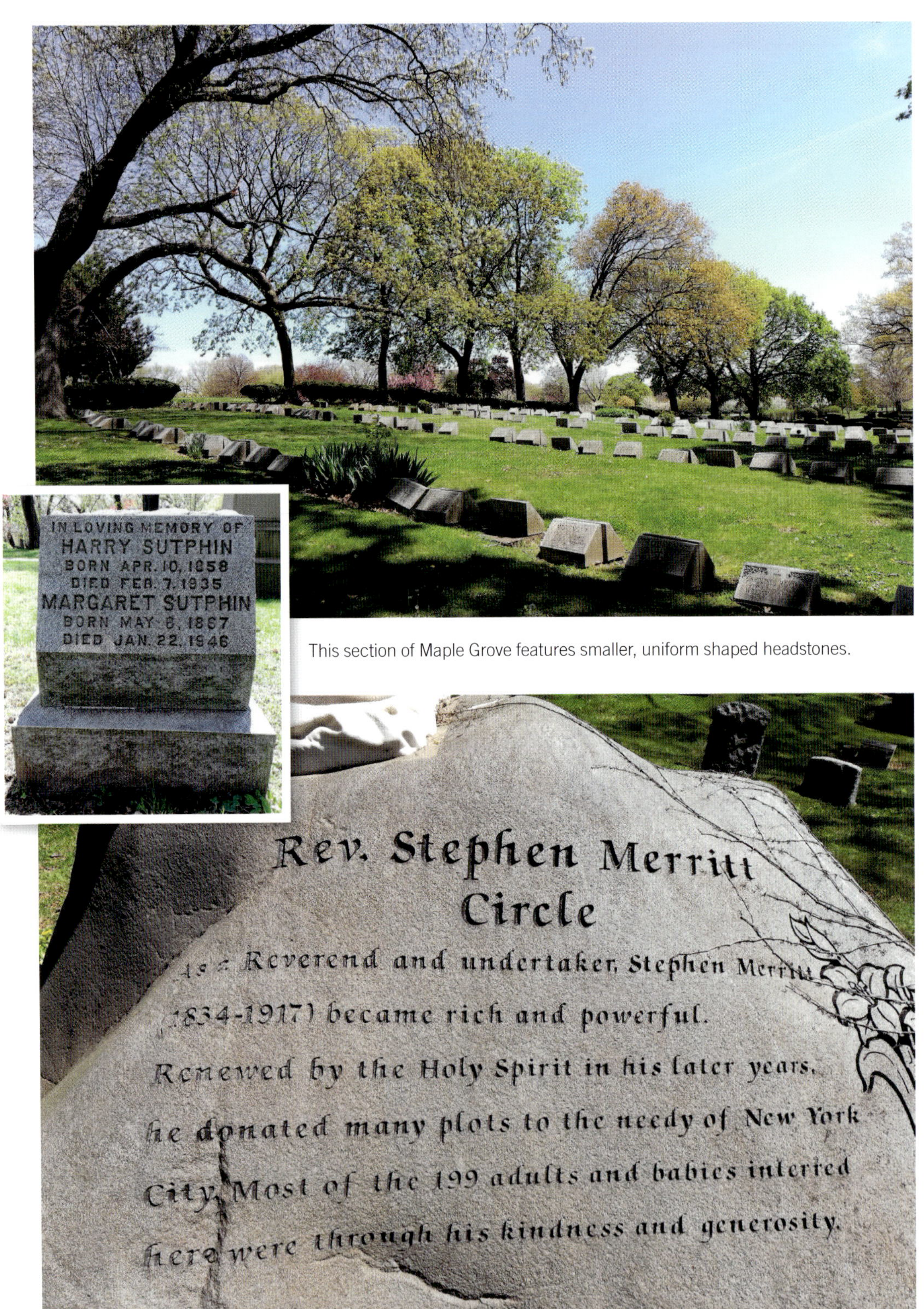

This section of Maple Grove features smaller, uniform shaped headstones.

A monument to Rev. Stephen Merritt, who paid for the burials of 199 poor adults and babies in Maple Grove. *Inset:* A headstone for members of the Sutphin family, after whom Sutphin Boulevard in Jamaica is named.

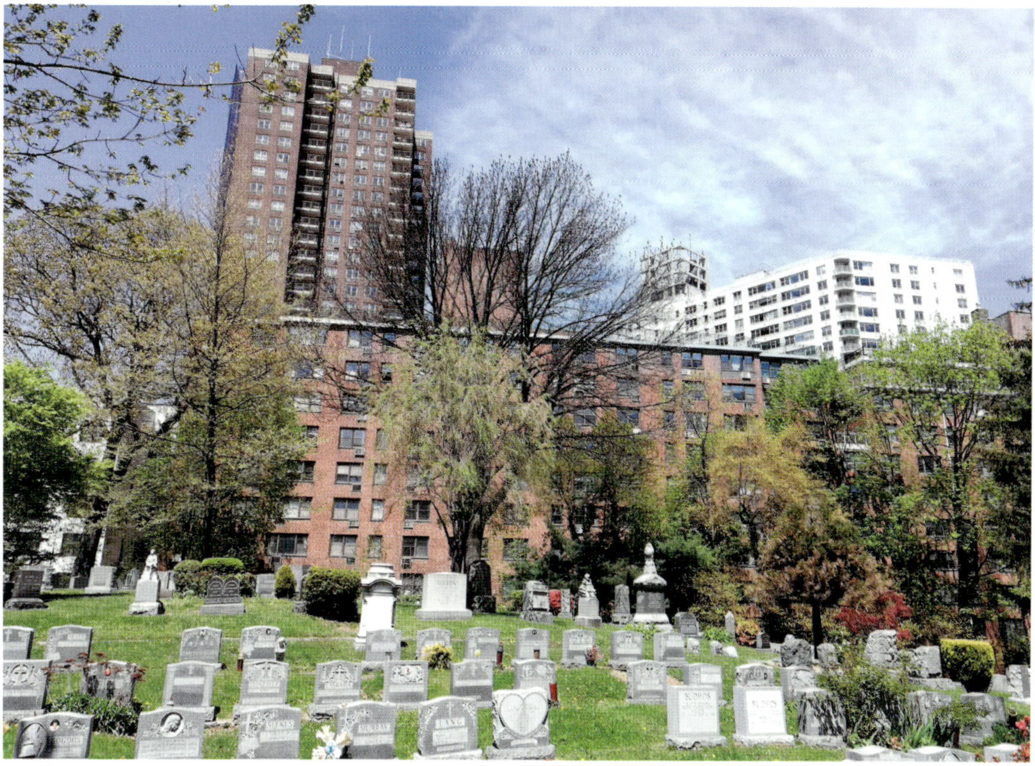

Parts of Maple Grove are across the street from apartment buildings.

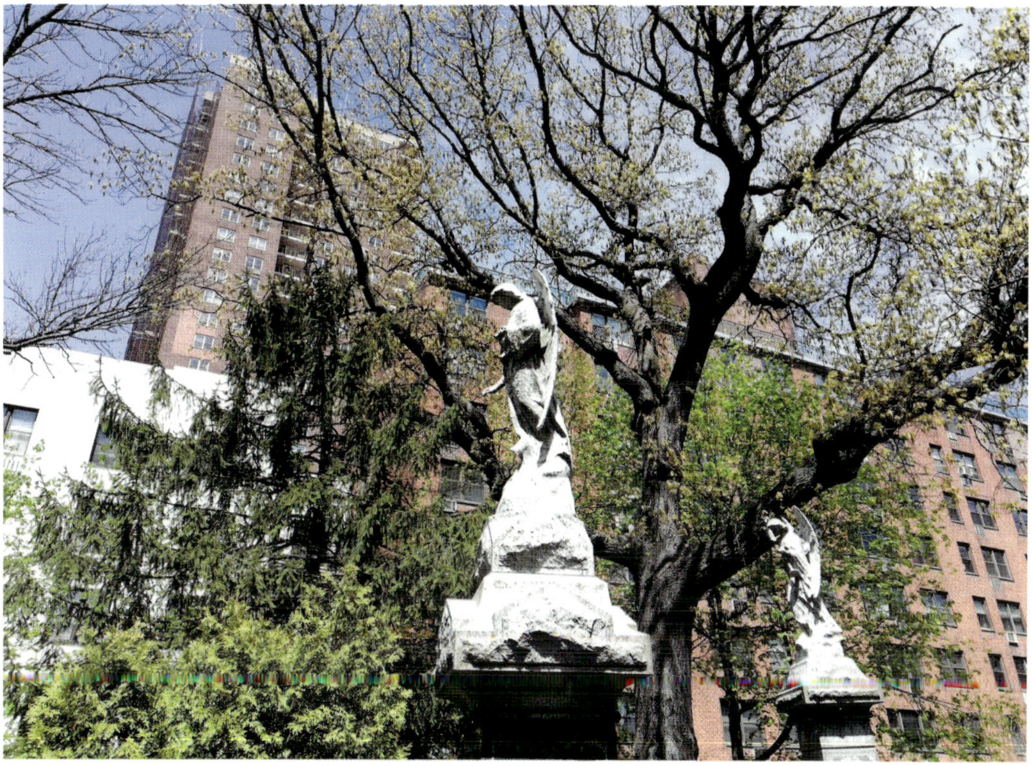

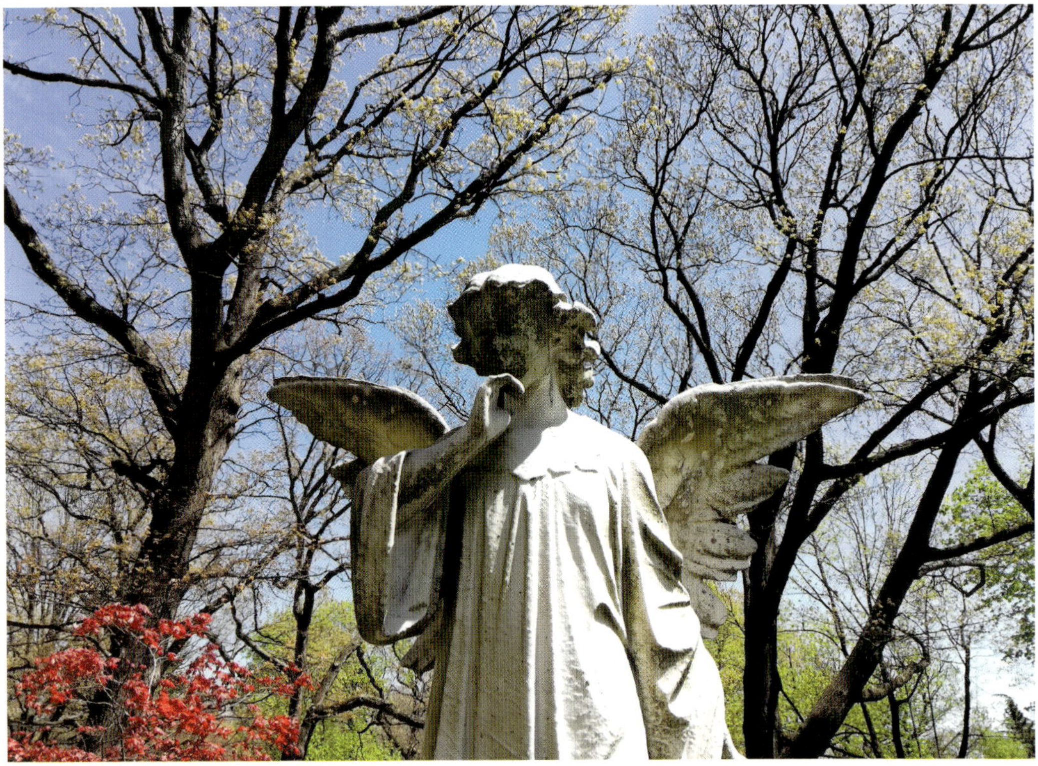

Two of the many statues and tall monuments at Maple Grove.

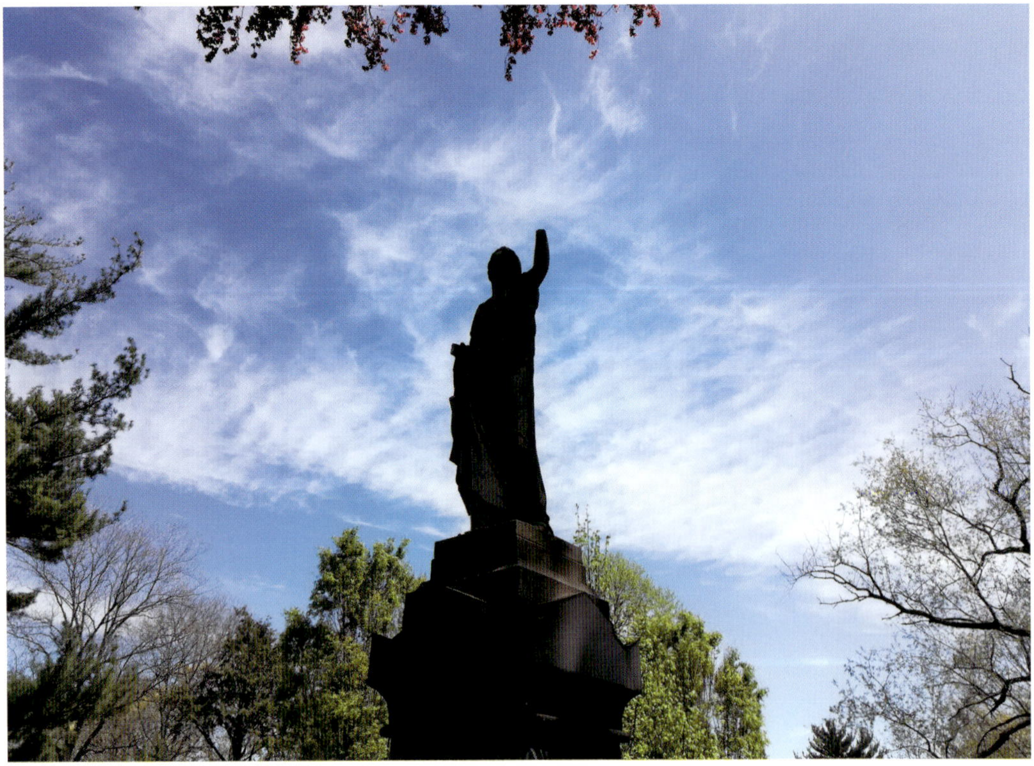

12

MONTEFIORE CEMETERY

121-83 SPRINGFIELD BLVD, QUEENS, NY 11413

In operation since 1908, Montefiore Cemetery, also known as Springfield Cemetery, is a Jewish cemetery with more than 160,000 burials over 114 acres. Notable graves include some members of the Amberg mobster family, actors Fyvush Finkel (*Picket Fences*) and Herb Edelman (*Golden Girls*), artist Barnett Newman, and Menachem Mendel Schneersohn, the seventh Lubavitcher Rebbe. Gravestones here are often impressive in size but also closely packed, making for an interesting visual. Located in the southern Queens community of Springfield Gardens (with a PO Box mailing address in St. Albans), this large cemetery runs along Springfield Boulevard between 121st Avenue and 130th Avenue, all the way east to Francis Lewis Boulevard (a distance of fifteen blocks). During the 1920s, this cemetery expanded to another site in Suffolk County, the New Montefiore Cemetery in West Babylon.

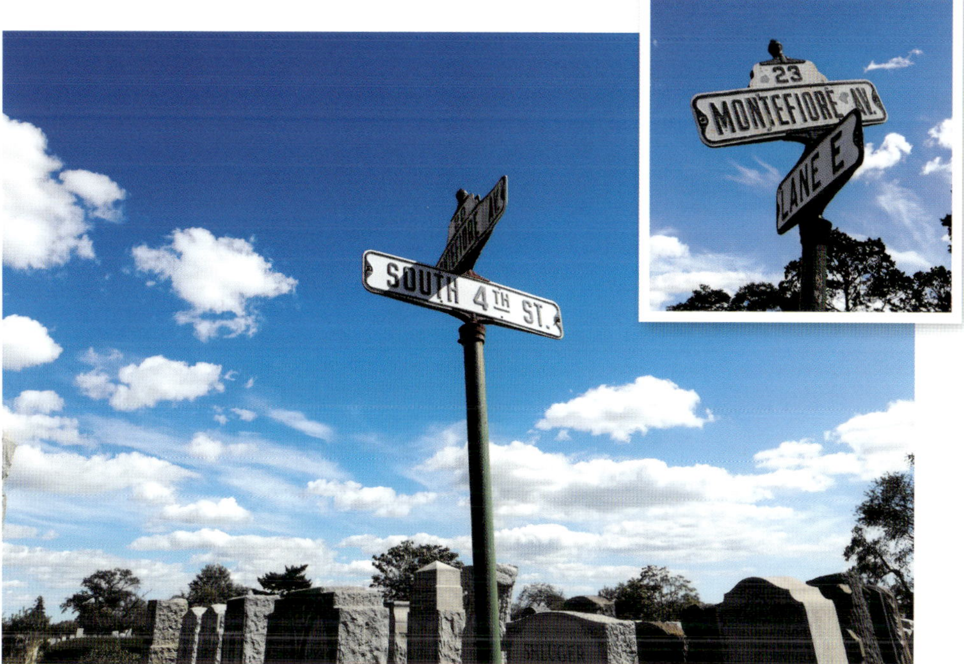

Street signs are always helpful in navigating through cemeteries.

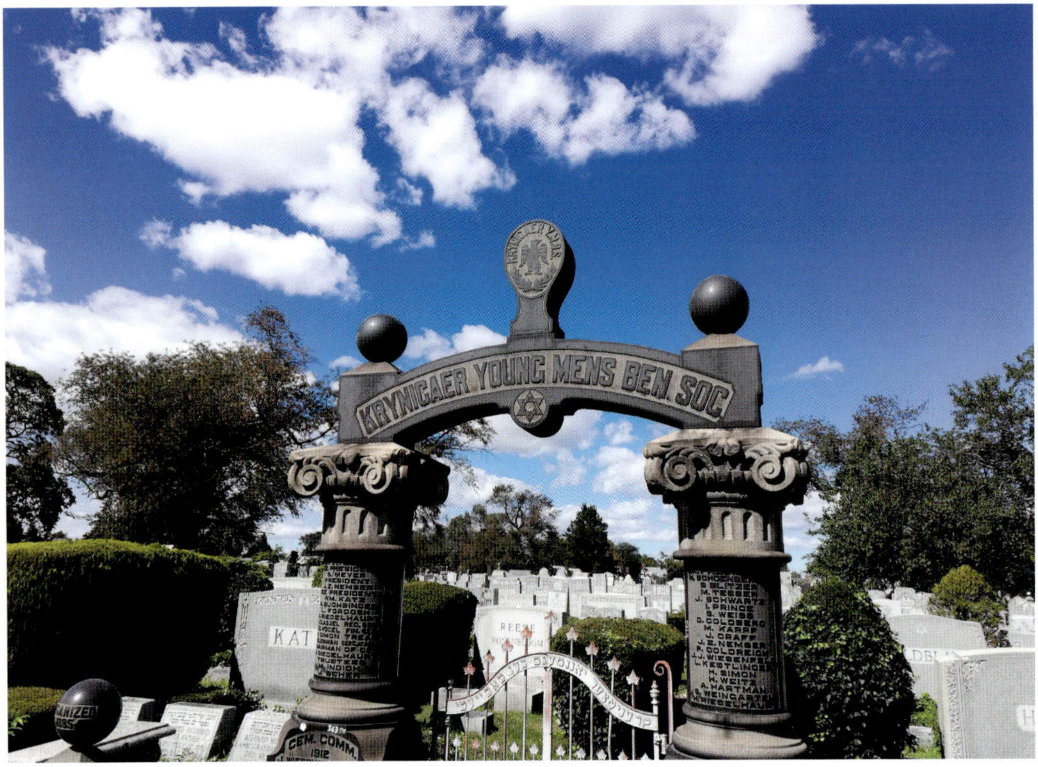

Societies and associations often have impressive memorial entrance gates to their sections within Jewish cemeteries.

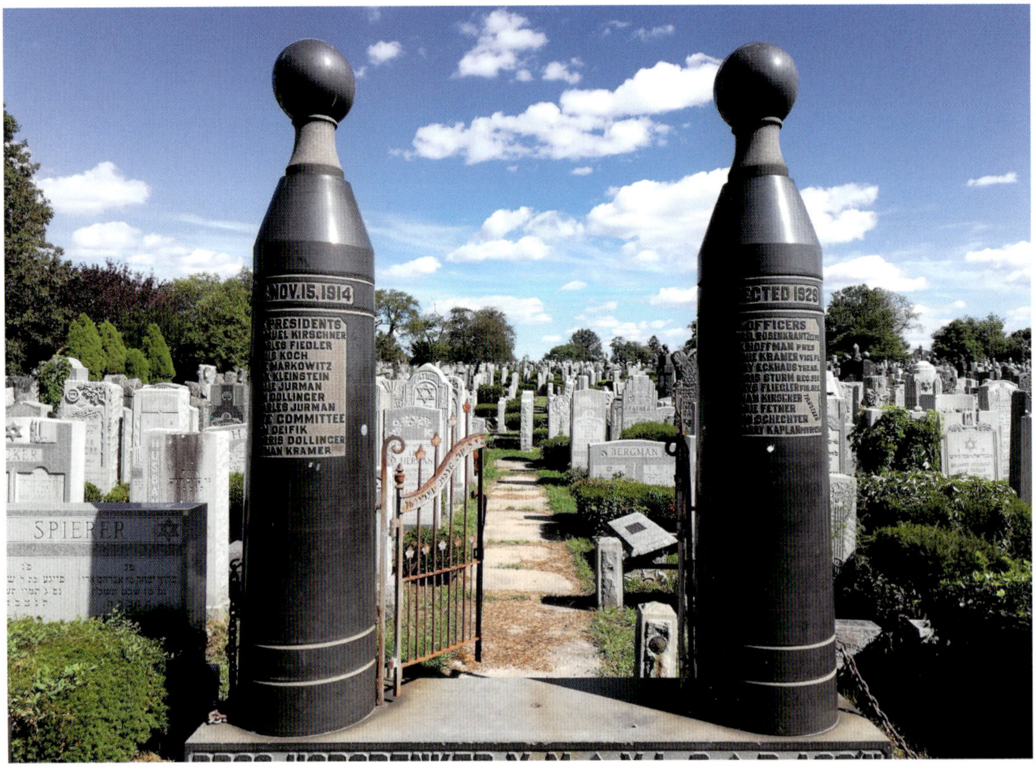

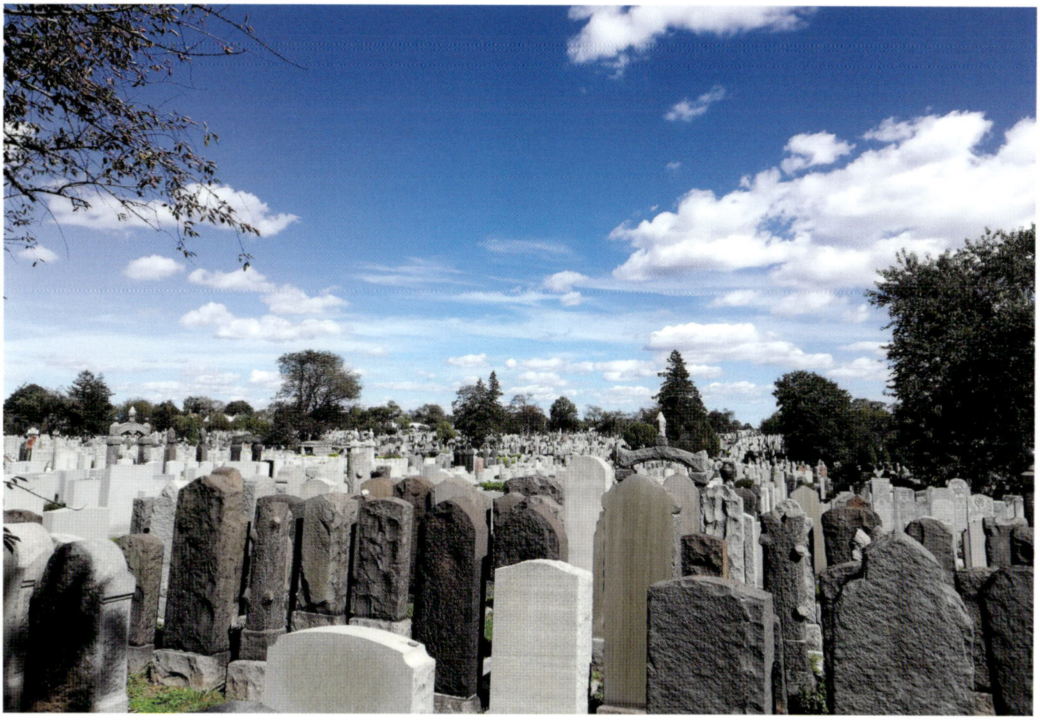

Looking out into a sea of gravestones at Montefiore.

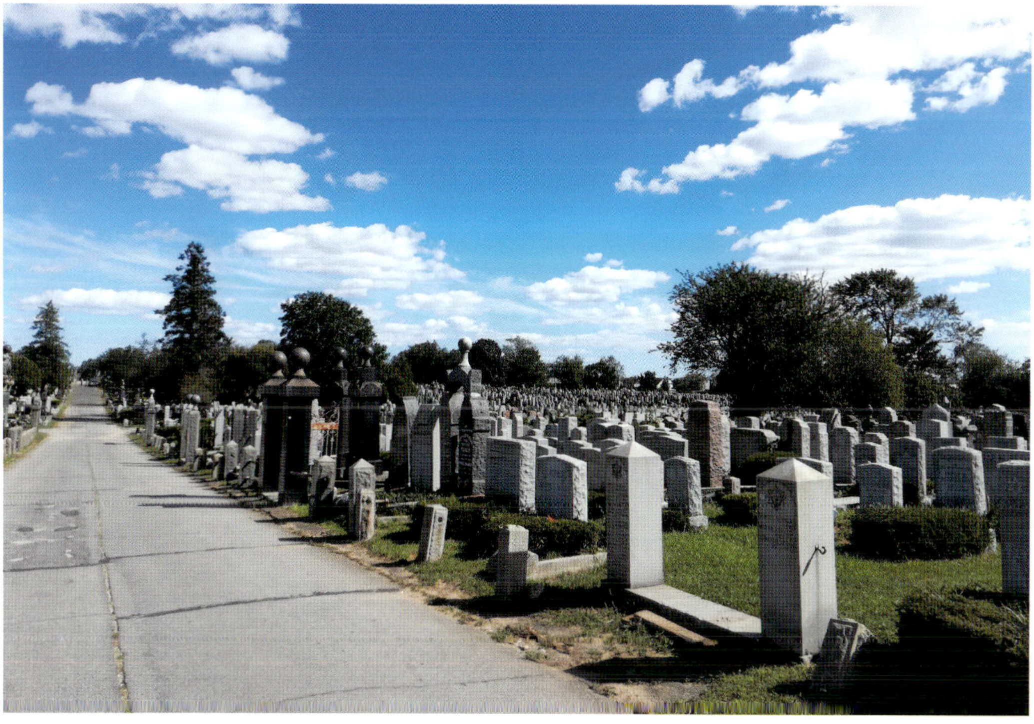

The street infrastructure of Montefiore is grid-like, making navigation easier than other Queens cemeteries that have winding roads.

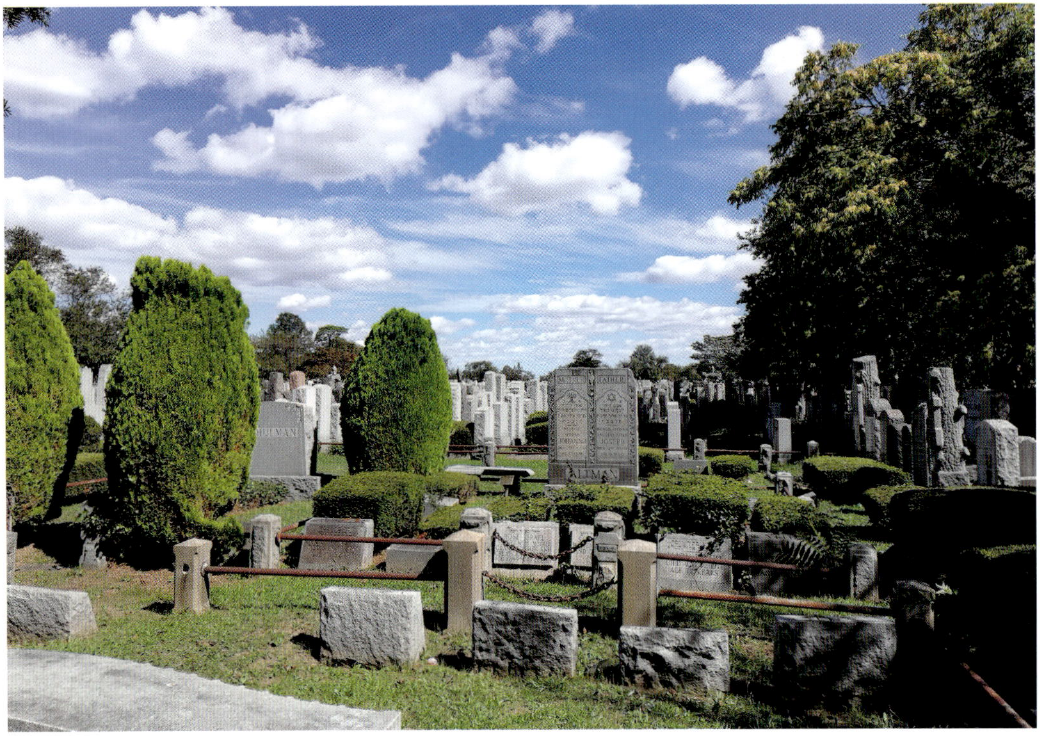

Text on stones in Montefiore are in Hebrew, English, or sometimes both Hebrew and English.

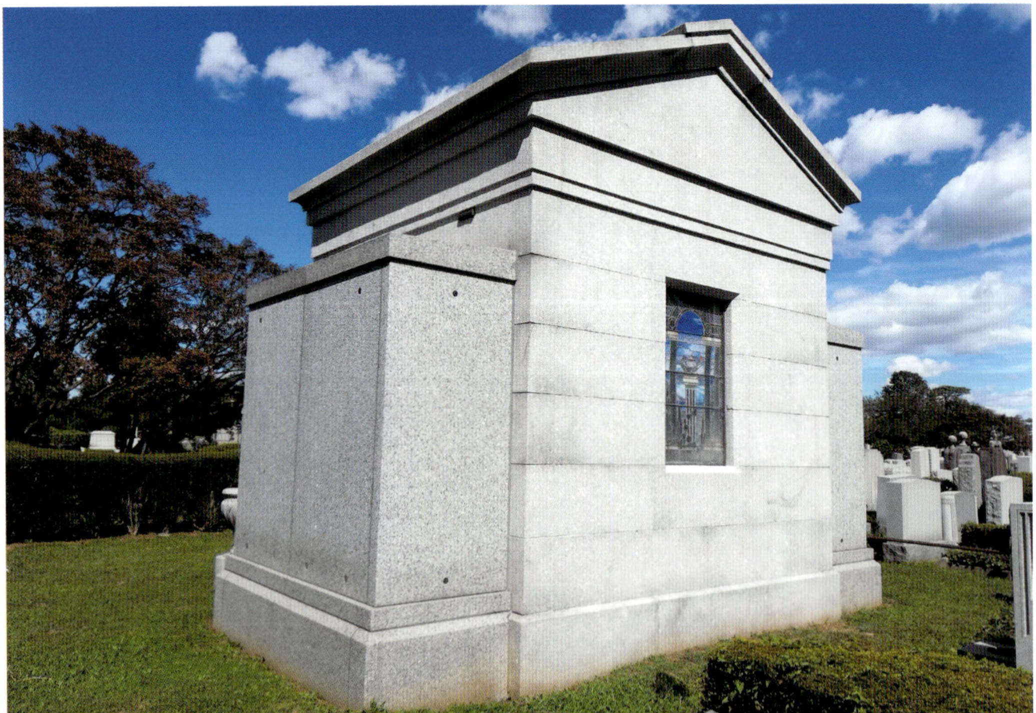

A mausoleum with a stained-glass window.

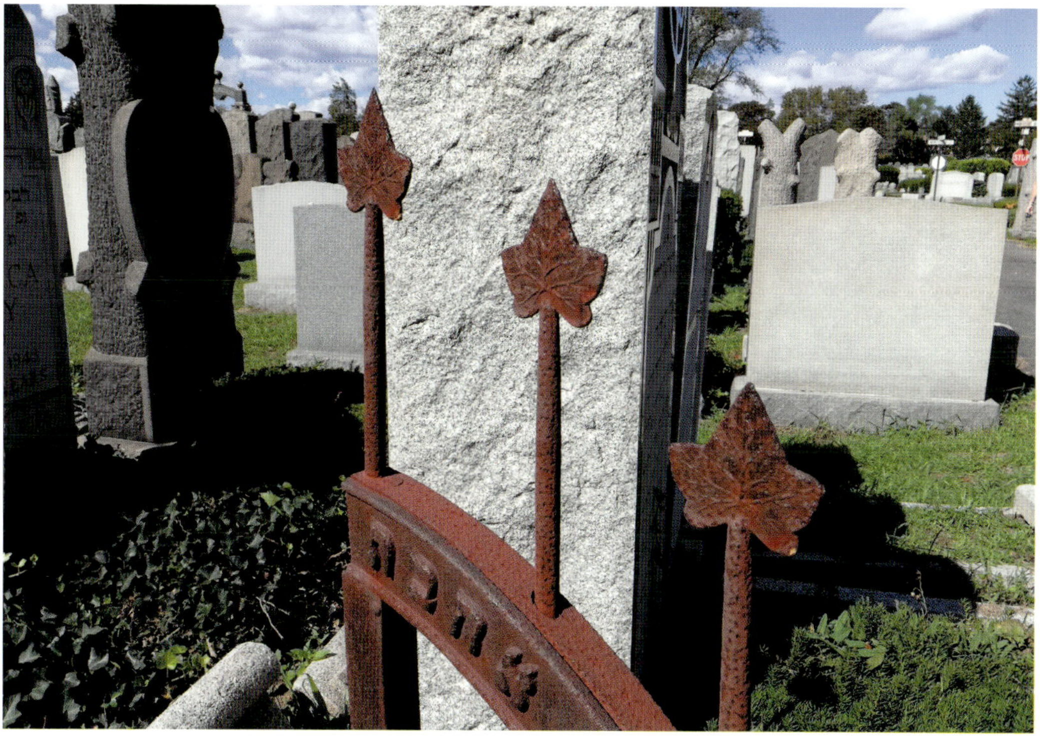

Leafy details on a rusted iron gate.

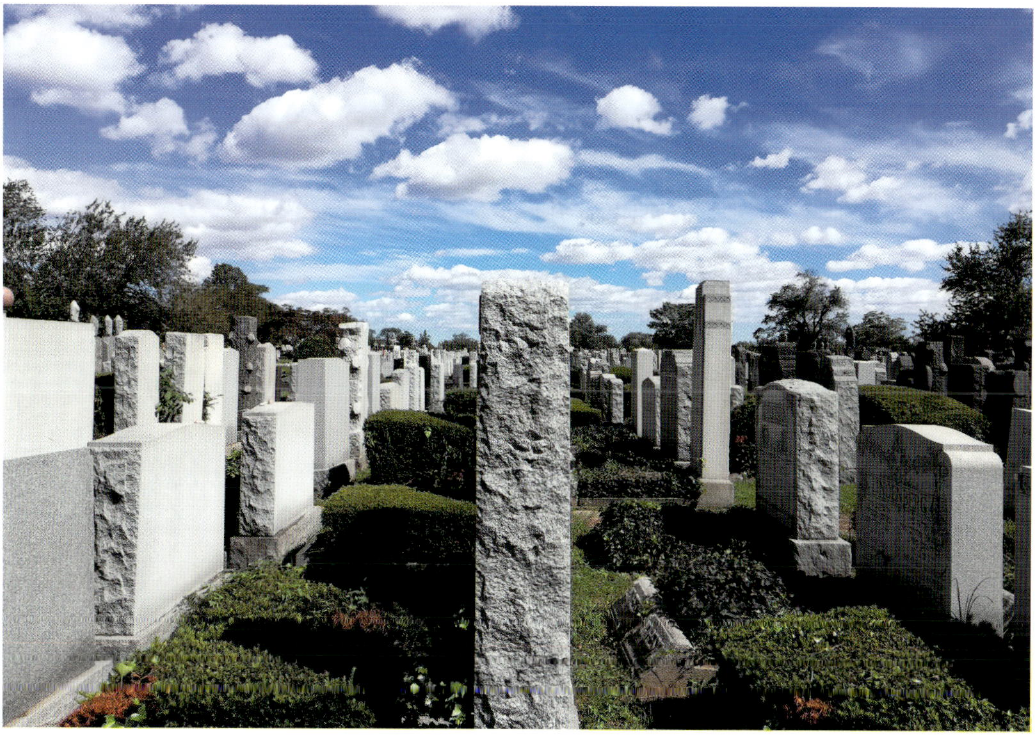

Though many of the stones are tightly packed, most are adorned with little shrubs and plants.

13

Moore Burial Grounds–Elmhurst

(Moore Homestead Cemetery at Broadway & 45th Avenue/ 82nd Street, Elmhurst, NY 11373 and Moore Cemetery Newtown, 56 Avenue and 92 Street, Elmhurst, NY 11373)

The Moore family of Newtown was one of the most prominent in Queens between the seventeenth and nineteenth centuries. Not only were the Moores credited with growing the first Newtown Pippin, a world-famous apple that was favored by Benjamin Franklin, George Washington, and Thomas Jefferson (and which is currently used to make Martinelli's brand apple juice), one of their descendants was none other than Clement Clarke Moore, the author of *A Visit from St. Nicholas*. There are at least three cemeteries in Queens associated with the family. Two of them are in Elmhurst, and retain no sign of the original headstones—one on the site of the Newtown Playground across from the Queens Center Mall (where more than 100 burials occurred), and the other on the site of the Moore Homestead Playground along Broadway, which is where the Moore house stood from the 1660s until 1929 when subway construction on the IND line led to its demolition.

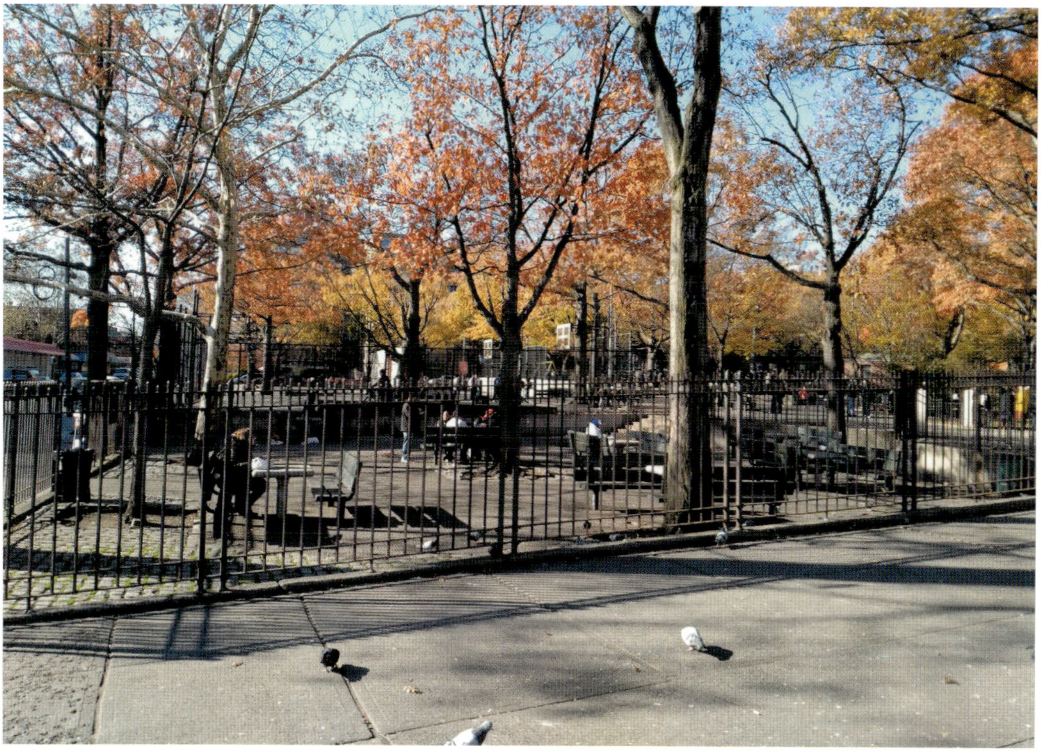

This playground on Broadway in Elmhurst, where the author played as a toddler, was once a burial ground for the seventeenth-century Moore family.

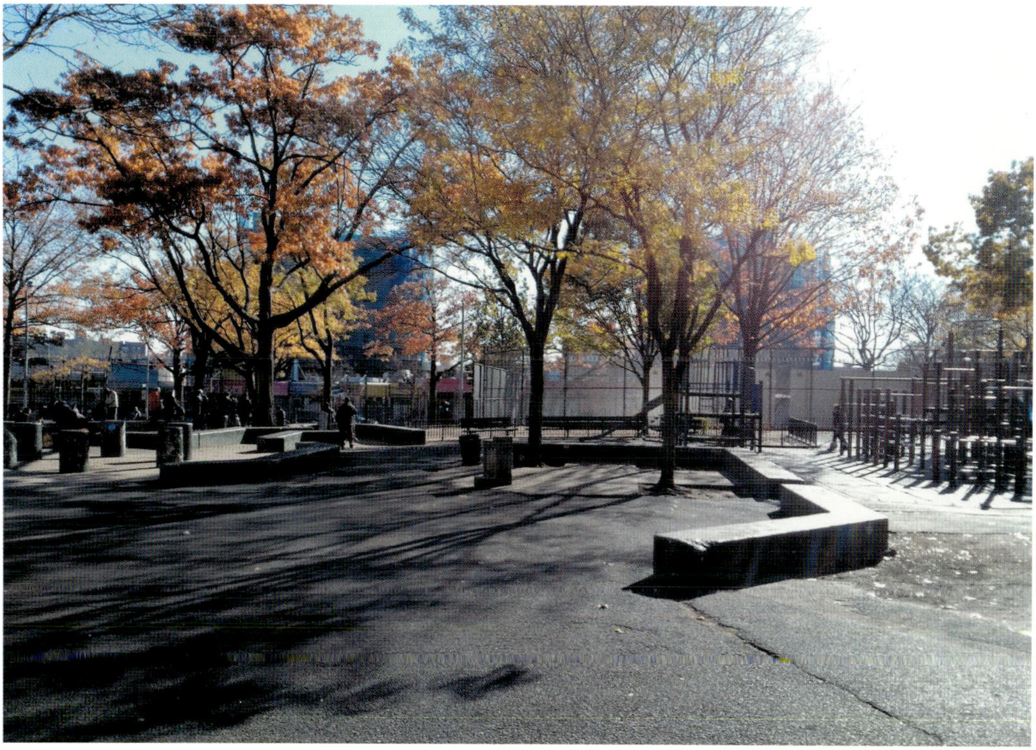

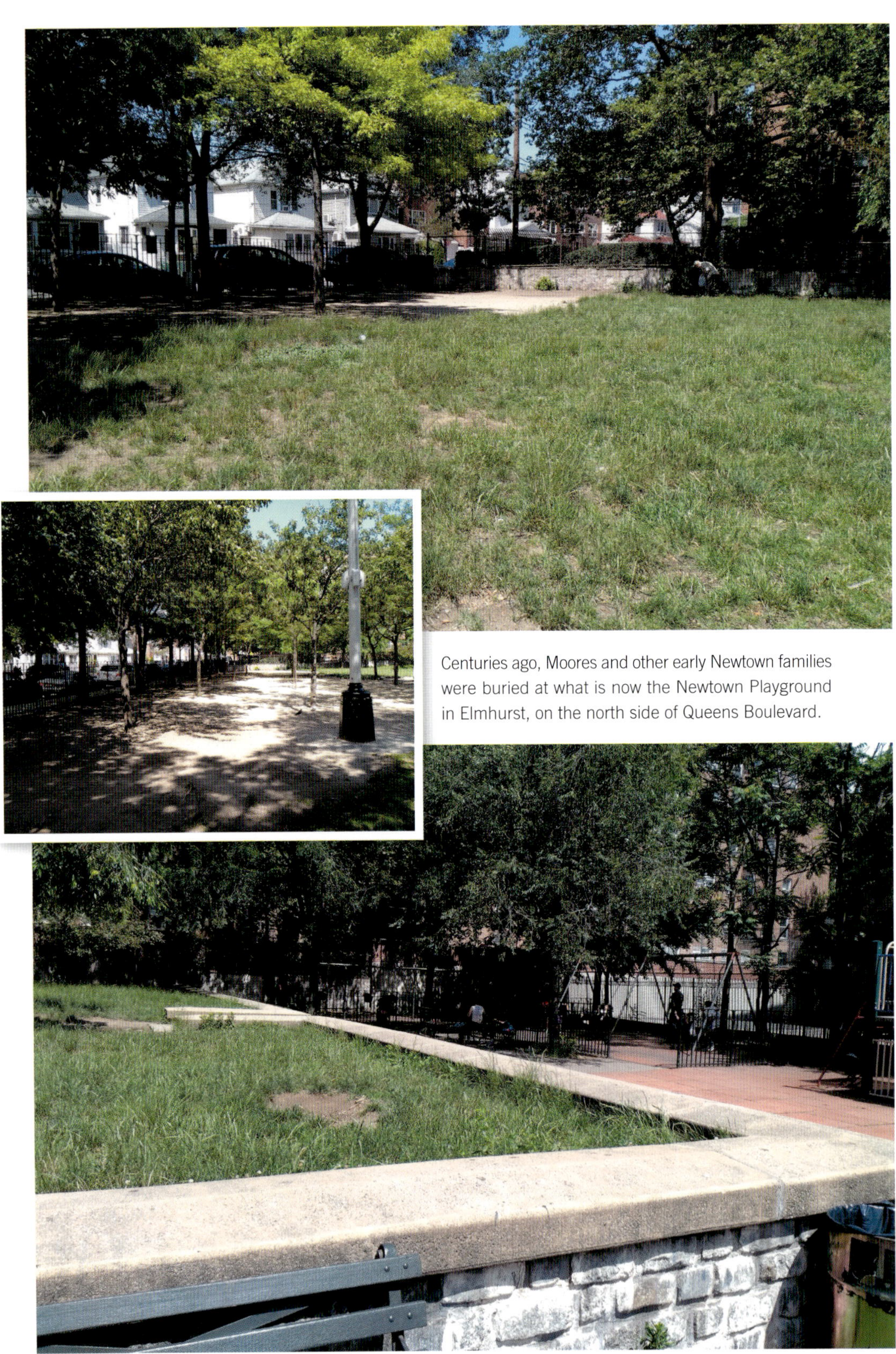

Centuries ago, Moores and other early Newtown families were buried at what is now the Newtown Playground in Elmhurst, on the north side of Queens Boulevard.

14

Moore-Jackson Cemetery

31-30 to 31-36 54th Street, Woodside, NY 11377

Located at 31-30 to 31-36 54th Street in Woodside (between 31st and 32nd Avenues and 54th and 51st Street—which was known as Bowery Bay Road back then), the Moore-Jackson Cemetery dates to 1733, and survived long after the other parts of the Moore family property were sold. The cemetery was forgotten by the early twentieth century and rediscovered in 1919. The site was declared a NYC landmark in 1997, so is protected from destruction. It is currently owned by the Queens Historical Society. There are fifteen headstones in the cemetery, some legible and others not so much (though a nineteenth-century survey found forty-six of them and a 1919 survey found forty-two). There have been a few attempts at restoration and clean-up, including in 1936, when a WPA project stripped away all the undergrowth leaving a very bare looking cemetery. What you see today does not represent the actual arrangement of the original stones. The remaining stones have been re-erected and placed on a 40 x 50 plot facing 54th Street. It makes for a fascinating and eerie reminder of the colonial past in the middle of a crowded residential neighborhood.

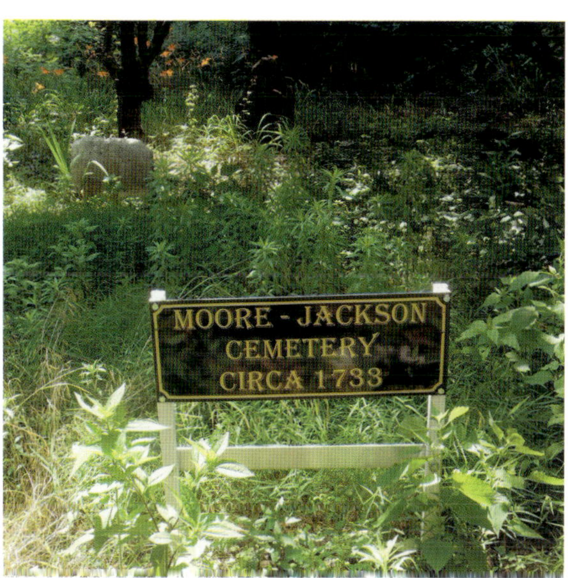

A small sign marks the Moore-Jackson Cemetery in Woodside.

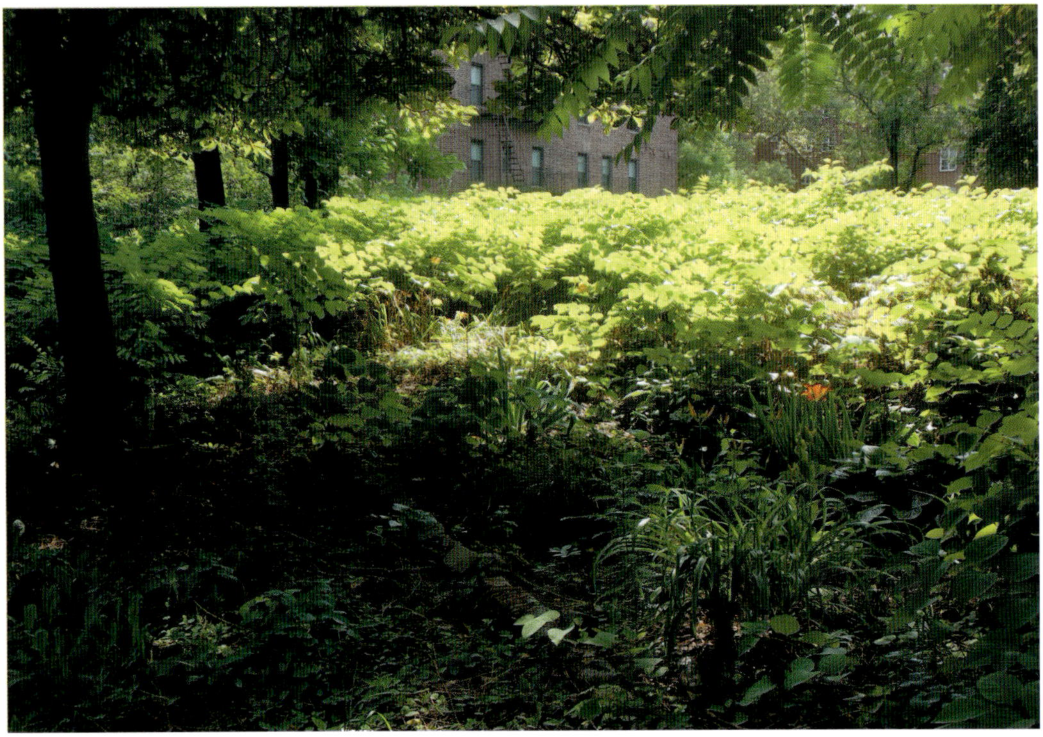

This parcel of land remains undeveloped and undisturbed.

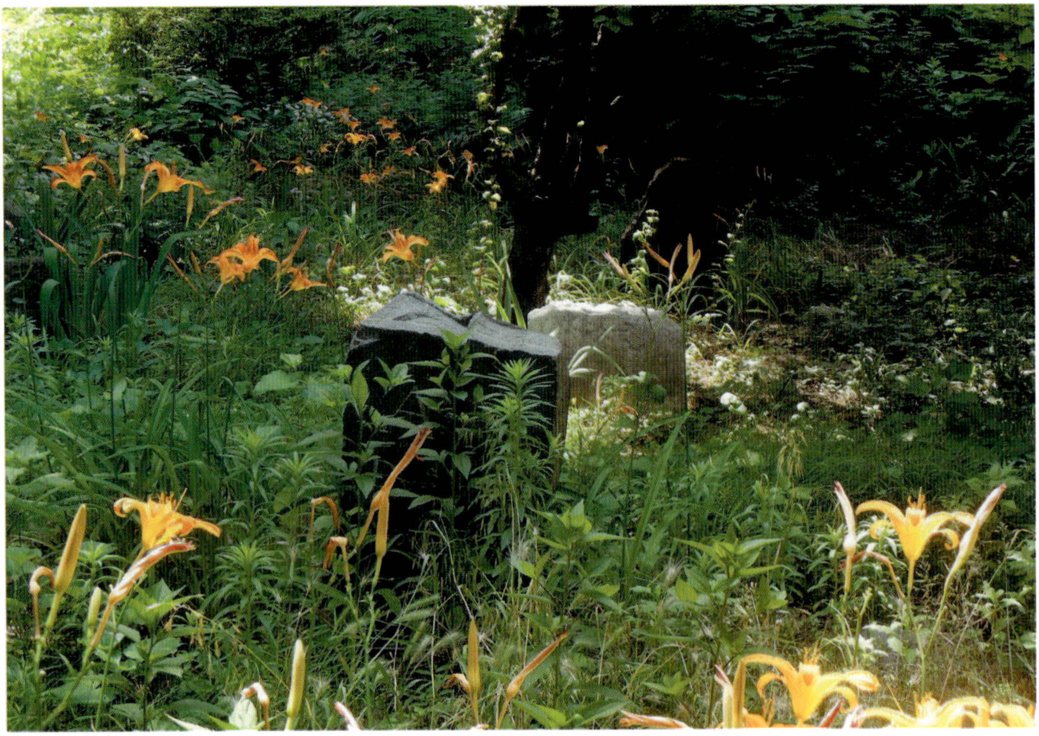

Several original headstones are visible from the sidewalk along 54th Street.

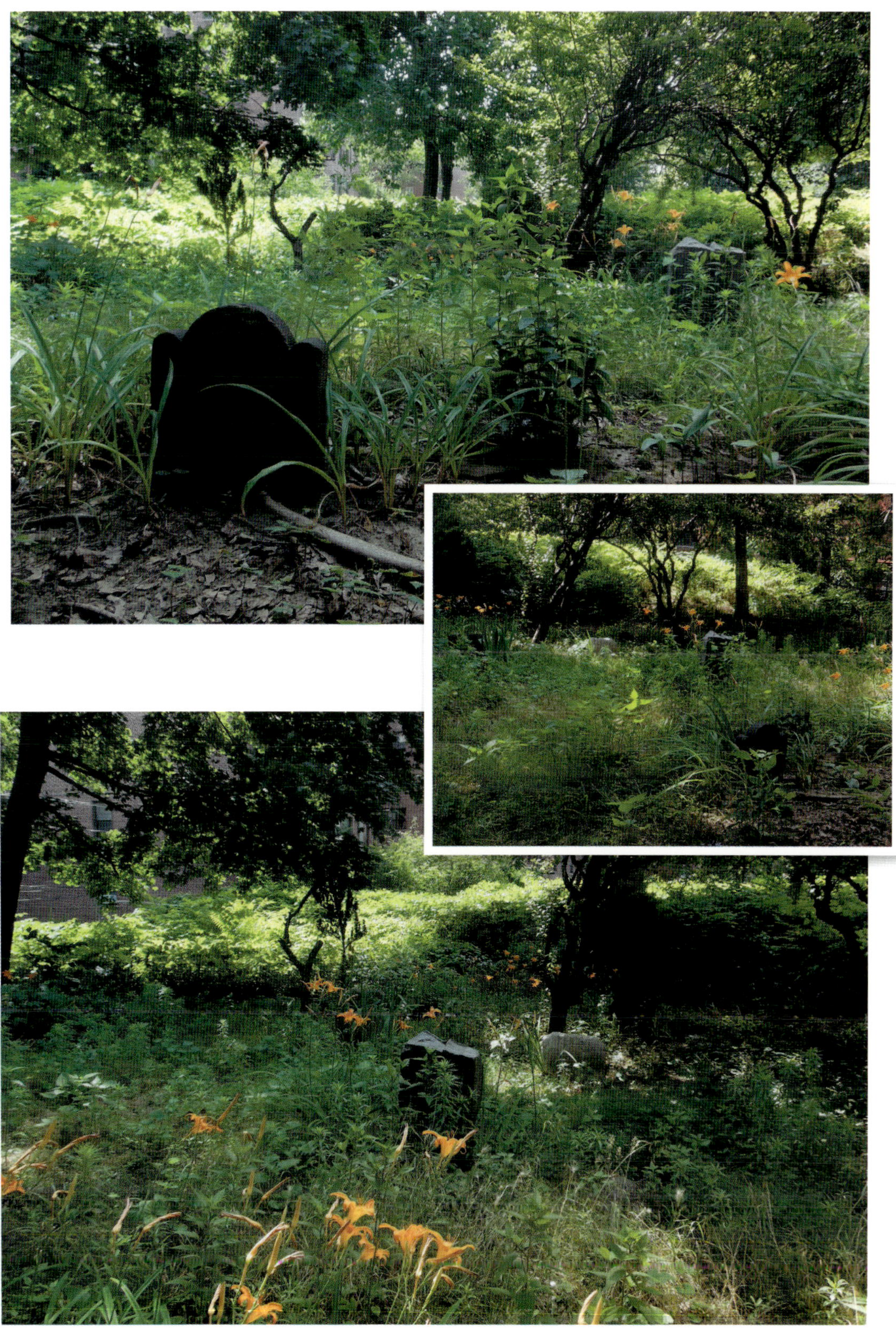

15

Mount Carmel Cemetery

83-45 Cypress Hills Street, Glendale, NY 11385

The Jewish Mount Carmel Cemetery was founded in 1906 in Glendale and its more than 100 acres are broken into Section 1 (Old Mount Carmel), Sections 2 and 3 (New Mount Carmel), Section 4 (the former Hungarian Union Field), and Section 5 (former Knollwood Park). Sections 1-4 are in Glendale and Section 5 is in Ridgewood. There are 114,000 interments in Mount Carmel. One of its most famous interments is the Yiddish writer Sholem Aleichem (1859-1916; his pen name means "may peace be with you"), who was the writer behind what became *Fiddler on the Roof*. Though originally buried in neighboring Mt. Neboh Cemetery, his remains were relocated to Mount Carmel. A more recent famous burial is the comedian Henny Youngman ("take my wife, please … ").

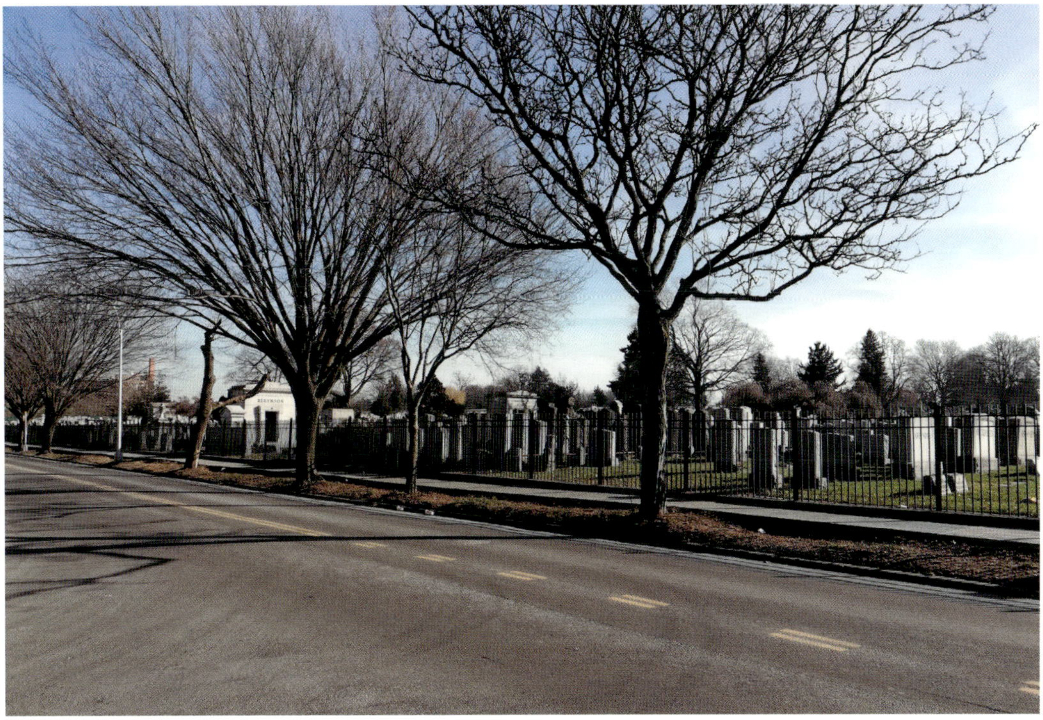

The New Mount Carmel section of the Mount Carmel Cemetery is adjacent to Cooper Avenue in Glendale.

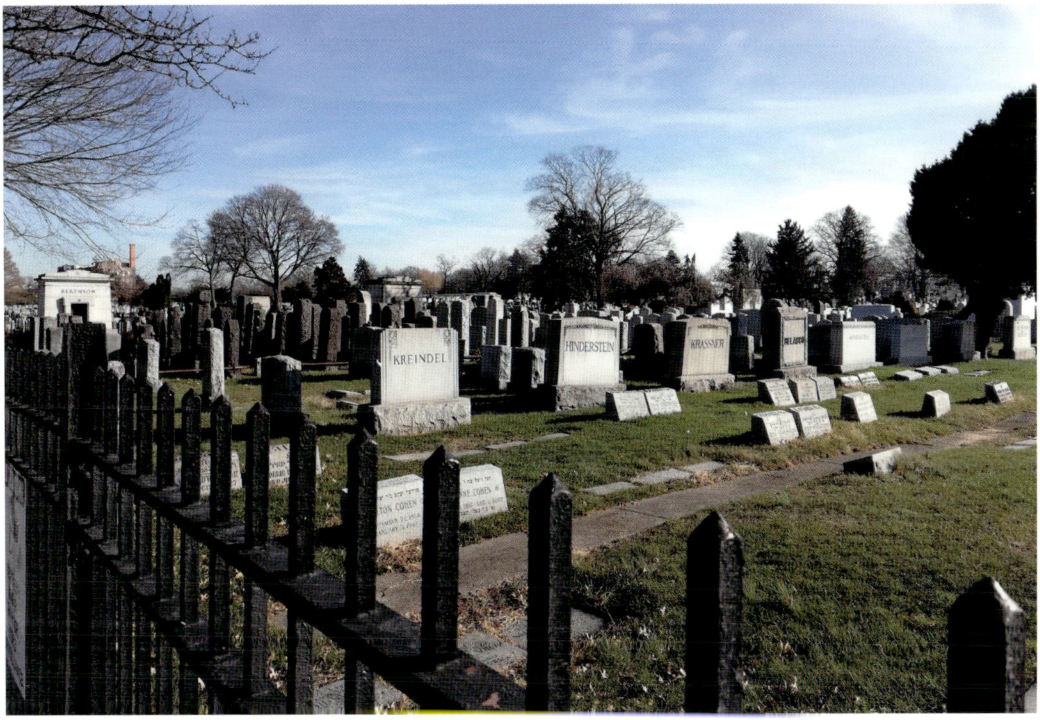

New Mount Carmel is the northern edge of a swath of cemeteries that runs south to Jamaica Avenue and extends from Forest Park Drive at the eastern edge to Bushwick Avenue in Brooklyn at the western edge.

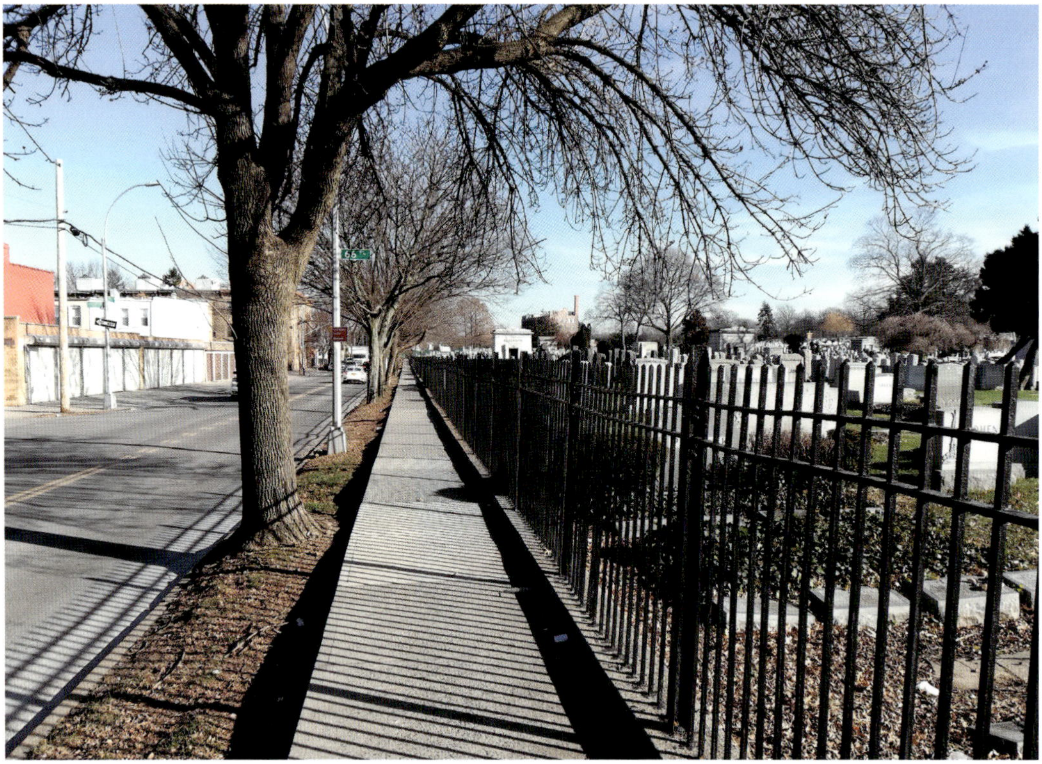

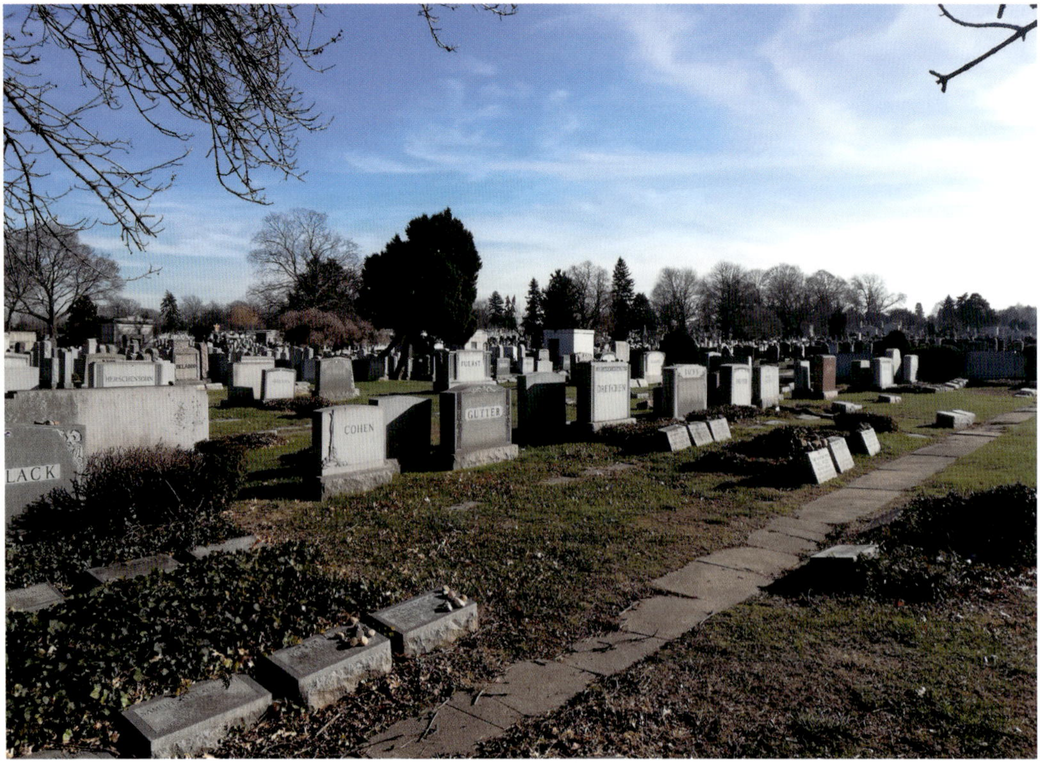

16

Mount Hebron Cemetery

130-04 Horace Harding Expressway, Flushing, NY 11367

Founded in 1909, this 114-acre Jewish cemetery opened just as Jewish immigration from Europe to New York was at its peak. With so many families arriving, there was a need for burial space in the city and several Queens Jewish cemeteries opened within a twenty-year period. There are 226,000 people buried at Mount Hebron, making it one of the largest Jewish cemeteries in the area. The cemetery's eastern edge faces Main Street and is directly across from Bowne High School and Queens College. As the cemetery's web site explains, in its early years, the cemetery sold about 80% of its space to Jewish societies whose members would then be buried in plots within the society's section. There are nearly 1,000 society sections within the cemetery (from the 1st Alexandria Woliner Benevolent Association to the Zwantchiker Podoler Young Men's Benevolent Association), each with dozens and sometimes hundreds of burials; the Austro-Hungarian Hebrew Free Burial Association contains 721 burials.

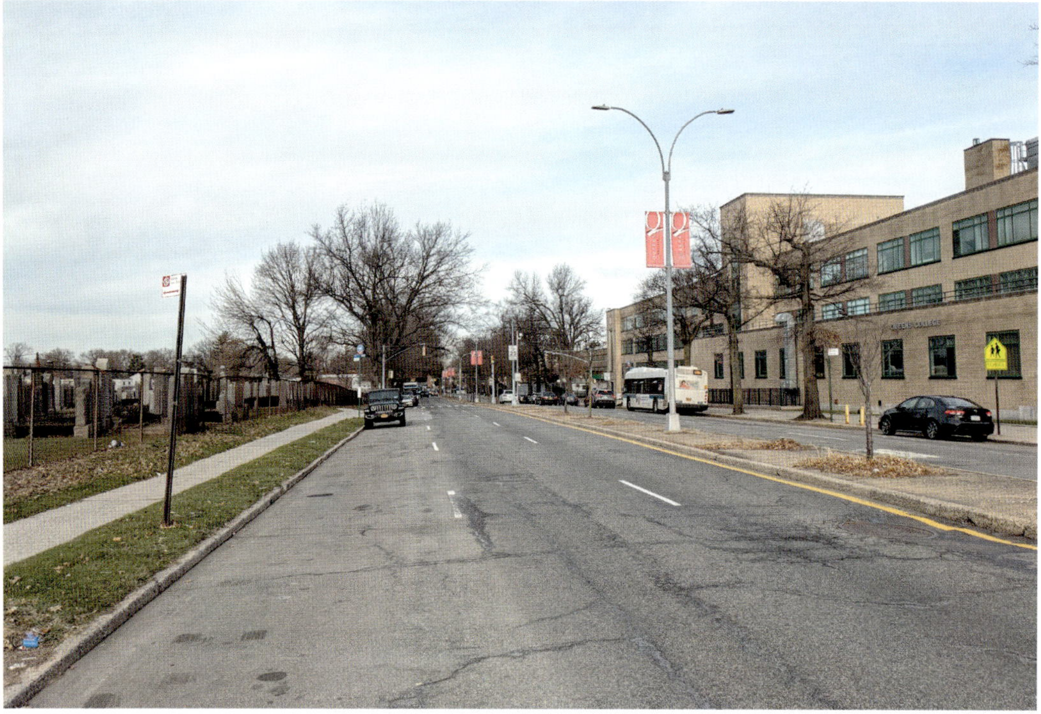

Looking north along Main Street in Flushing. The cemetery is on the left; Queens College and beyond it, Bowne High School are on the right.

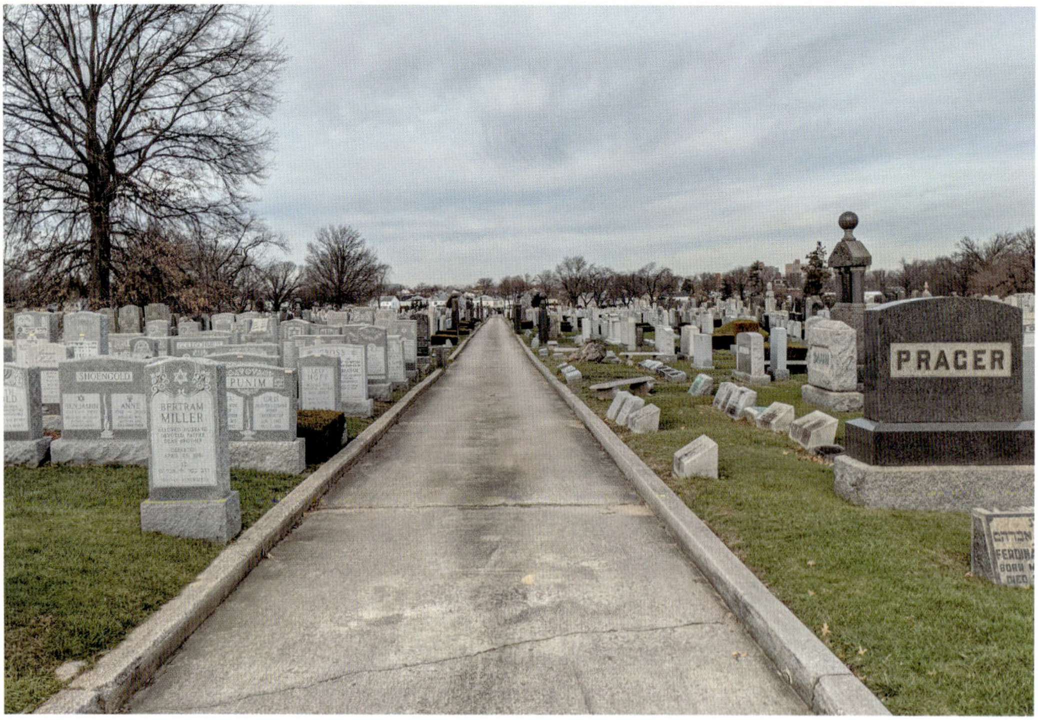

Looking north toward the northern edge of the cemetery. Houses along 64th Avenue are visible in the distance.

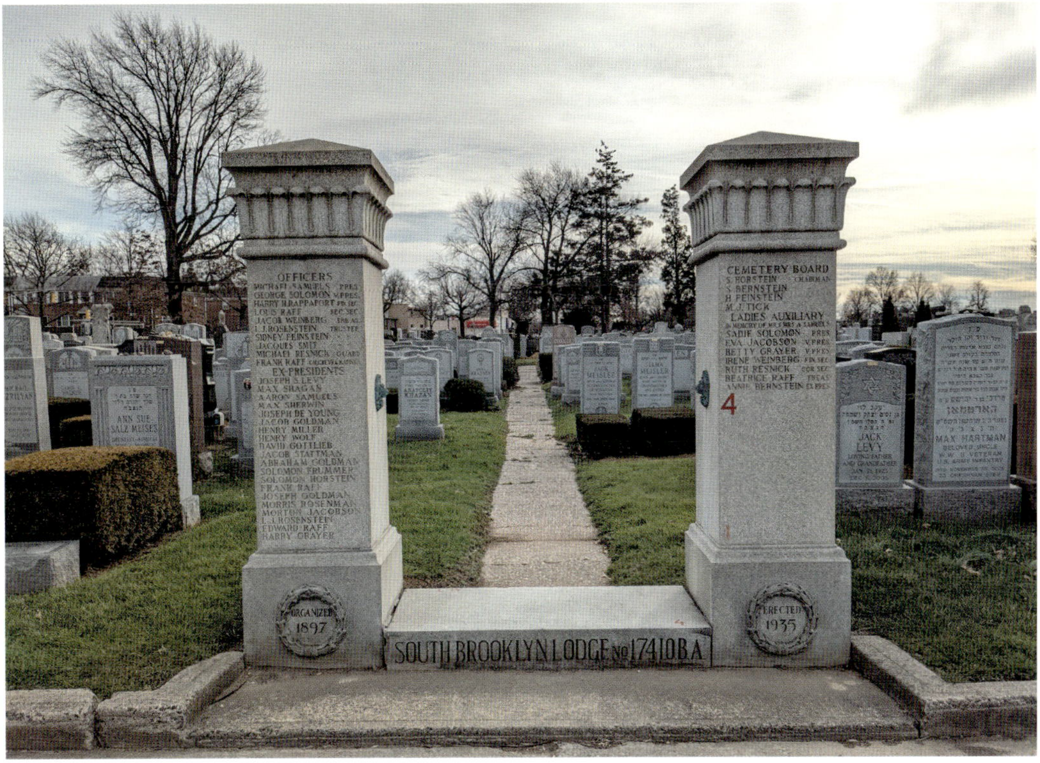

Entrances to two of the many association sections within Mount Hebron.

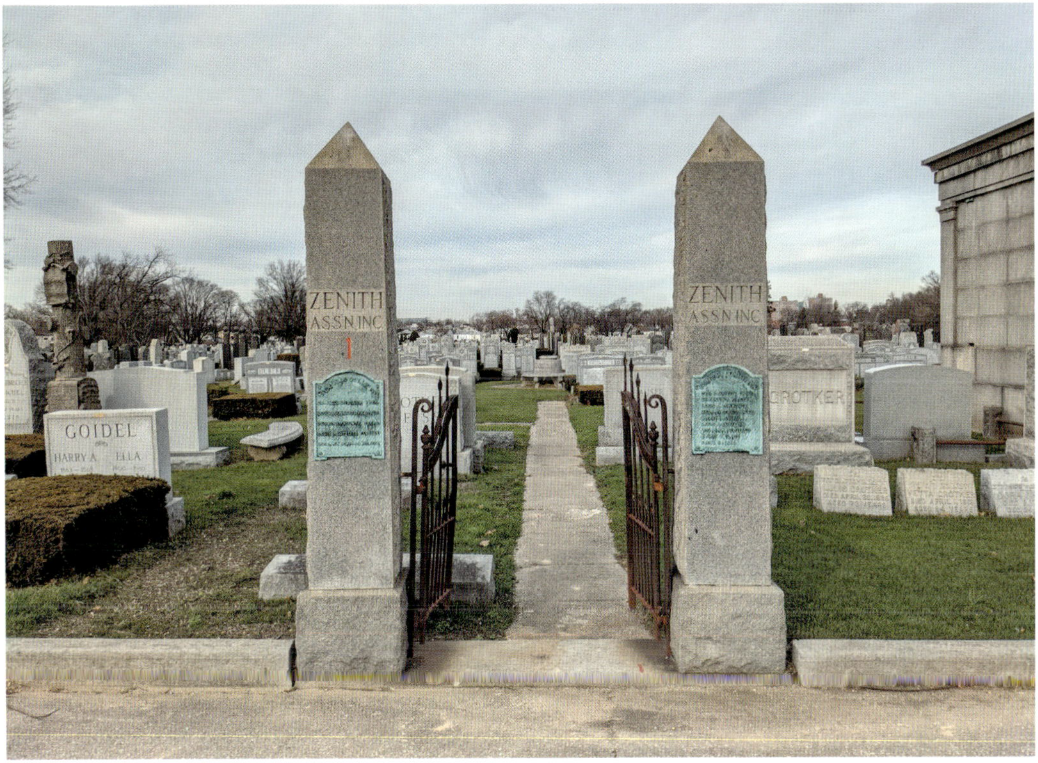

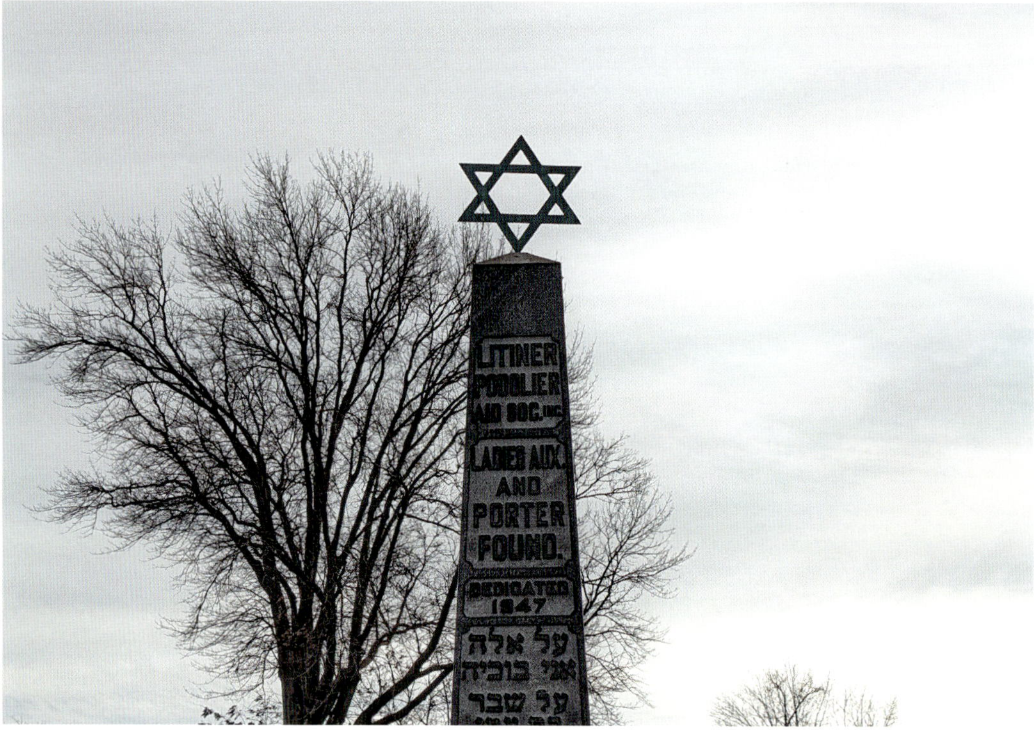

A Star of David atop one of the monuments at Mount Hebron.

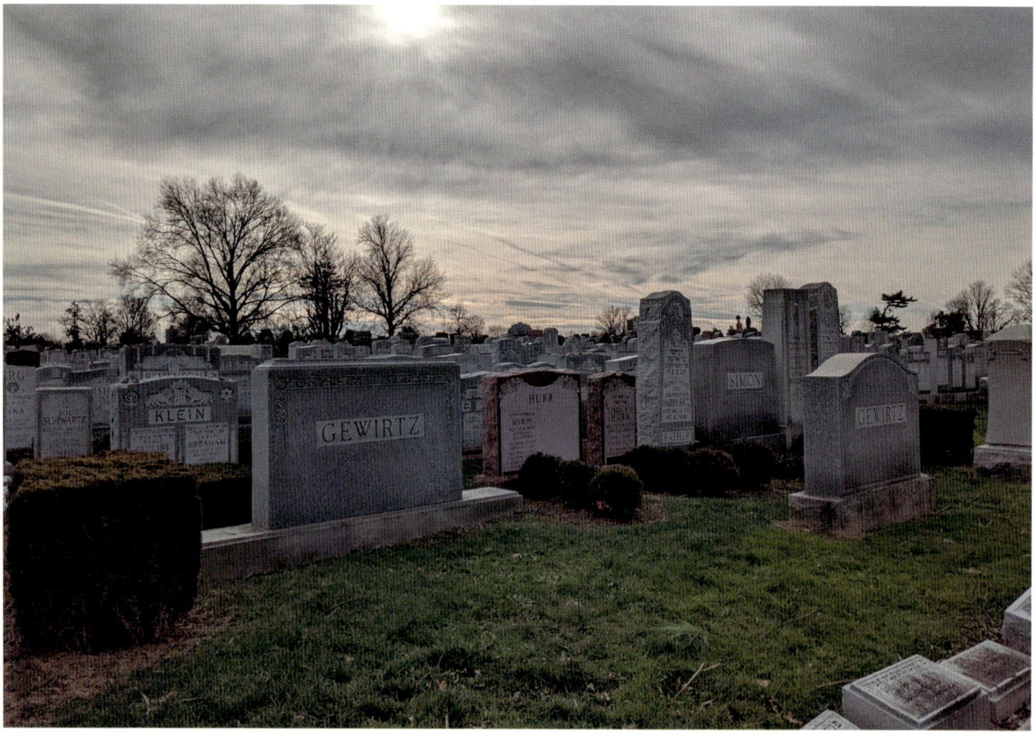

Looking southwest from the eastern edge of the cemetery off Main Street.

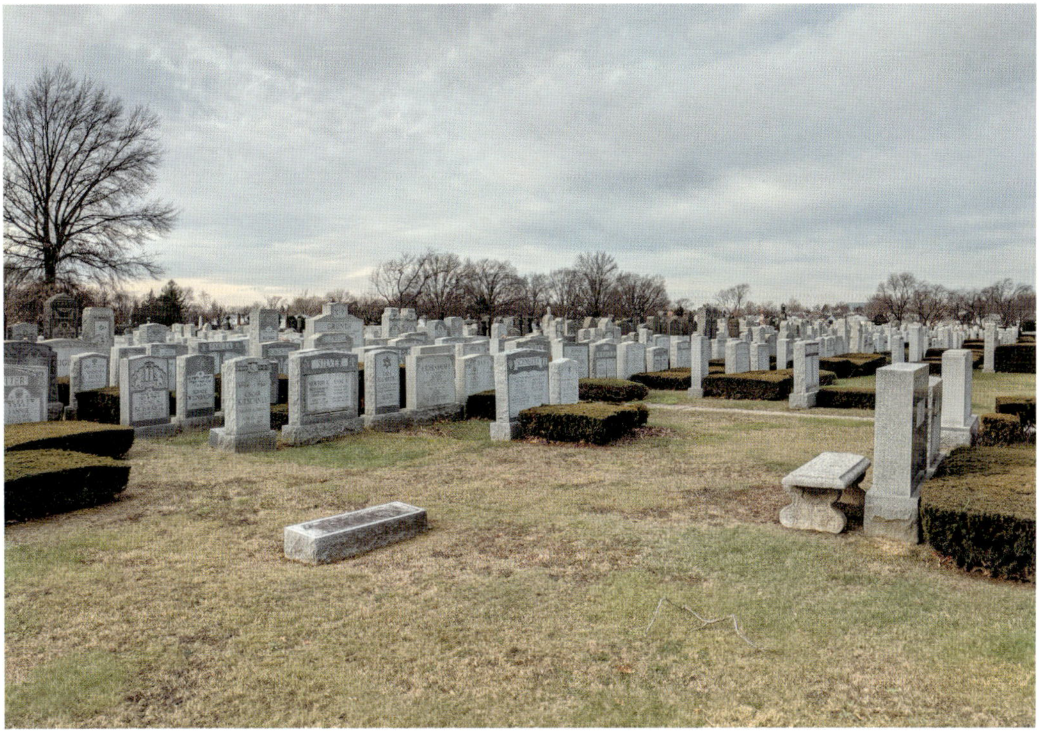

Some of the newer stones in the cemetery.

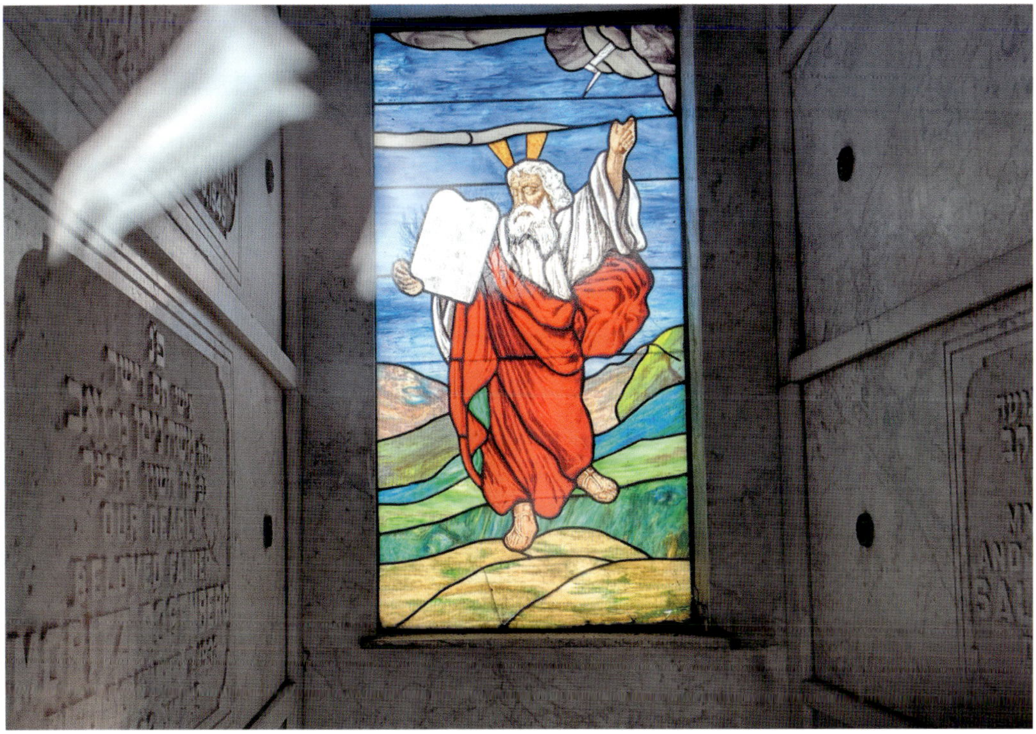

A peek inside a mausoleum reveals a colorful depiction of Moses.

17

Mount Olivet Cemetery

65-40 Grand Ave, Maspeth, NY 11378

The Mount Olivet Cemetery in Maspeth offers one of the best views of any cemetery in Queens. With its main entrance located along Grand Avenue, the main drag in Maspeth, the cemetery advertises itself as a "Beautiful Garden Cemetery Since 1850" and that is an accurate description. Nestled in a residential enclave with private homes surrounding it on three sides, this 71-acre cemetery's hills provide vistas of Manhattan. The "garden" aspect of the cemetery lies in its flowering trees (dogwood, weeping cherry, magnolia, redbud, and crabapple) that are especially spectacular in springtime. The high point of the cemetery is 165 feet above sea level. Formed just after the Rural Cemetery Act was enacted, the cemetery was originally 42 acres and expanded over the years with additional land purchases of 16 and 12 acres. The portion of the cemetery fronting Eliot Avenue is directly across the street from the All Faiths Cemetery.

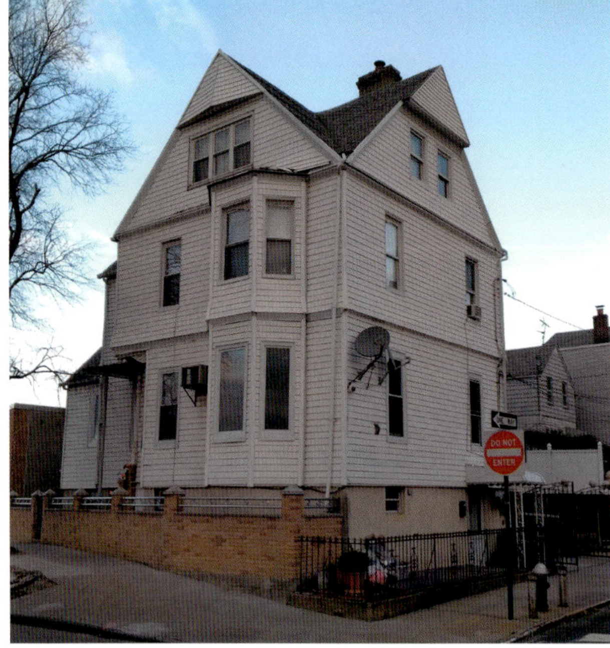

The James Maurice (a prominent local citizen and future congressman) House in Maspeth is where the first meeting to discuss the formation of Mount Olivet Cemetery was held in 1850.

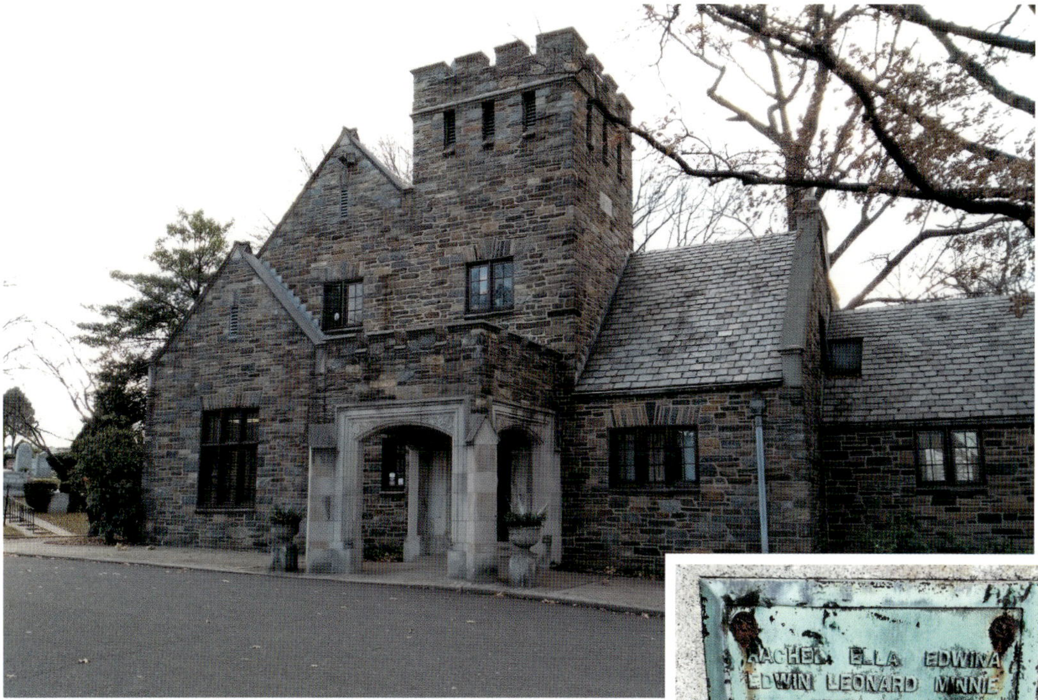

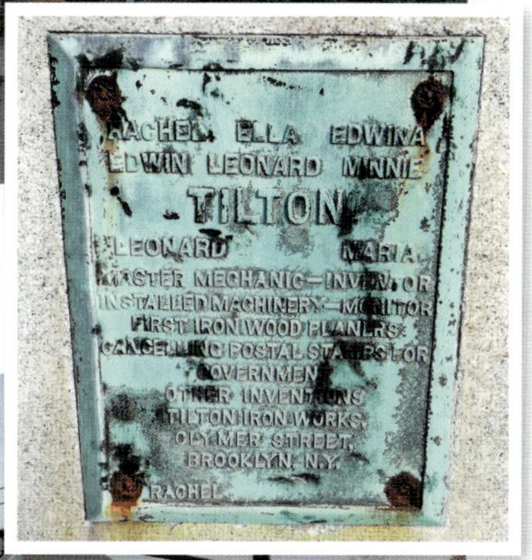

Administration building at the entrance to Mount Olivet on Grand Avenue in Maspeth. *Right:* An interesting plaque celebrates the achievements of an inventor named Leonard Tilton.

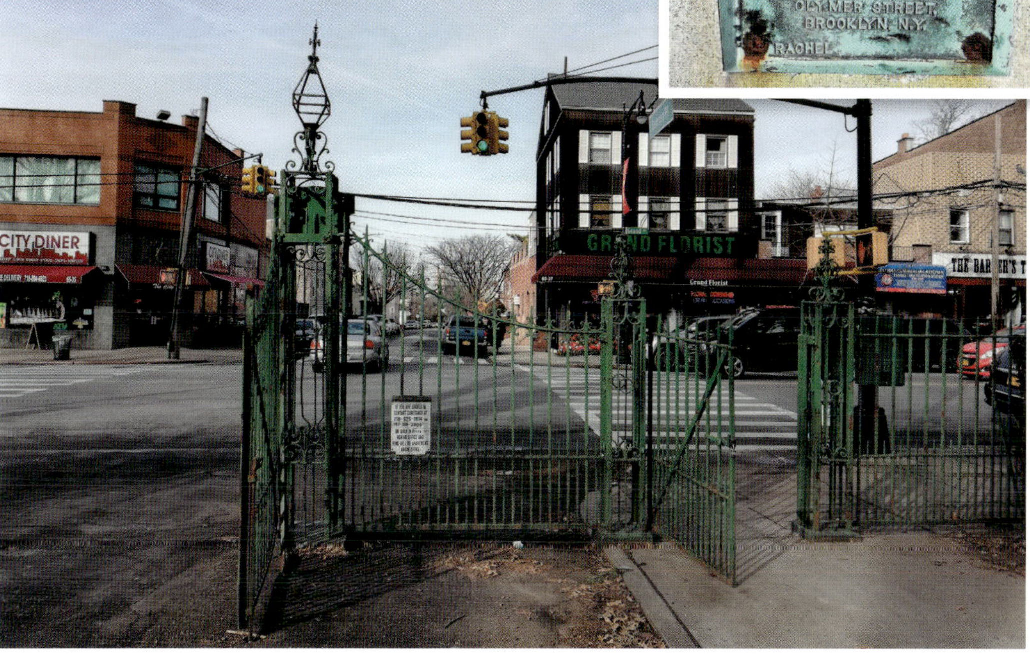

Looking toward Grand Avenue from inside the cemetery at the ornate old main gate.

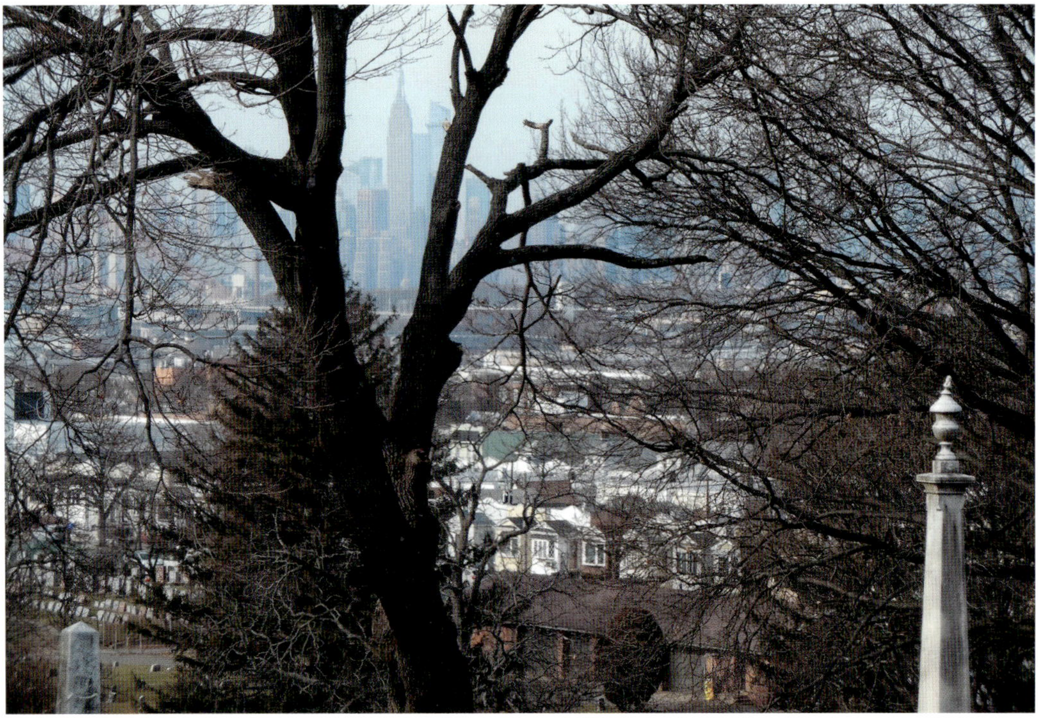

Stunning views of the New York City skyline are visible from the high points in Mount Olivet.

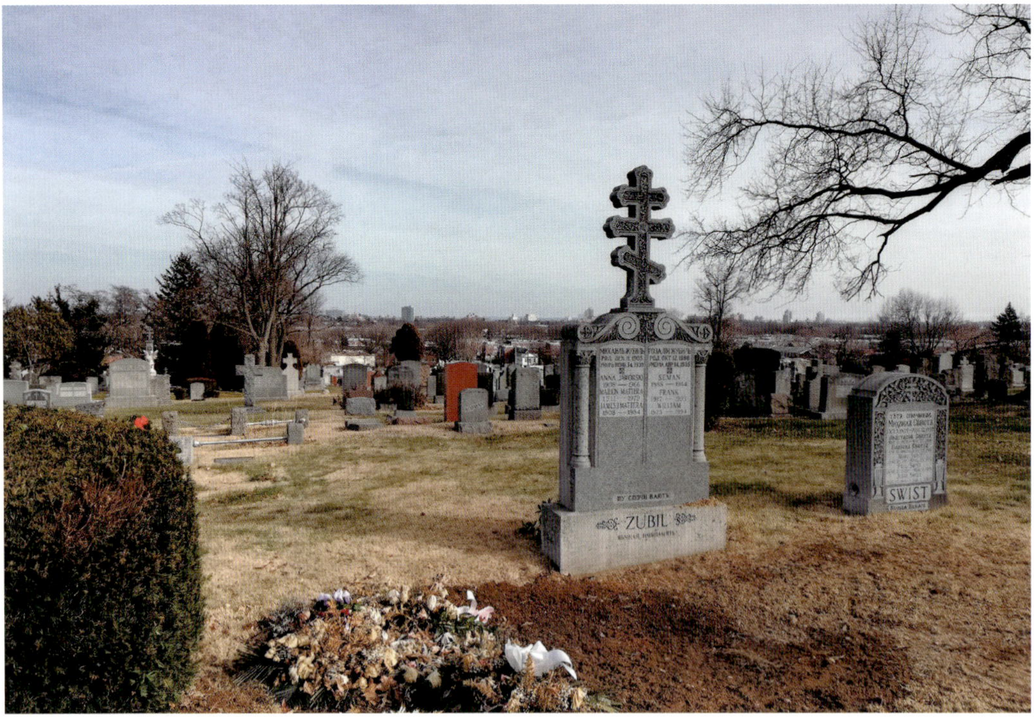

Views of Queens are also pretty from the higher parts of the cemetery.

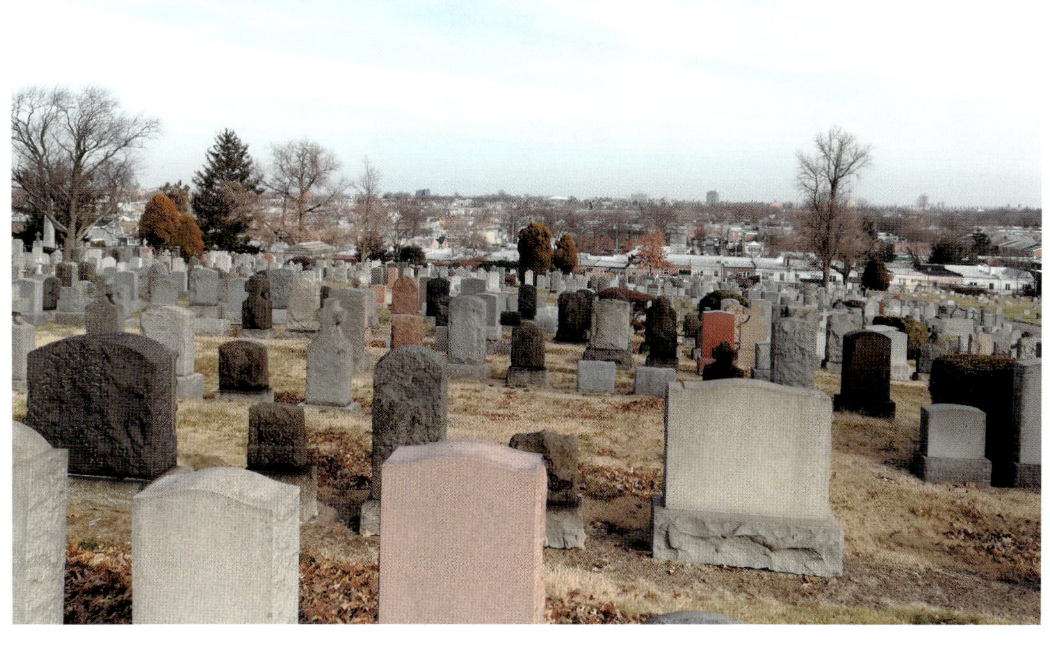

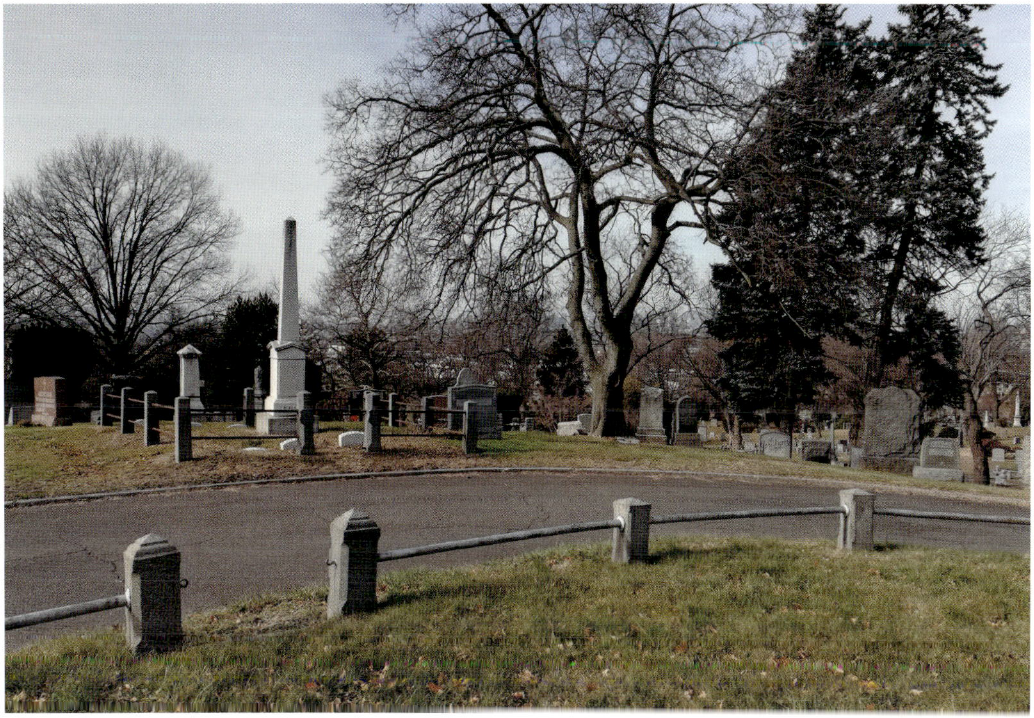

So many of the cemeteries in Queens have the ability to transport the visitor to another world, and Mount Olivet is no exception. From busy Grand Avenue, you enter someplace quite tranquil.

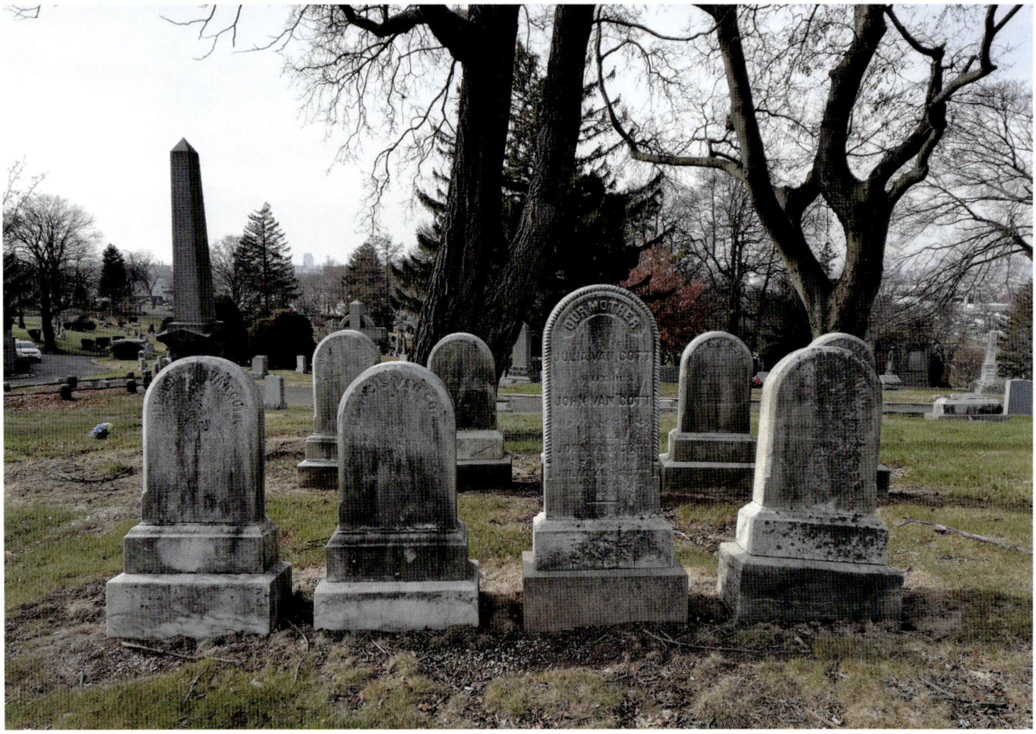

Nine nineteenth-century headstones are grouped together in this section of Mount Olivet.

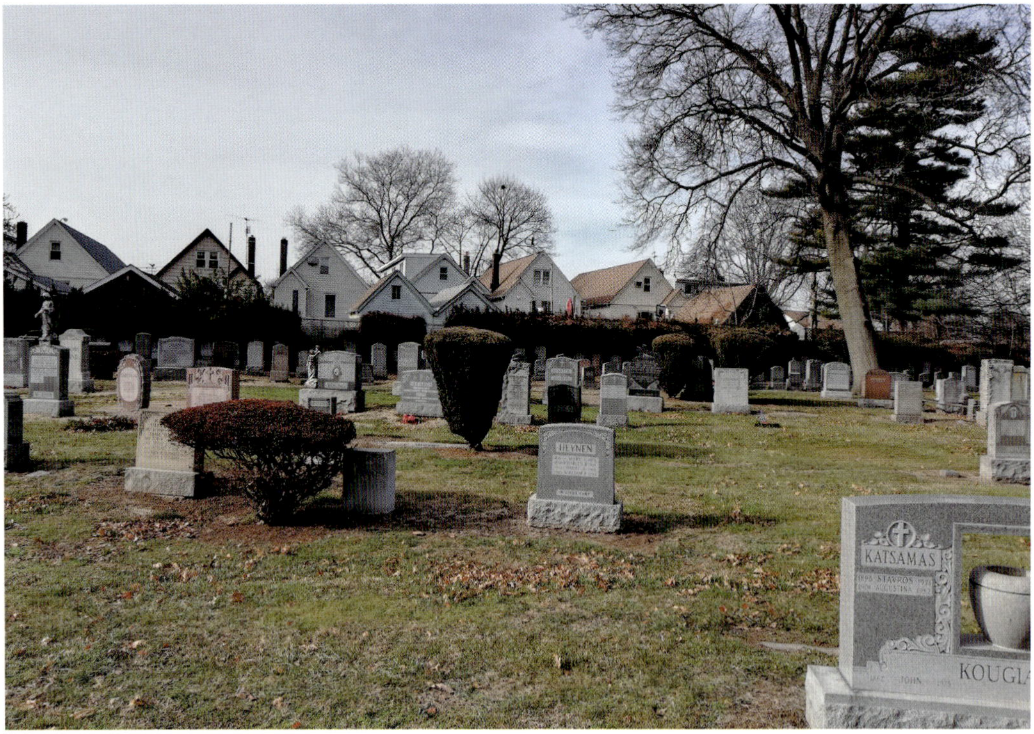

Maspeth homes are visible from the many parts of the cemetery's periphery.

18

Mount St. Mary Cemetery

172-00 Booth Memorial Ave, Flushing, NY 11365

The smaller of two Catholic cemeteries of the Diocese of Brooklyn within Queens (the other being St. John—see page 112), Mount St. Mary is located on Booth Memorial Avenue in the southernmost part of Flushing, across from the Kissena Park Golf Course and Francis Lewis High School, and just north of the Long Island Expressway. The first six acres of this cemetery were consecrated in 1863 by John Loughlin, the first Bishop of the Diocese of Brooklyn at a time when Catholics presence in the area was finally amounting to more significant numbers, thanks to the thousands of Irish immigrants who came here due to the Potato Famine. Expansion over time brought the total holdings of the cemetery to almost 54 acres. Remains from nearby St. Michael's (the first Catholic parish founded in Queens, in 1833) churchyard were relocated to Mount St. Mary.

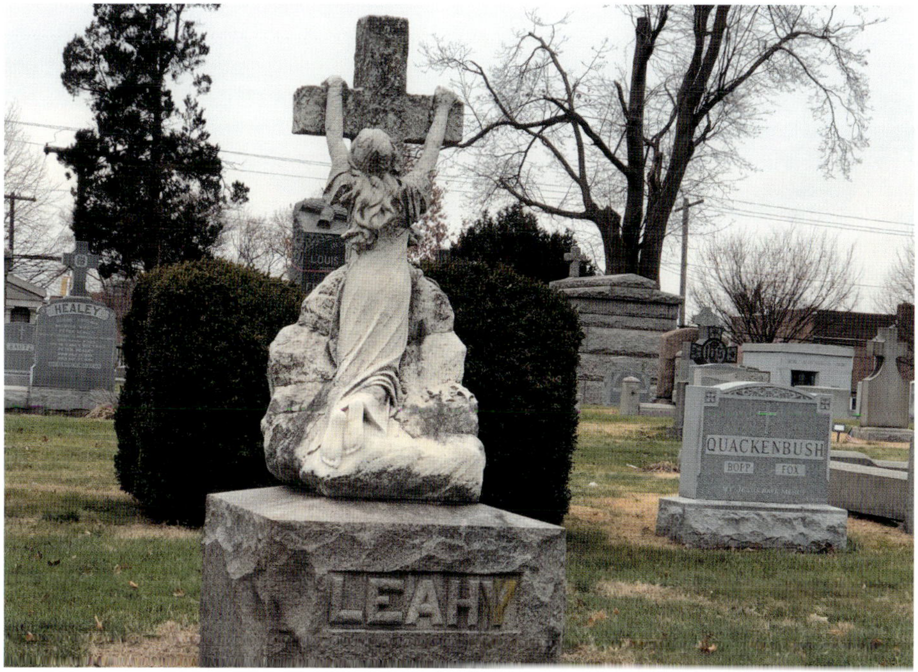

Some headstone statuary is eye catching and makes you pause for a moment and ponder

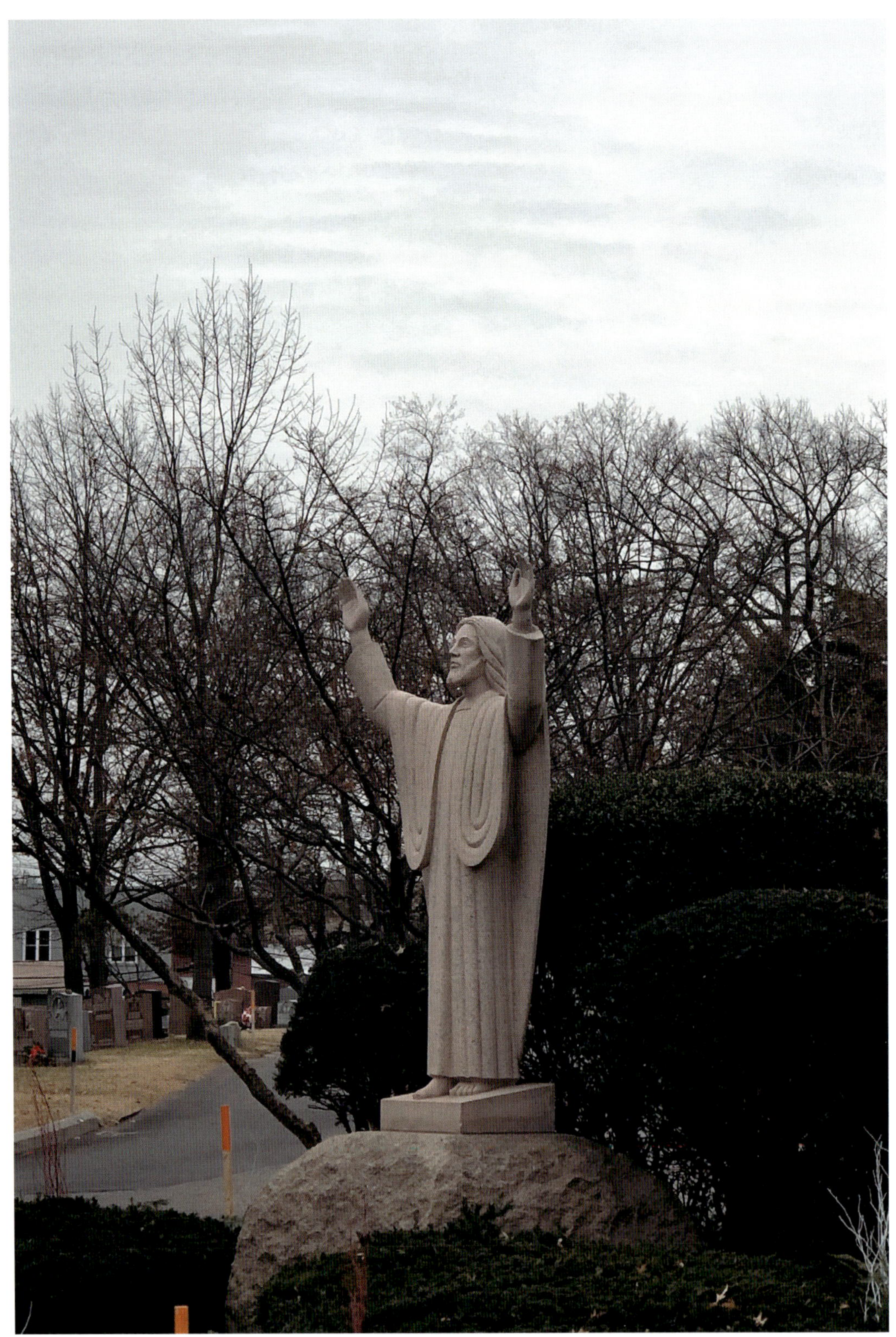

This statue of Jesus greets visitors near the main entrance.

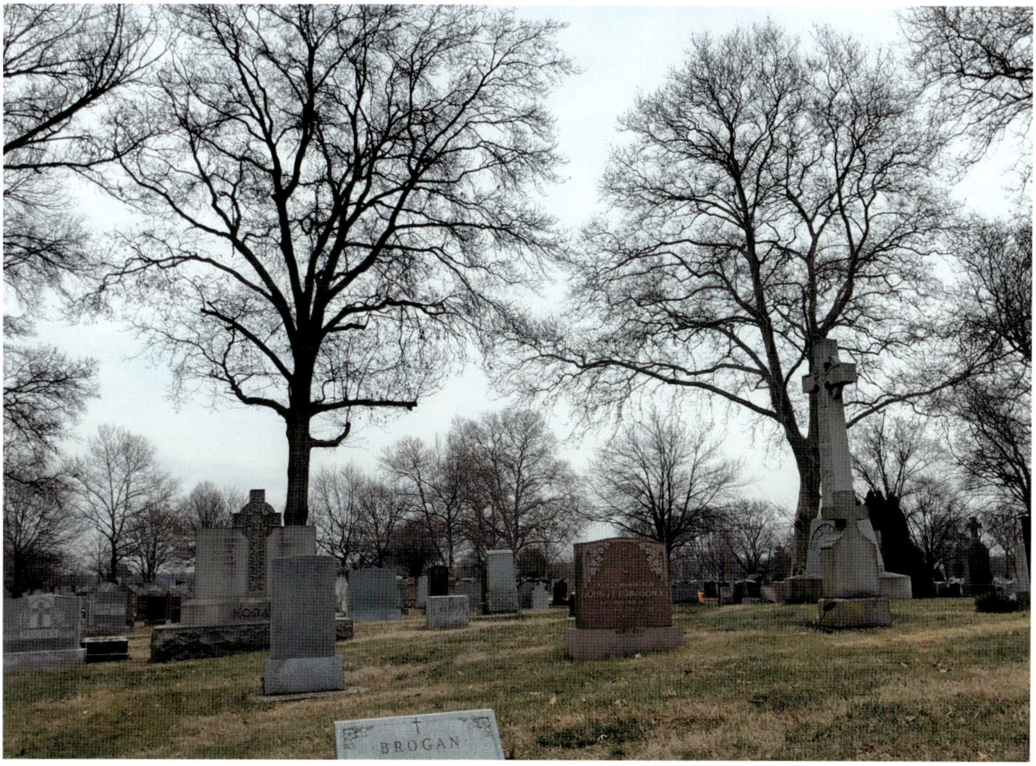

Winter plus an overcast day can make for eerie, gloomy cemetery views.

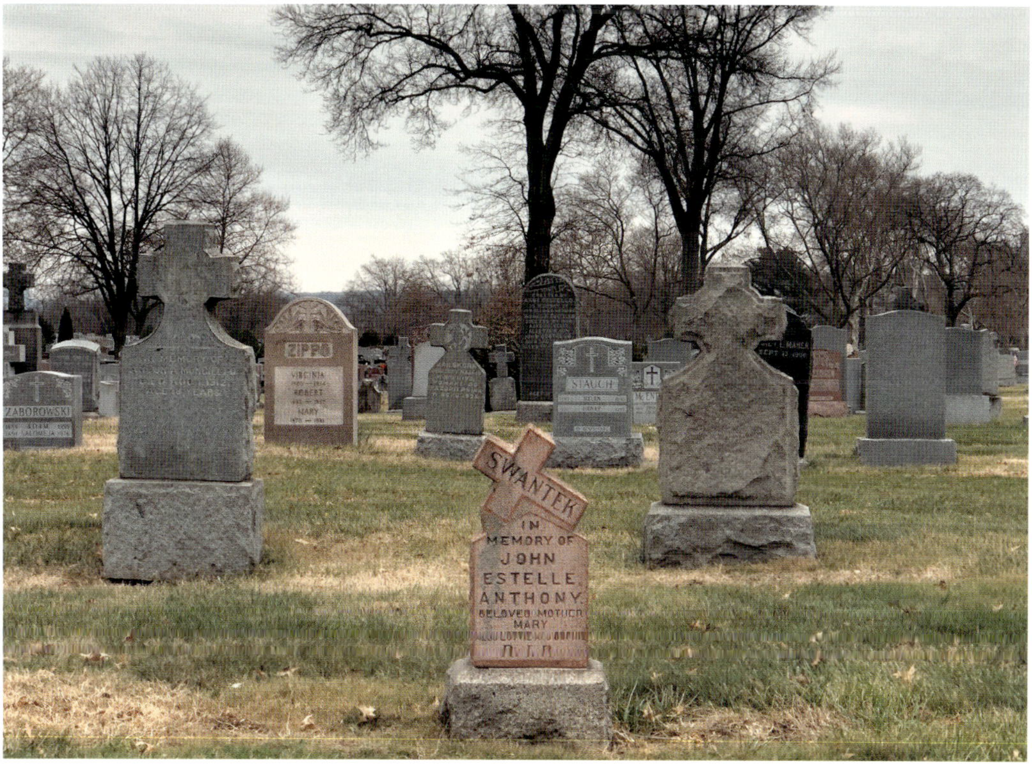

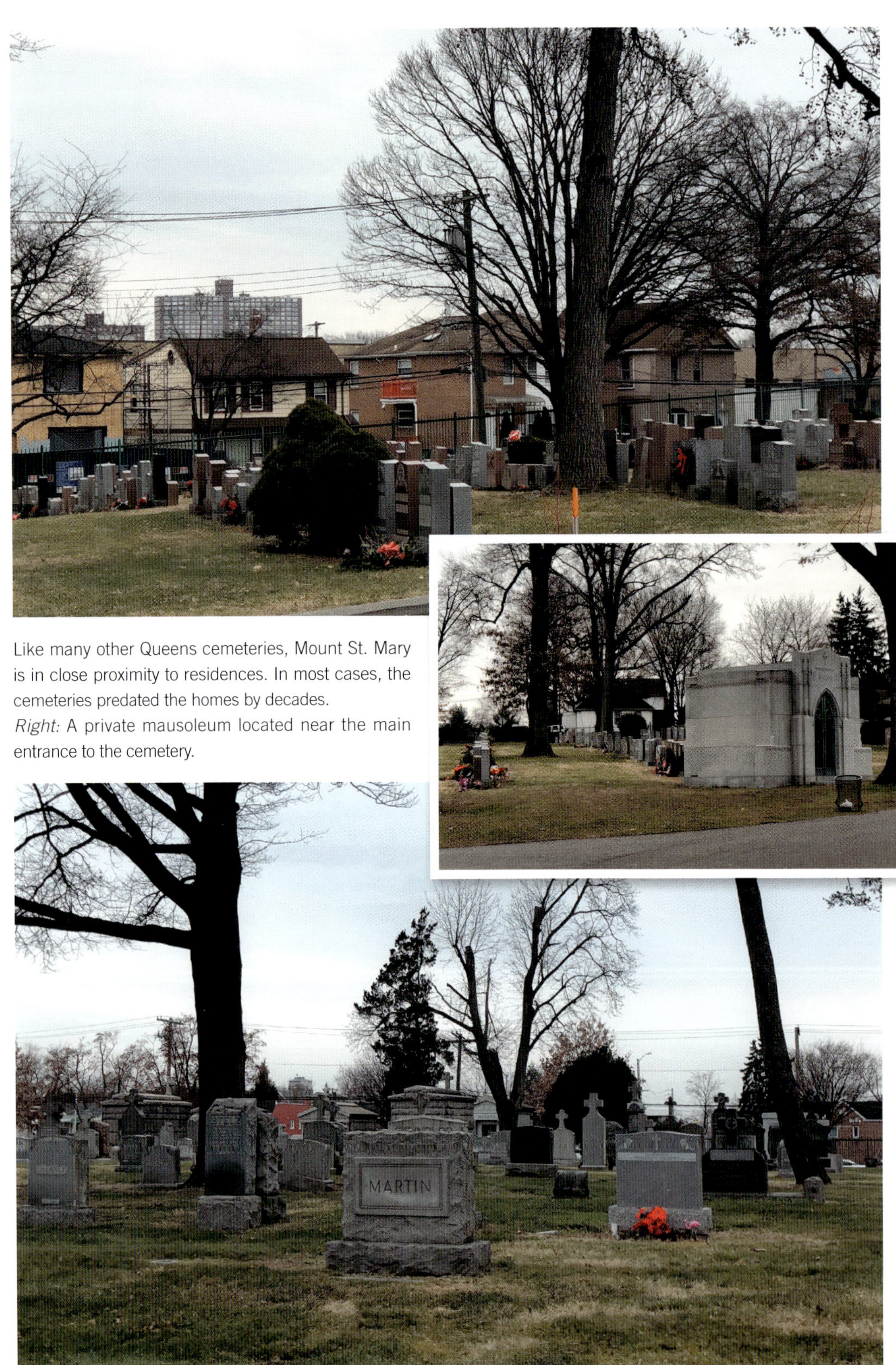

Like many other Queens cemeteries, Mount St. Mary is in close proximity to residences. In most cases, the cemeteries predated the homes by decades.

Right: A private mausoleum located near the main entrance to the cemetery.

19

MOUNT ZION CEMETERY

59-63 54TH AVE, MASPETH, NY 11378

Located in Maspeth, the 78-acre Mt. Zion Cemetery has an eclectic array of neighbors. Bordering a heavily industrial area (though bordered on the north side by a residential area), the western side of this Jewish cemetery is adjacent to the much larger Calvary Cemetery, which lies directly across 58th Street. Looking west, all that you will see is an endless sea of gravestones. The Brooklyn-Queens Expressway lies just to the north and the Long Island Expressway just to the south. The cemetery dates to 1893 and has more than 210,000 burials, many of them packed tightly together. Mount Zion was named after the biblical term for the City of David (though Mount Zion now refers to a hill in Jerusalem).

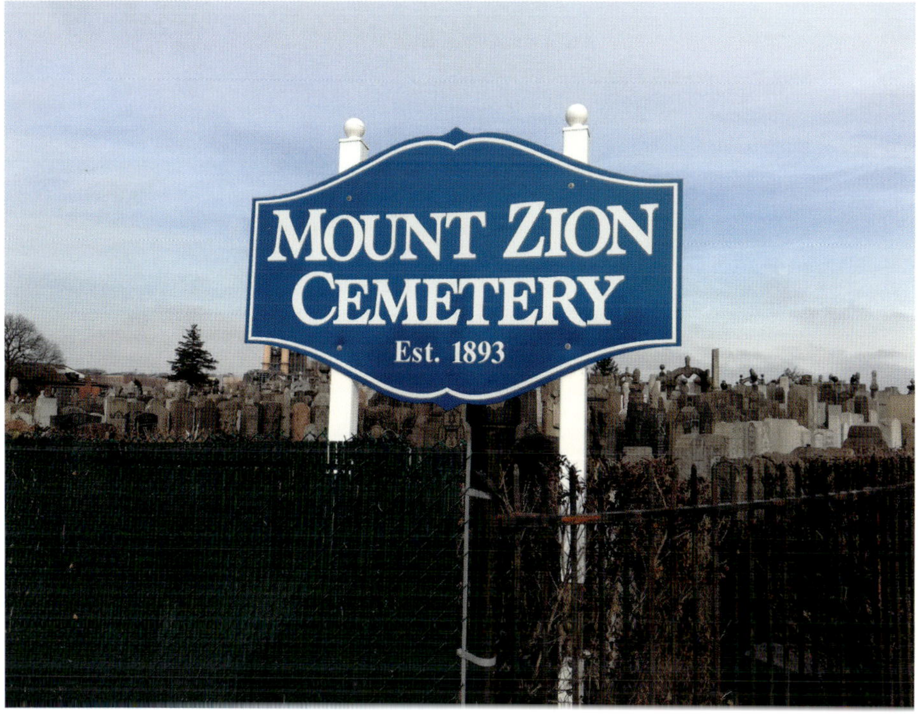

A sign for Mount Zion Cemetery at the corner of Maurice and 54th Avenues

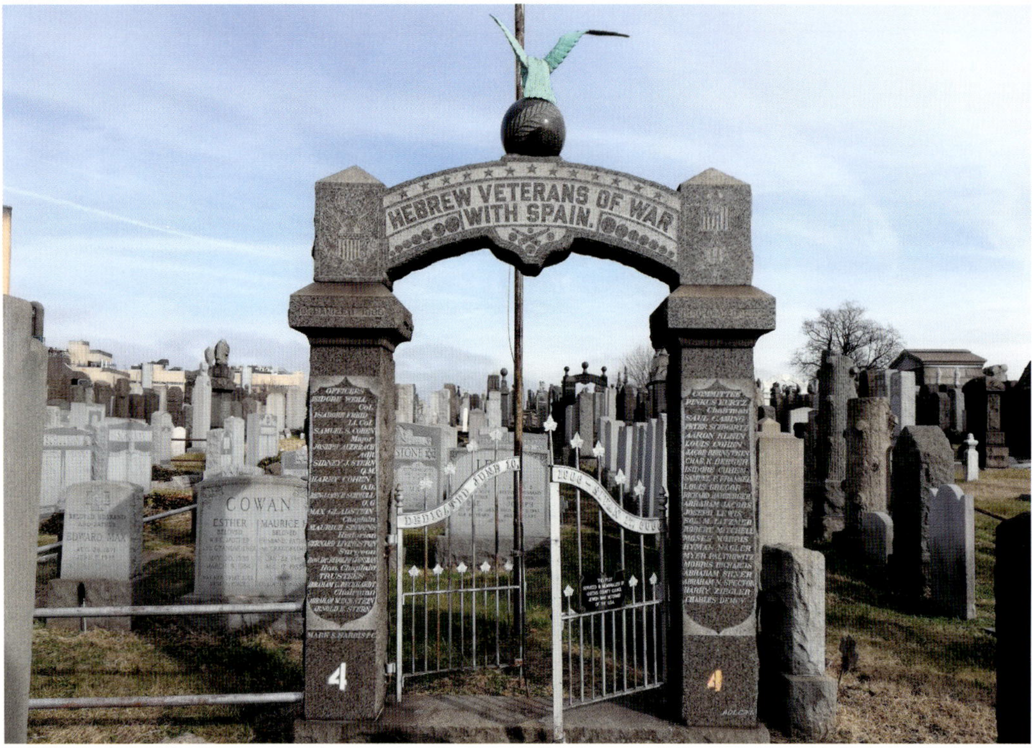

Two of the many association sections within the cemetery, where specific groups of people who belonged to various societies are buried.

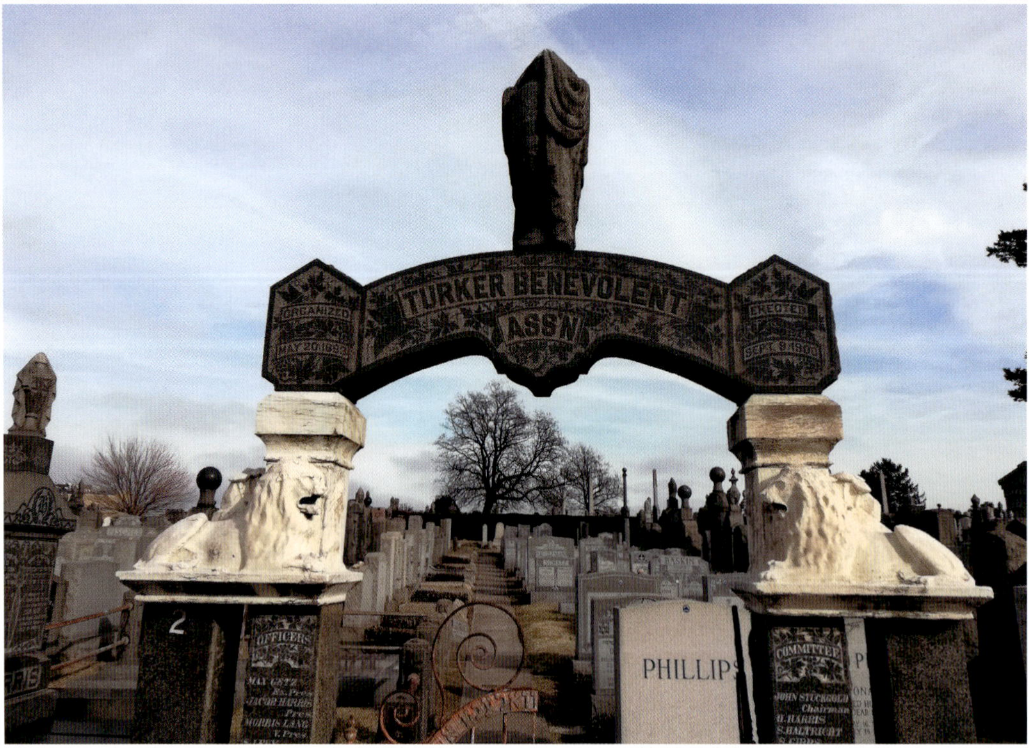

Right: A lion adorns the post for a Jewish association's burial section.

Below: A touching poem on a stone for a twenty-seven-year-old man.

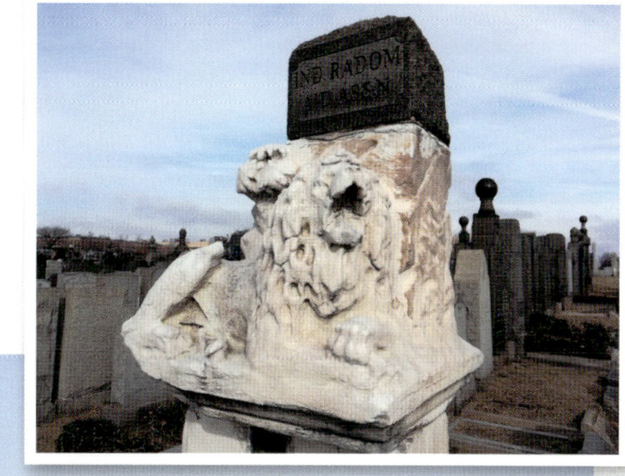

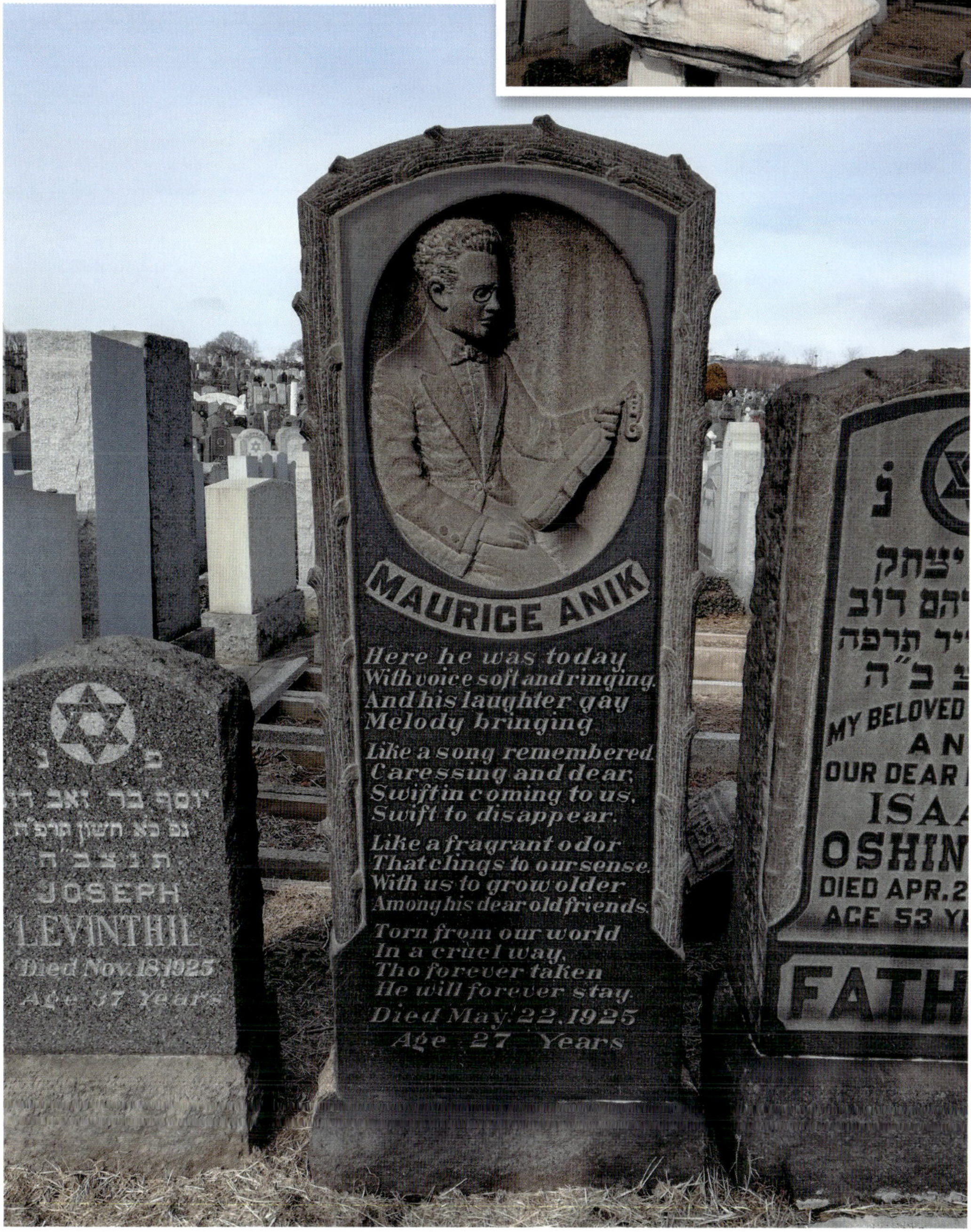

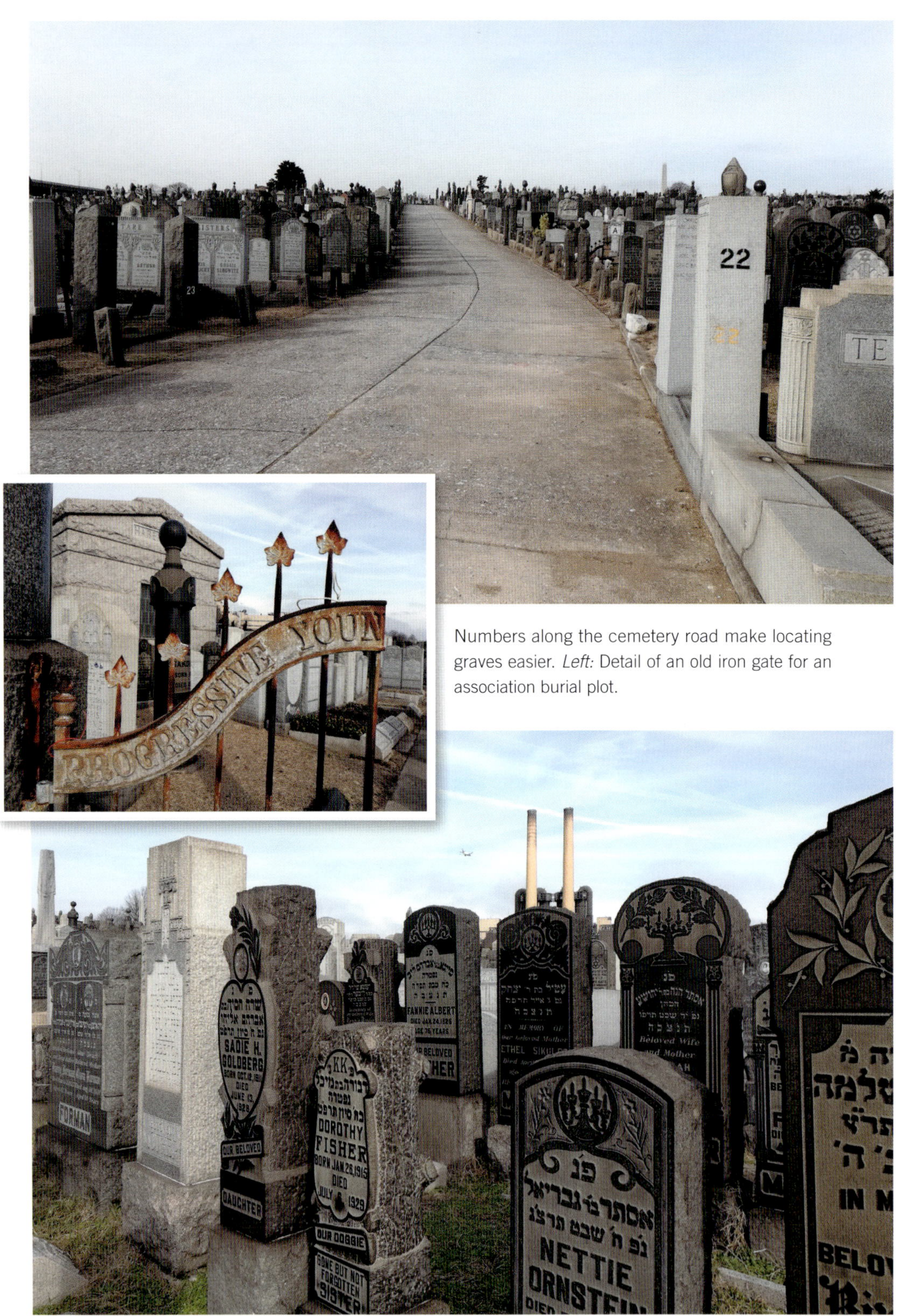

Numbers along the cemetery road make locating graves easier. *Left:* Detail of an old iron gate for an association burial plot.

The smokestacks in the background are a reminder of the area's industrial nature.

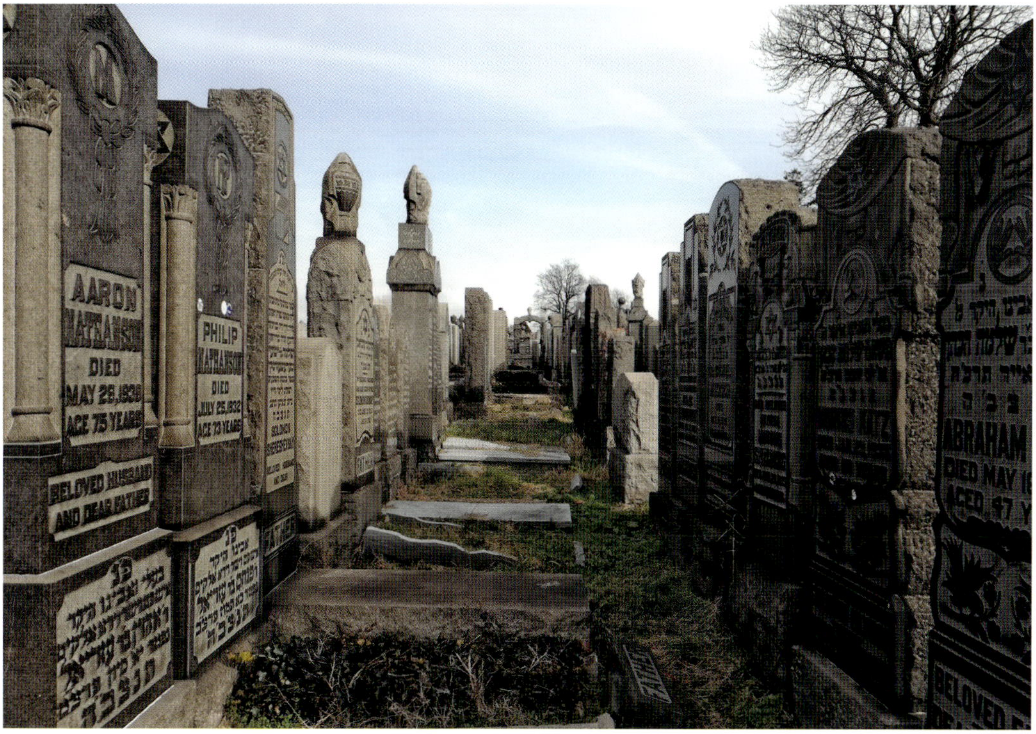

Most of the gravestones in this section have text in both English and Hebrew.

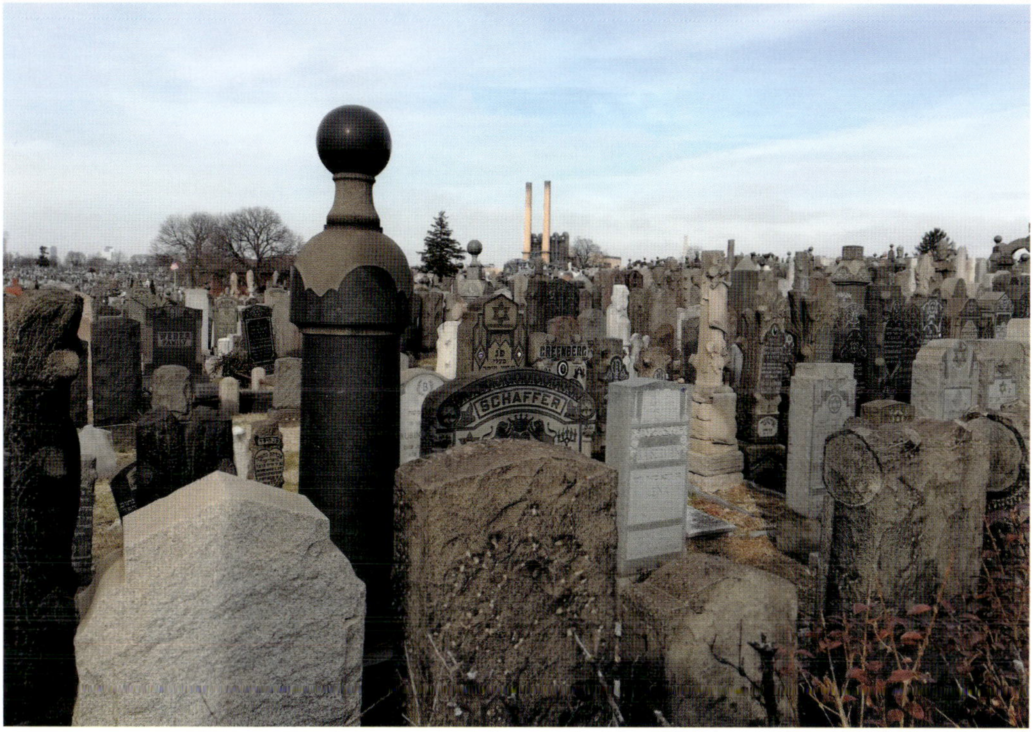

To the west of Mount Zion lies the expansive Calvary Cemetery.

20

The Olde Towne Burial Ground of Flushing

46th Avenue & 164th Street & 165th Street, Flushing, NY 11358

This cemetery, located on 46th Avenue directly across the street from the much larger Flushing Cemetery, was formed in 1840 by the town of Flushing to create a public burial ground to house victims of a cholera epidemic. The cemetery, originally known as "Paupers' Burial Ground," was in use for a dozen or so years and then again starting in 1881, when it was used as a burial site for African Americans and Native Americans. By the time it was closed in 1898, there were between 500 and 1,000 burials in the cemetery. The Queens Department of Parks acquired the property in 1914. The four remaining headstones, marking burials of members of the local African American Bunn family, were removed by the Parks Department. In 1936, the Works Progress Administration (WPA) converted part of the site into a playground with a wading pool, baseball field, and swings. In the process, the historic significance of the park was downplayed. It was only recently that the city placed more emphasis on the cemetery as a hallowed ground. A 2006 project relocated the playground and placed it on special foundations in order to not disturb the burials. The site was renamed The Olde Towne of Flushing Burial Ground in 2009.

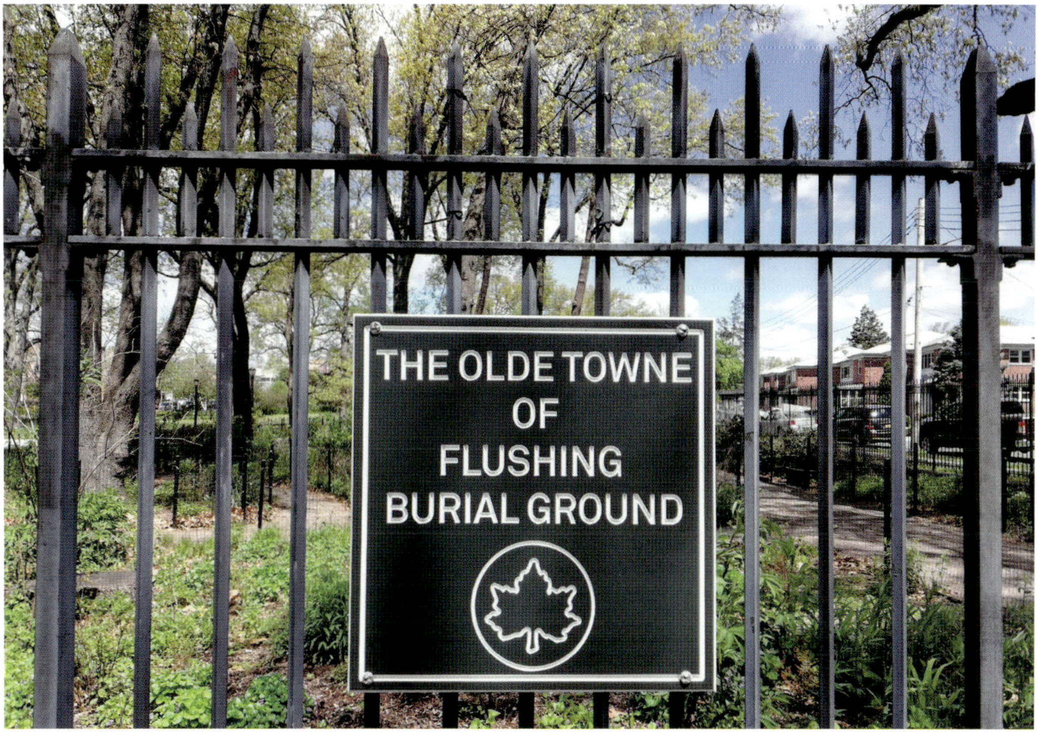

A recently placed sign marks the site of the burial ground.

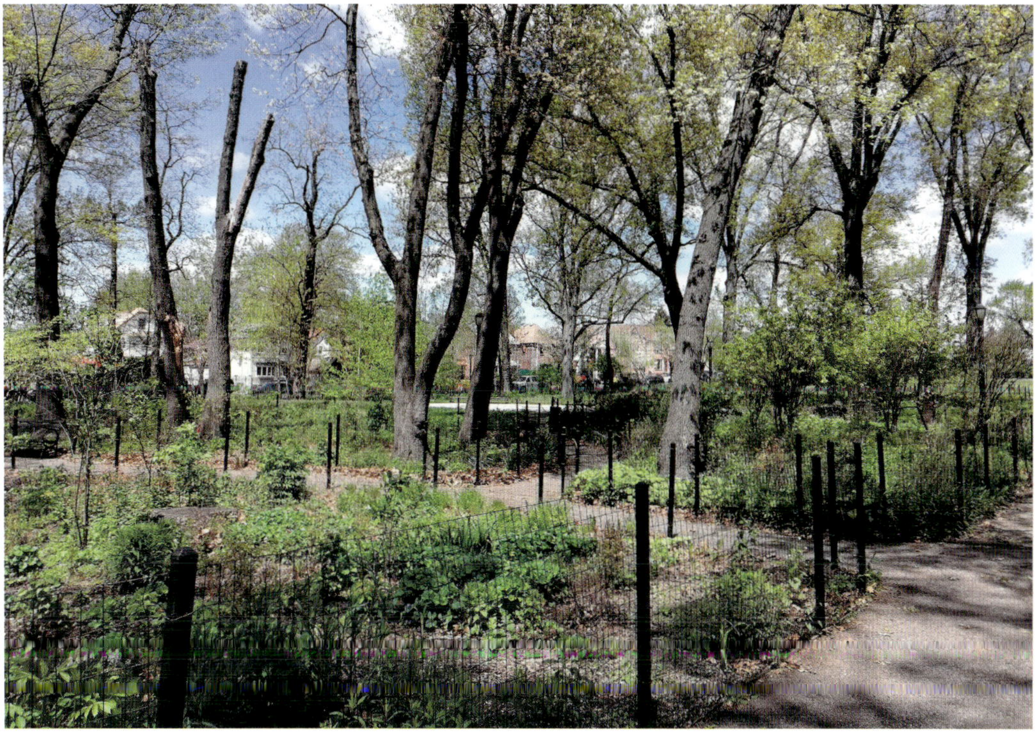

The cemetery feels hallowed despite the lack of headstones.

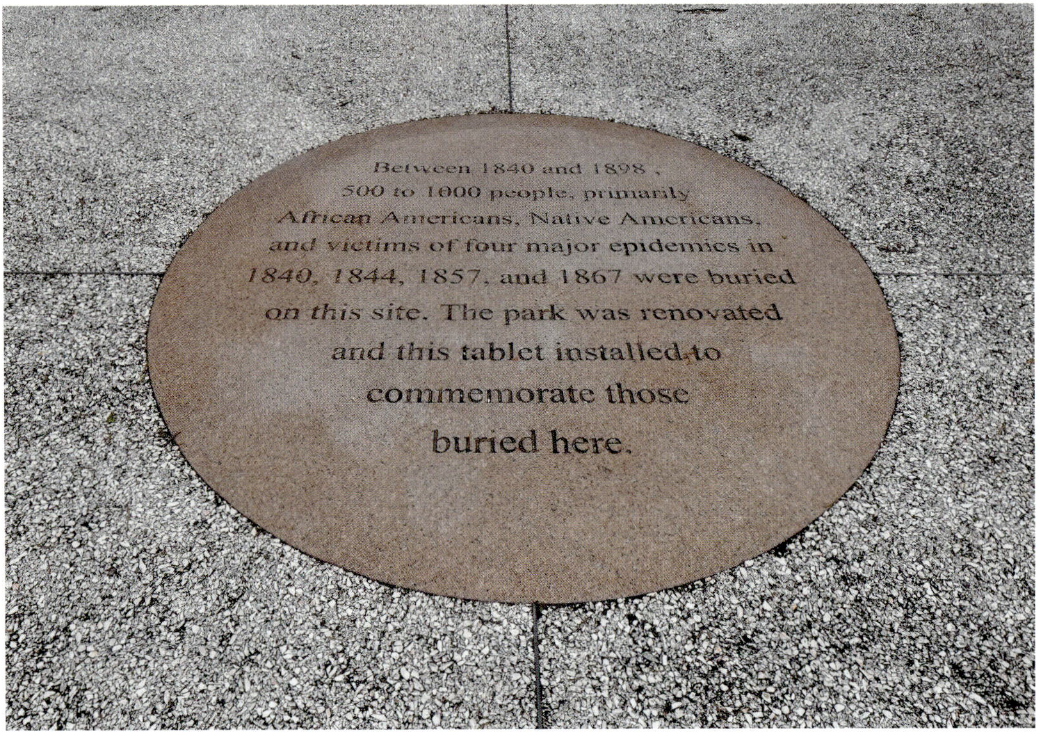

A stone plaque explains the history of the burial ground.

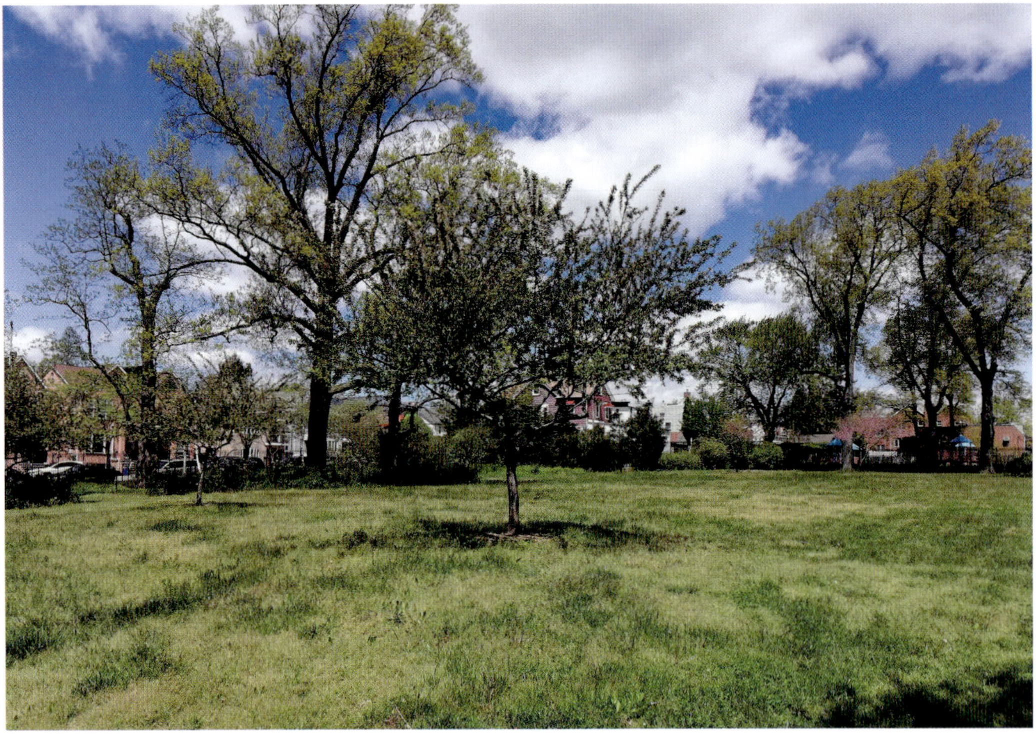

Part of the burial ground has footpaths, but another section is a grassy field.

21

Old Springfield Cemetery

Springfield Boulevard, Laurelton, NY 11413

The non-sectarian Springfield Cemetery, located on Springfield Boulevard in Springfield Gardens, dates to about 1670, making it one of the oldest in Queens. Oddly, the 5.5-acre cemetery is actually part of the Montefiore Jewish Cemetery, which surrounds it on three sides (it does have its own entrance and is fenced to separate it from the Jewish cemetery). Recent burials are mixed among the much older ones, but overall, the cemetery has the feel of a place time left behind, unlike its much larger and busier neighbor. Old local families such as Nostrand (104 burials) can be found here.

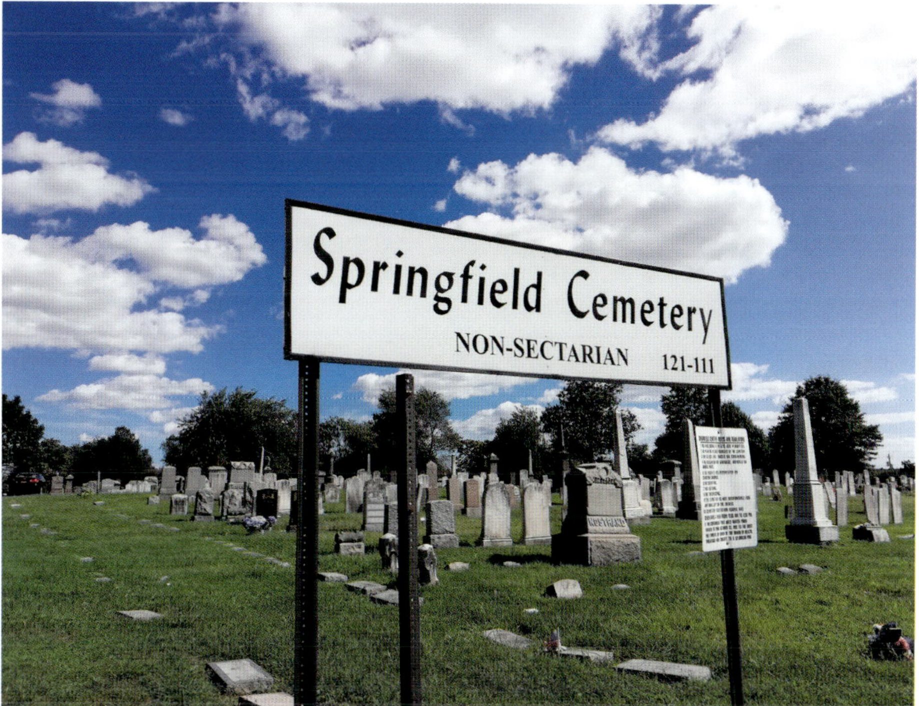

This small seventeenth-century non-sectarian cemetery is also one of Queens' most interesting in both its age and its location within a Jewish cemetery.

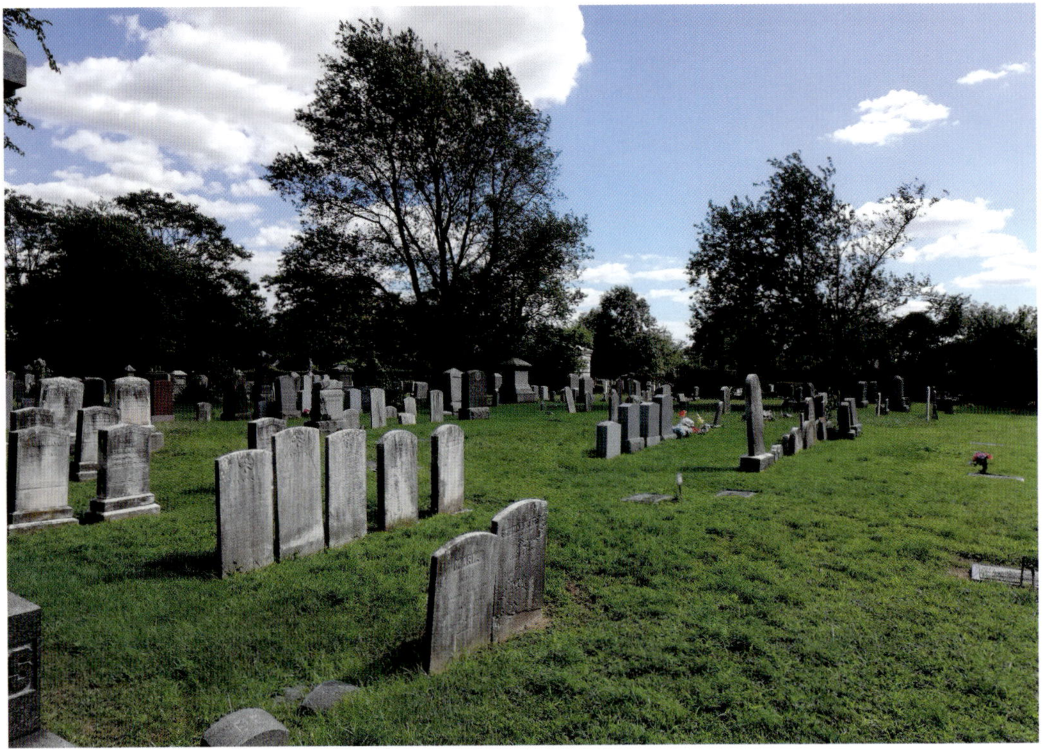

The Old Springfield Cemetery has a mixture of vintage and newer headstones, with many dating to the nineteenth or early twentieth centuries.

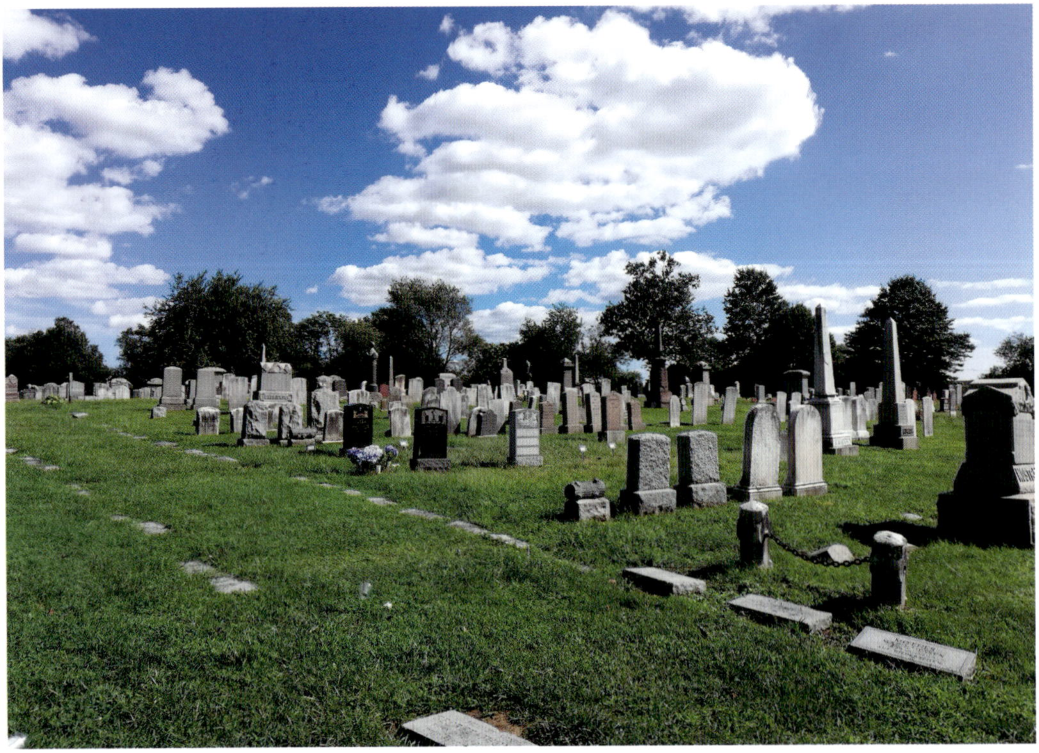

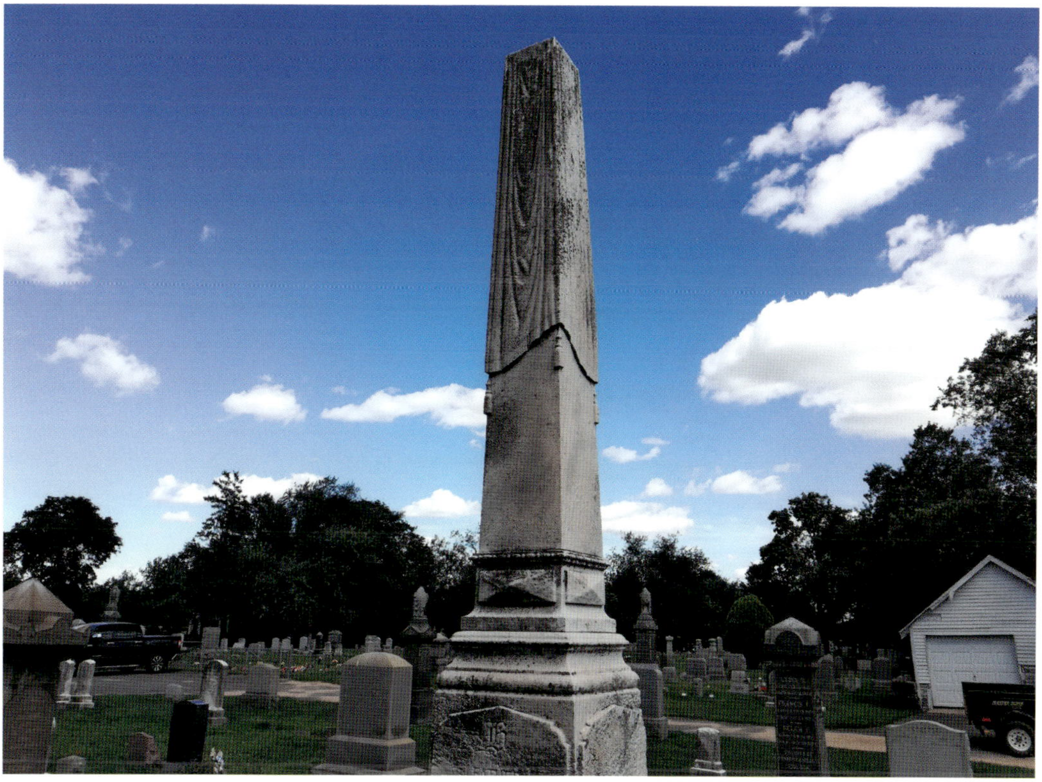

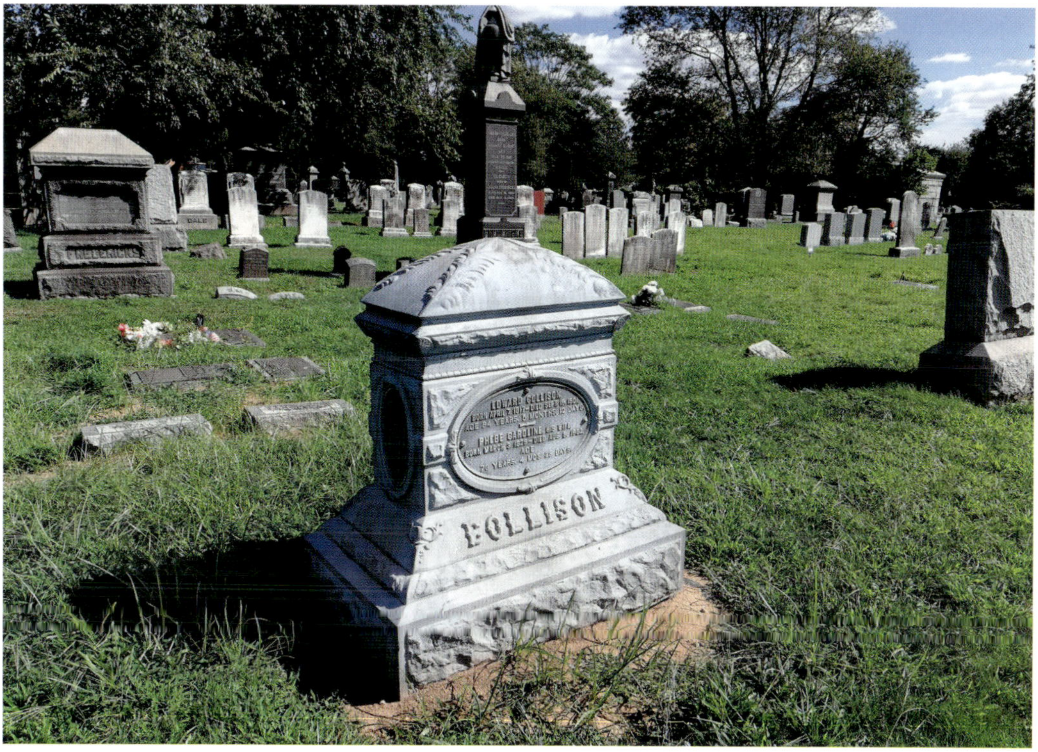
PHEBE CAROLINE
COLLISON

22

Prospect Cemetery

94-15 159th Street, Jamaica, NY 11433

The oldest cemetery in Queens may be one of its least well known. Located in the heart of old Jamaica village, Prospect Cemetery was founded in 1665 as the town burial ground. Located just south of the Long Island Rail Road tracks, the Prospect Cemetery sits adjacent to the remains of St. Monica's Church and the York College campus. The earliest surviving stone dates to 1709. The names in the cemetery are like a roadmap to Jamaica's history, literally. The Sutphins, Van Wycks, and Merricks all have roads in Jamaica named after them. The most visually impressive feature of the cemetery did not even exist until the mid-nineteenth century. In 1856, Nicholas Ludlam, a longtime Jamaica resident, purchased three acres of land to enlarge the cemetery to Prospect Street (now 159th Street). He built a Romanesque Revival stone chapel with two stained glass rose windows on the eastern edge of the cemetery, in remembrance of his three deceased daughters. His intent was not purely personal; the Chapel of the Sisters was to be used as a place of reflection and commemoration for any Prospect Cemetery funeral. By the twentieth century, the cemetery was already overgrown and showing signs of neglect. A 1910 book about the cemetery said that, "It is sad to record that many old stones have been used to form a walk and new graves are being made over the old ones." Prospect Cemetery was designated as a NYC landmark in 1977. The last burial there was in 1988.

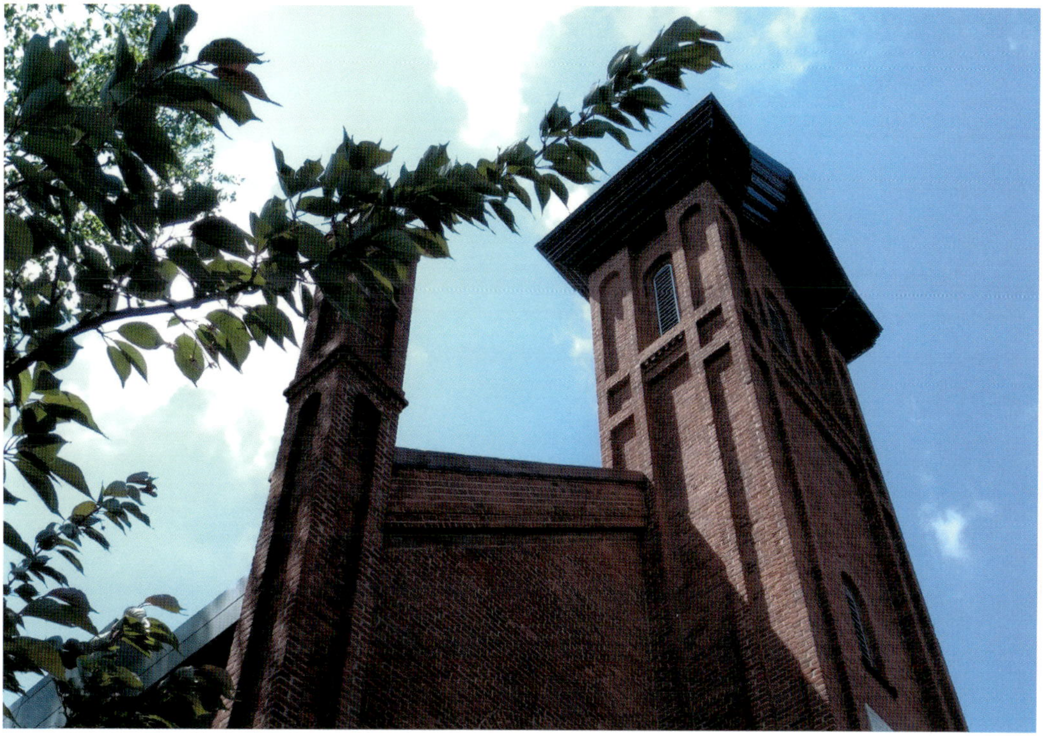

Prospect Cemetery is located adjacent to what used to be St. Monica's Church.

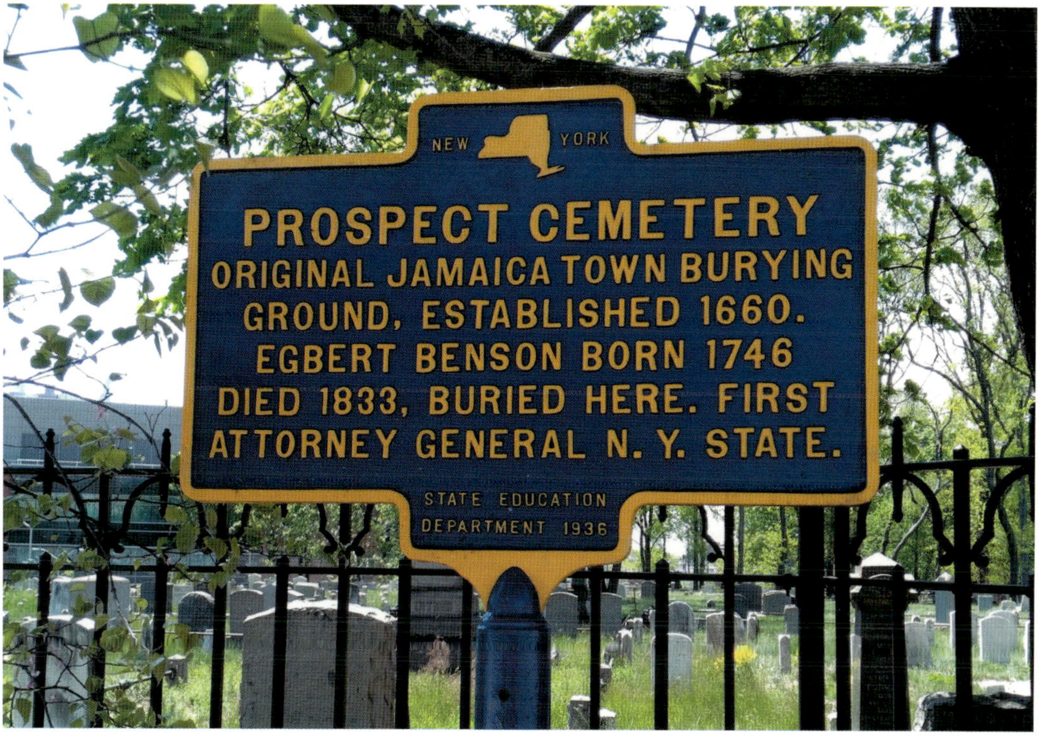

A historic marker celebrates the importance of the cemetery.

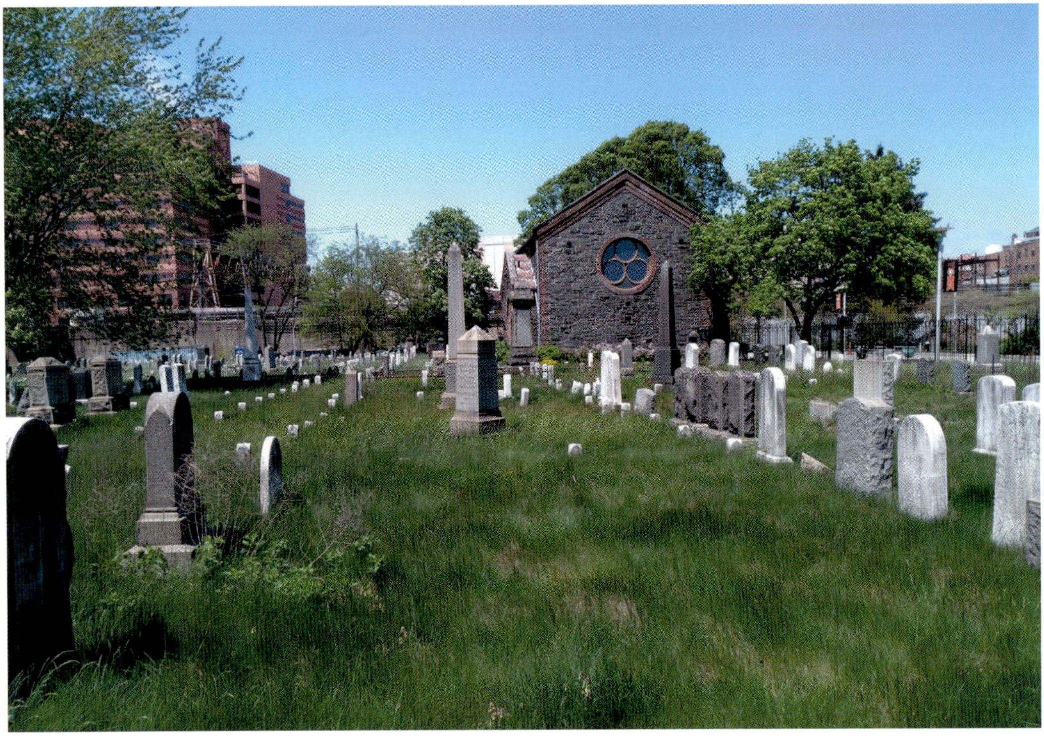

A Jamaica office building and the Chapel of the Sisters are in the background in this image.

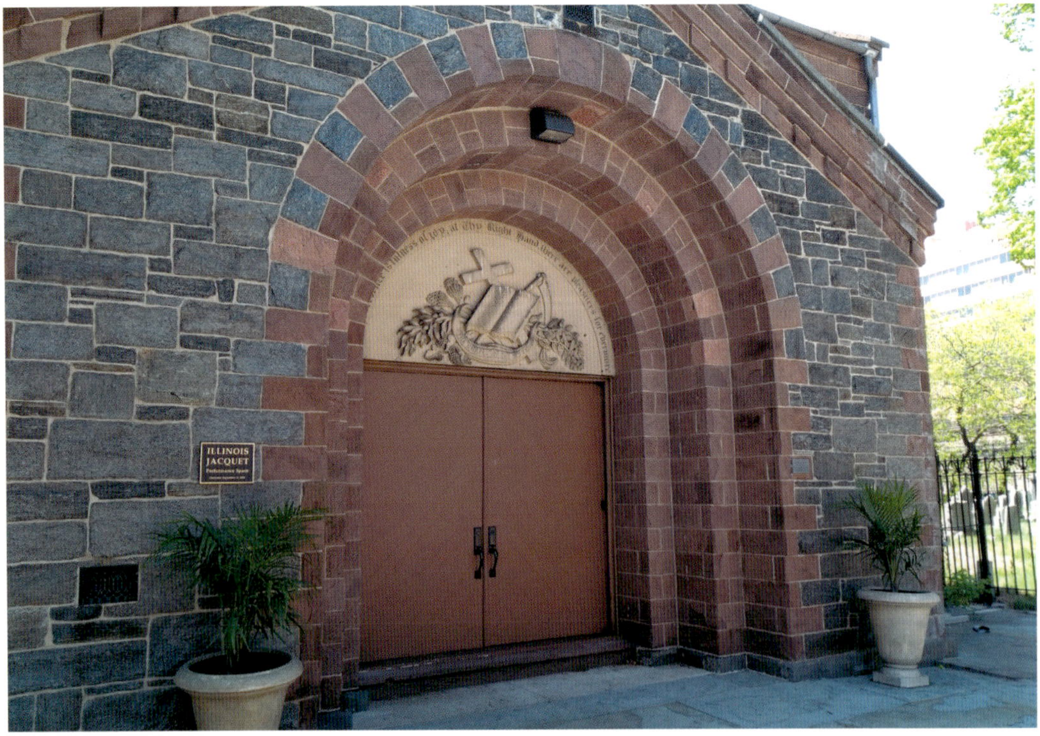

The nineteenth-century Chapel of the Sisters is a beautiful Victorian stone building.

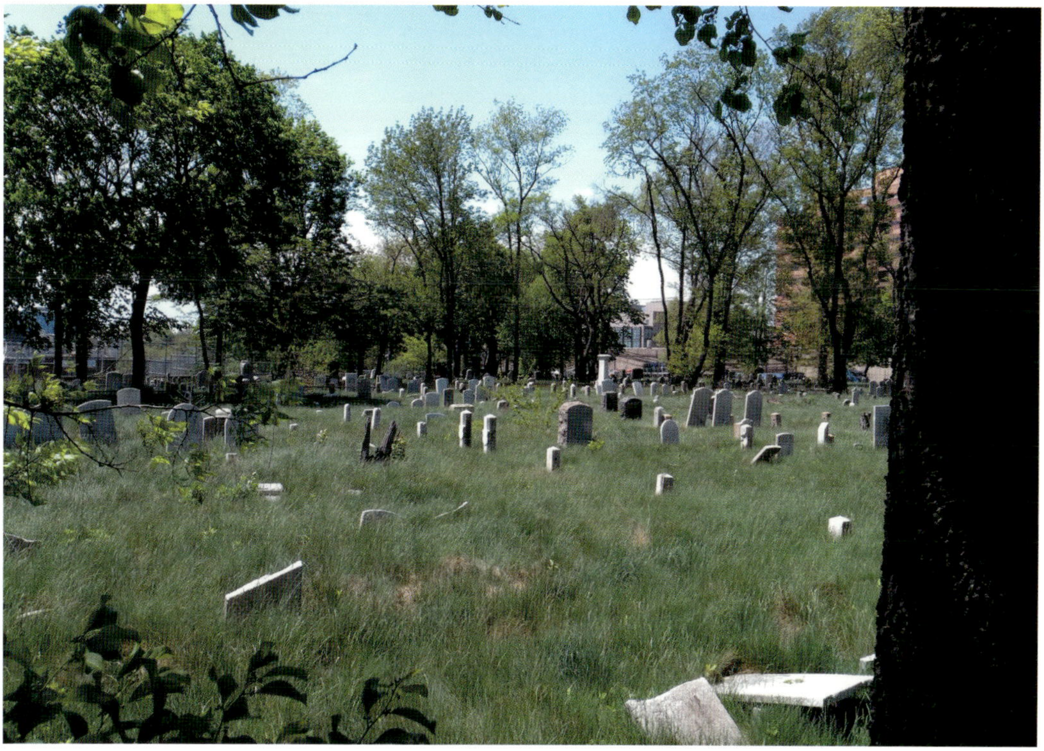

The burials in this cemetery represent some of the oldest Queens names; it is one of a few cemeteries in Queens that date to the seventeenth century.

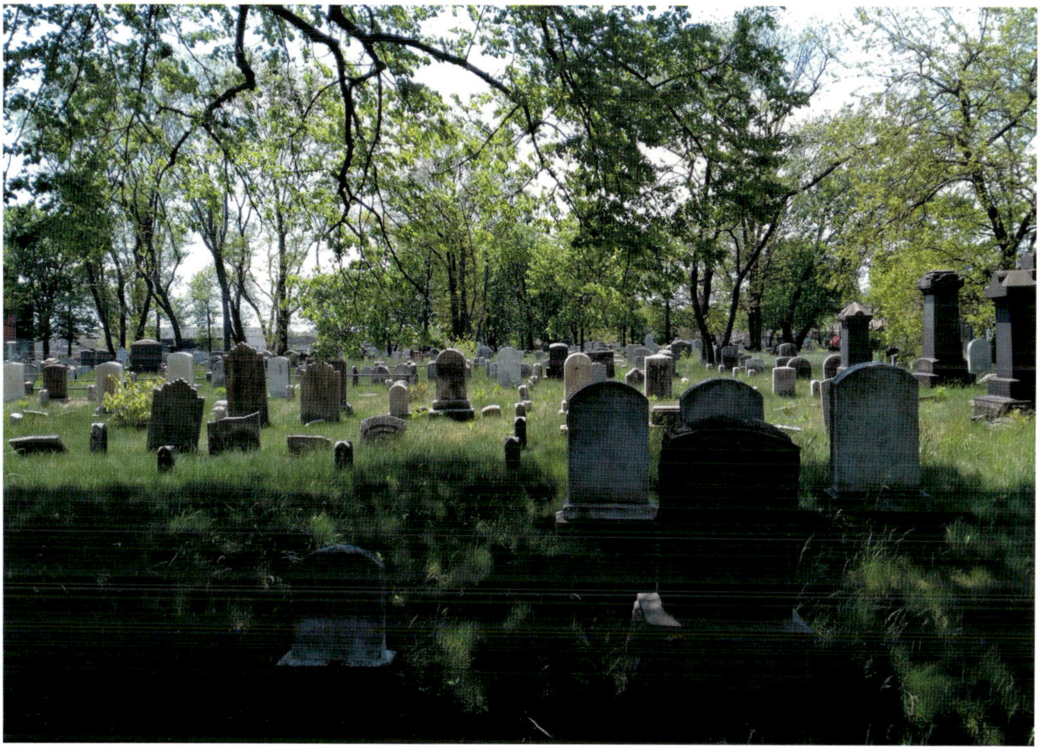

23

Pullis Family Cemetery

Juniper Valley Park, Middle Village, NY 11379

A few minutes to the southwest of the Remsen Cemetery is another preserved small family cemetery. This one is located near the northwestern corner of Juniper Valley Park in Middle Village (much of which was swampy land in the 1700s), on North 63rd Street near 81st Street. The Pullis Farm Cemetery (seven graves) was begun in 1846 on what was then the 32-acre farm of Thomas Pullis, to bury a child. Thomas Pullis (born 1778) was buried there in 1854. His will prohibited the sale of the cemetery and so it still stands today. The park was created in 1938 and incorporated the cemetery, while the rest of the farmland was sold off. Part of the property went to the St. Margaret's parish, which built a Catholic church in 1860 on what was called Pullis Road (now 79th Street). I sometimes went to Juniper Valley Park as a kid but did not know about the existence of this hidden cemetery until a few years ago.

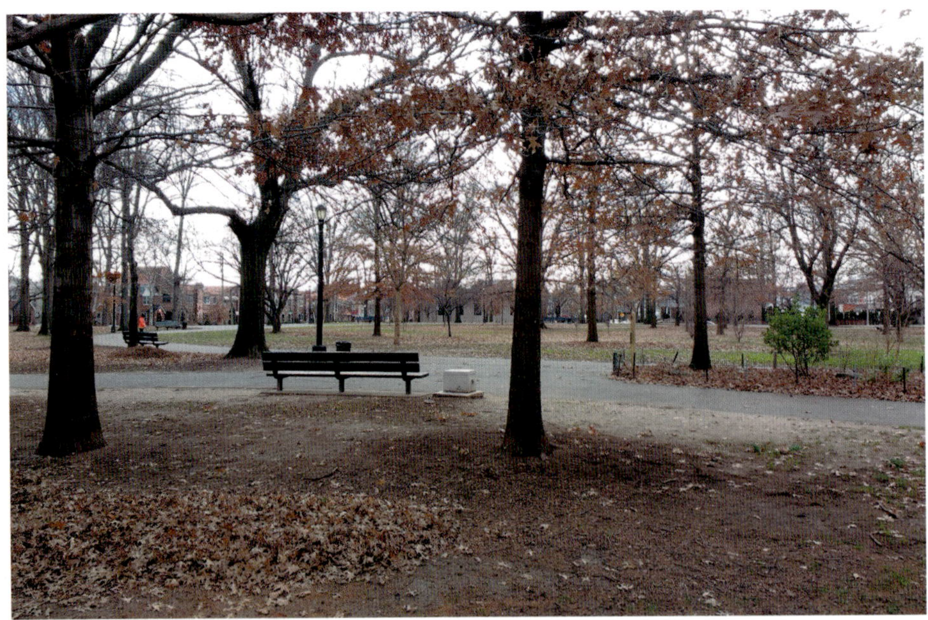

Juniper Valley Park is used by thousands of people every week. How many even know there is a cemetery within its limits?

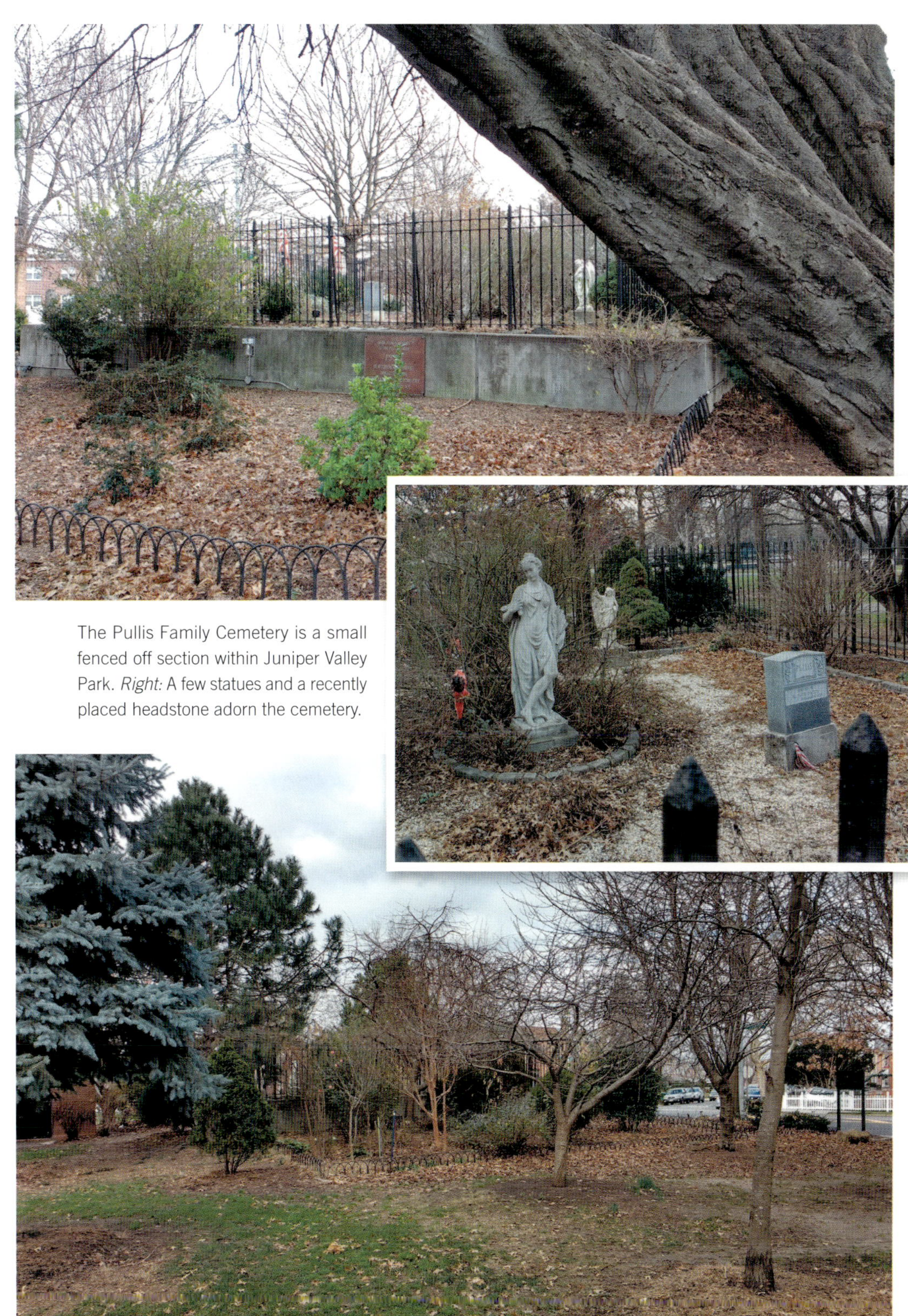

The Pullis Family Cemetery is a small fenced off section within Juniper Valley Park. *Right:* A few statues and a recently placed headstone adorn the cemetery.

You have to get pretty close to the burial ground to even notice it.

24

Queens Vietnam Veterans Memorial

57th Avenue &, Grand Avenue, Queens, NY 11373

The popular Elmhurst Park wedged between Grand Avenue and 57th Avenue in Elmhurst, opened in 2011 on a site that once held the ubiquitous (mainly from local traffic reports) and loved (interestingly) Elmhurst Gas Tanks, was selected as the site for a new memorial to remember the hundreds of Queens residents who lost their lives during the protracted Vietnam conflict. The stately Vietnam Veterans Memorial was opened in December 2019 within the busy park, which sees hundreds of visitors on any given day. As described on the NYC Parks web site, the memorial consists of: "Two semi-circular granite walls inscribed with honor roll of 371 names of those who died, historical timeline, bamboo motif, memorial name, and military crests, surrounding a sunken seating area and plaza inscribed with a map." The historical timeline is more in depth than what you might think reading the word "timeline"; it contains over 900 words of text explaining the history of the conflict. A glance at the list reveals the stunning ages of the deceased; the majority were between eighteen and twenty-two years old.

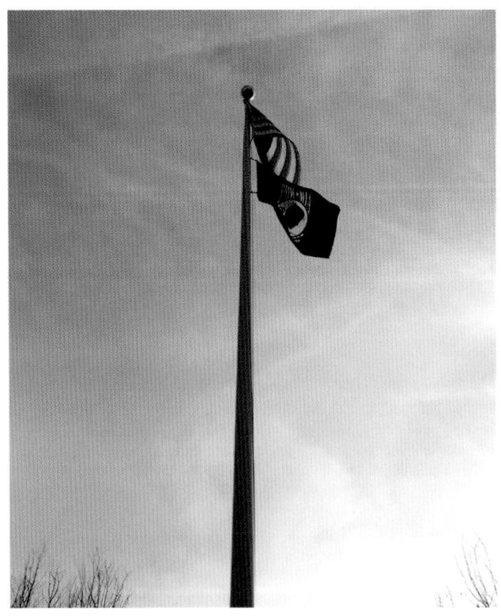

The American flag and the POW-MIA flag fly over the Vietnam Veterans Memorial in Elmhurst.

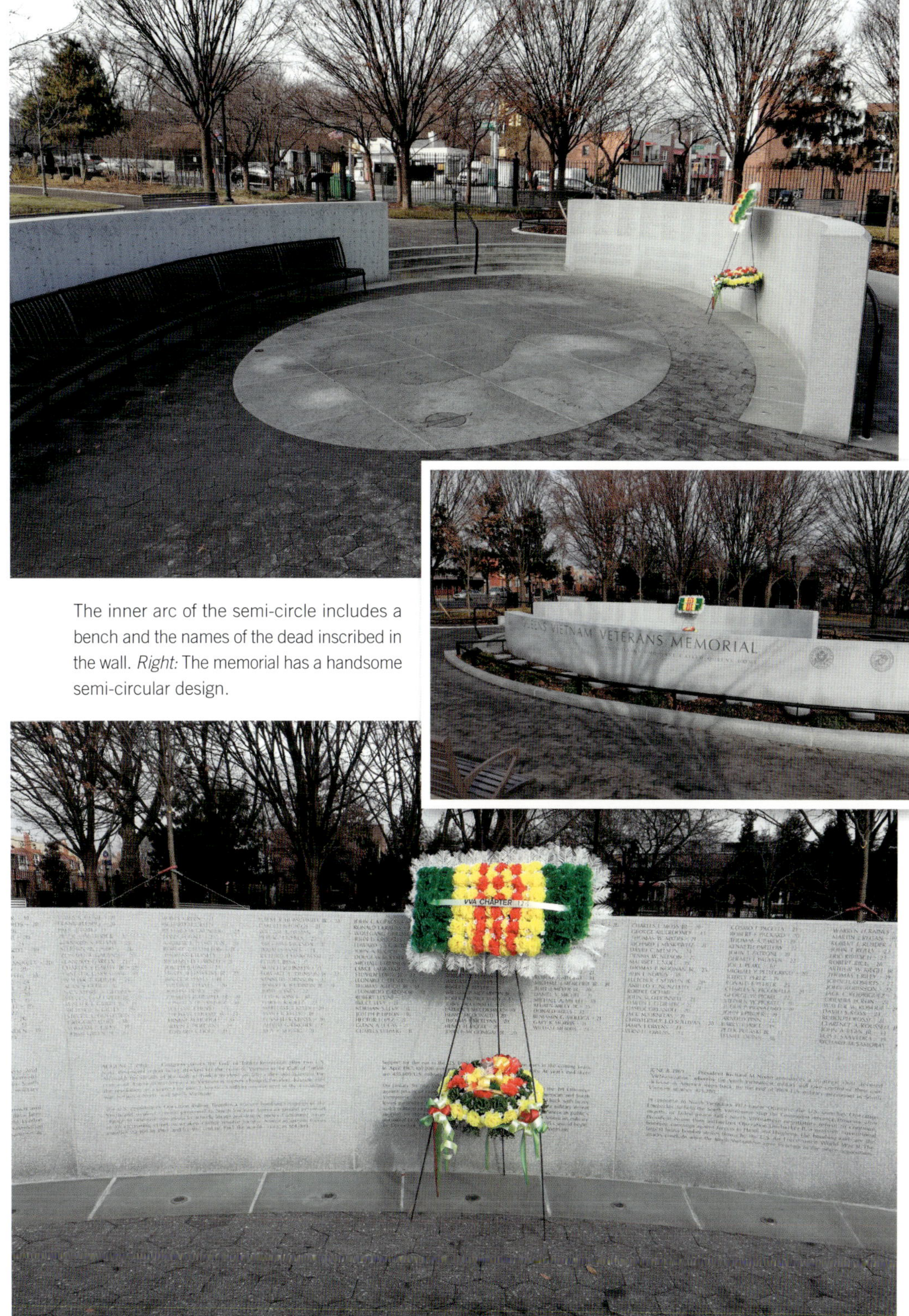

The inner arc of the semi-circle includes a bench and the names of the dead inscribed in the wall. *Right:* The memorial has a handsome semi-circular design.

25

Reformed Church of Newtown Cemetery

85-15 Broadway, Queens, NY 11373

Directly across the street from the St. James Cemetery is the Dutch Reformed Church, which dates to 1831 (with a fellowship hall that dates to 1858; the congregation itself was established in 1731 by Dutch settlers). This architectural gem, one of the finest examples of Greek Revival architecture in the city, is also one of the few remaining all-wood churches. The building was designated as a NYC landmark in 1966 (making it one of the city's first structures to be so honored) and was added to the National Register of Historic Places in 1980. There is a churchyard on its west side, featuring many nineteenth-century gravestones. As of 2021, the church is known as the Reformed Church of Newtown, and worship is conducted in English, Taiwanese, and Mandarin. It also offers a Chinese School. Many of the stones are badly weathered, but names and dates are visible nonetheless. Some of the old Queens (and specifically Newtown) names in the churchyard include Brinckerhoff, Rapelje (of which there are over forty burials), Lent, Polhemus, and Remsen. As one of the few churchyards left in Queens, it is definitely worth a visit. The Rapeljes (aka Rapelye) are part of family that traces its lineage back to the first European child born in what is now New York State.

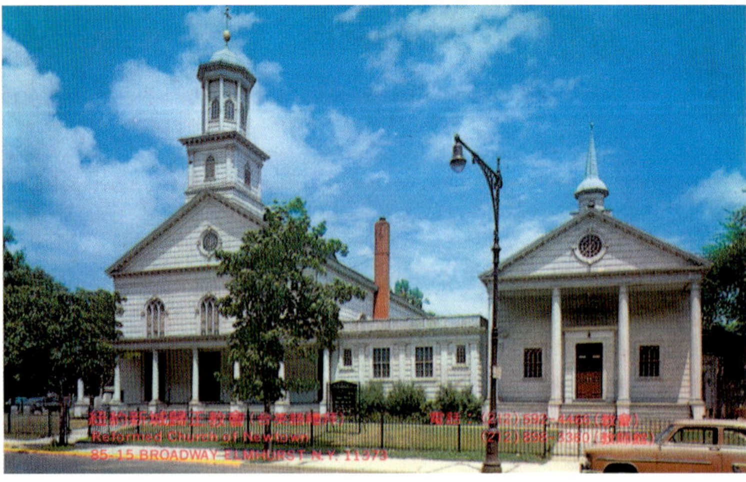

The nineteenth-century Dutch Reformed Church of Newtown (seen in a *circa*-1960s postcard) is a NYC landmark.

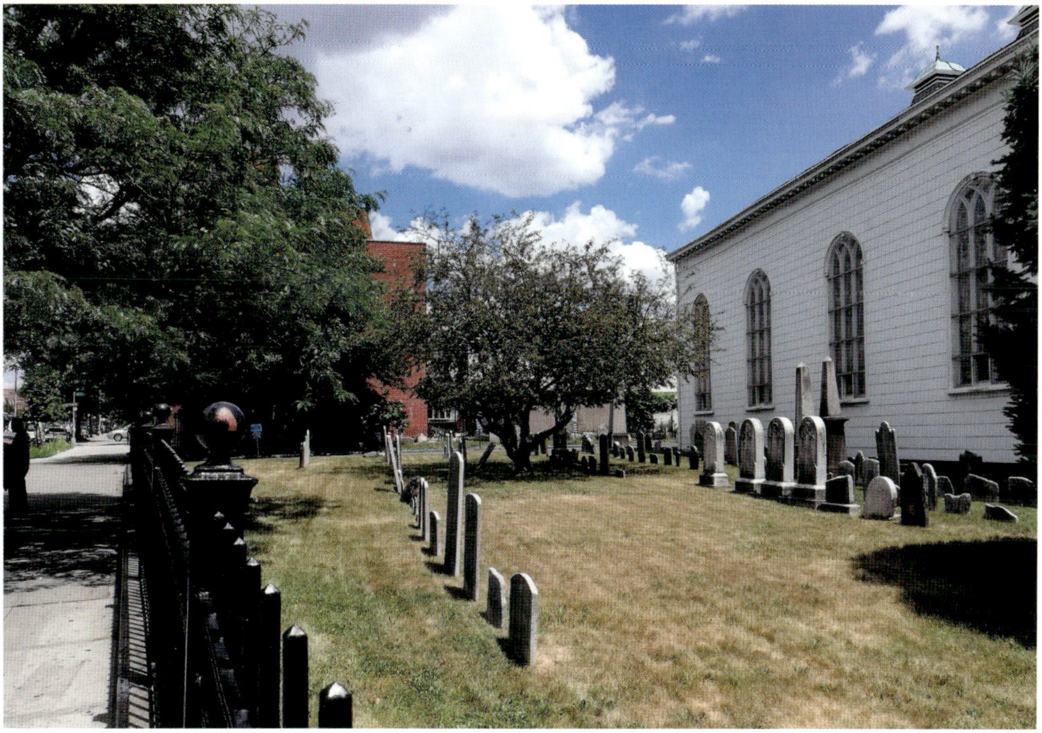

The churchyard is on the west side of the church, facing Corona Avenue.

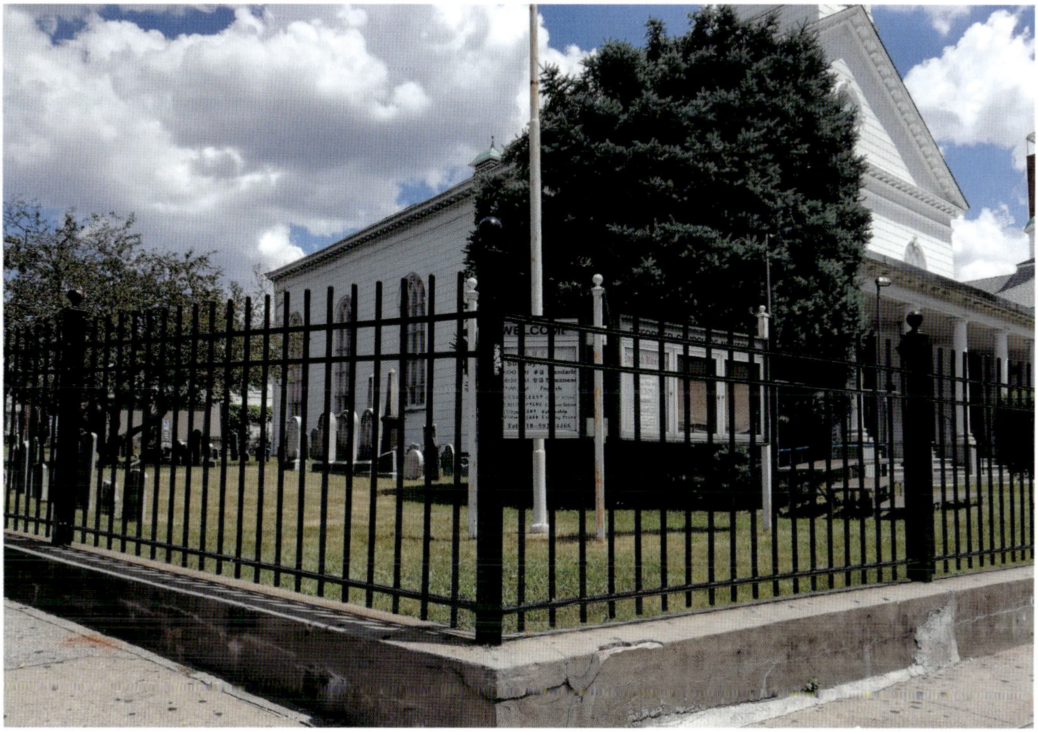

A vintage fence surrounds the church property.

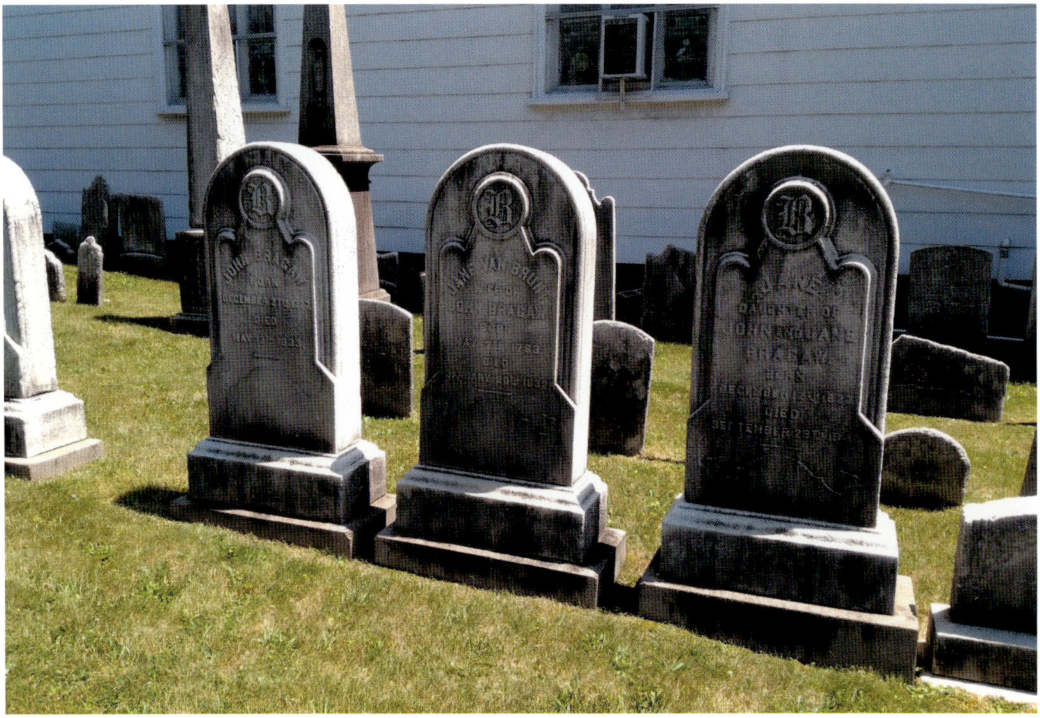

A trio of gravestones for members of the Bragaw family, with dates between 1832 and 1841.

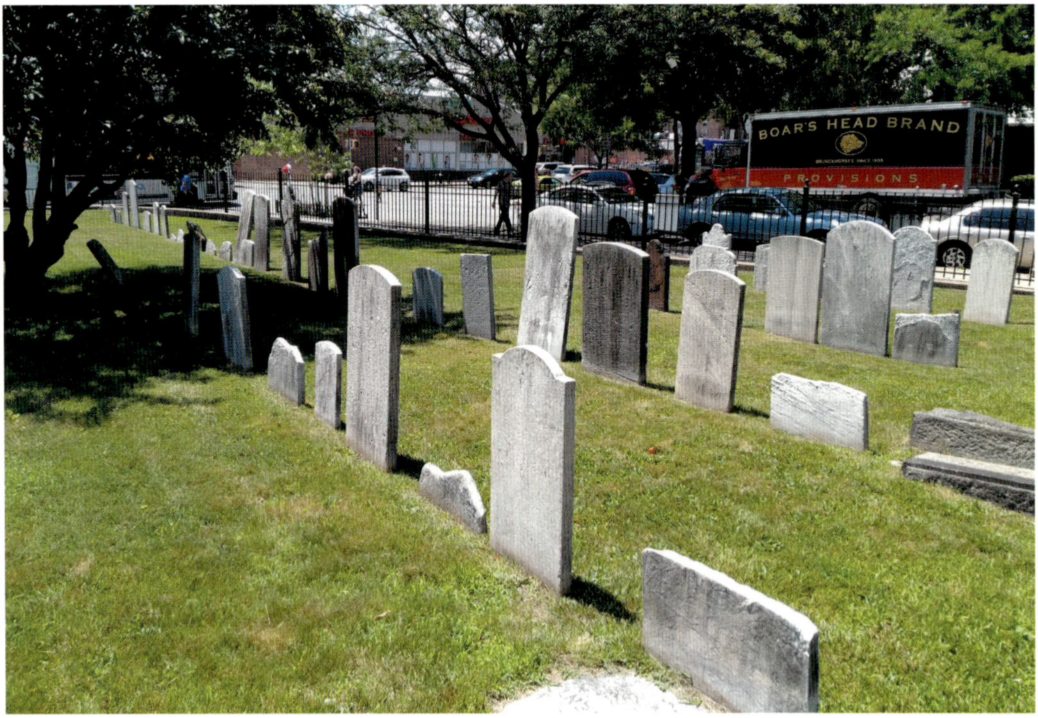

The age of these stones is evident in their lack of thickness.

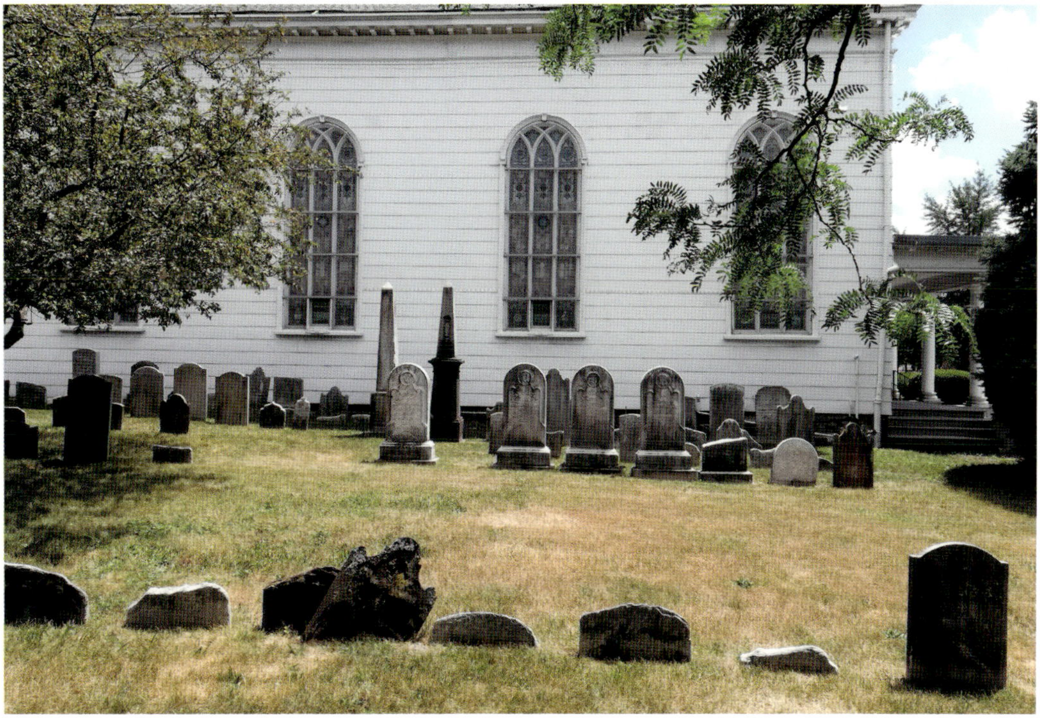

Some of the oldest stones are sunken or damaged.

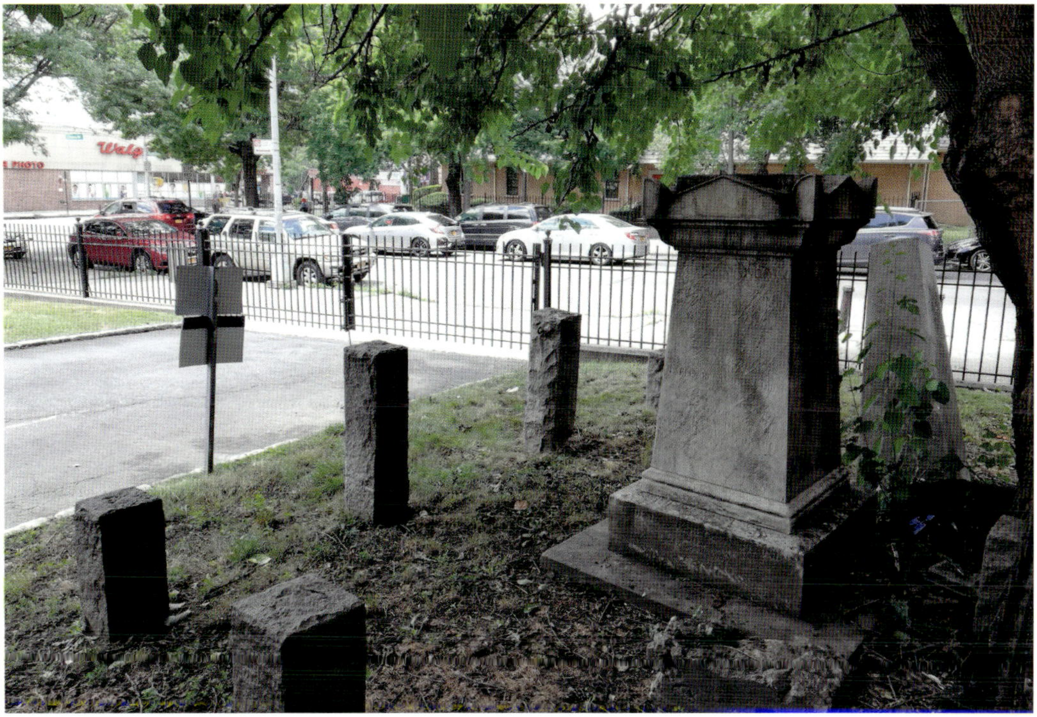

This may be the only spot in all of New York City where two churchyards are directly across the street from one another; the St. James Episcopal Church cemetery is on the other side of Corona Avenue.

26

Remsen Cemetery

Trotting Course Lane, Rego Park, NY 11374

Rego Park has changed dramatically from the settlement that was known as Whitepot centuries ago. One interesting vestige of the past dates to the eighteenth century, and it is tucked away, just off Trotting Course Lane, hidden in plain sight within a small triangle of greenery just steps away from homes and streets and a Home Depot—the Remsen Family Cemetery. The Remsen family, of German origins and originally called Van Der Beek, settled on Long Island in the late-seventeenth century. A member of that family, Jeromus Remsen, was a "Whig" during the American Revolution, as the patriots were known, and his army experience made him the perfect choice to lead up a regiment of militia soldiers. Remsen became a colonel and gathered a small group of men under his command in the summer of 1776, as the British massed in Staten Island preparing to attack. After the Americans were routed, he retreated to New Jersey and remained there until after the war. Remsen died in 1790 and he and at least seven of his family members are buried in this little cemetery. The cemetery, which became a NYC Landmark in 1981, is now owned by the City of New York. Because many of the original markers were destroyed over the years, new ones were erected in 1980 to honor those buried there.

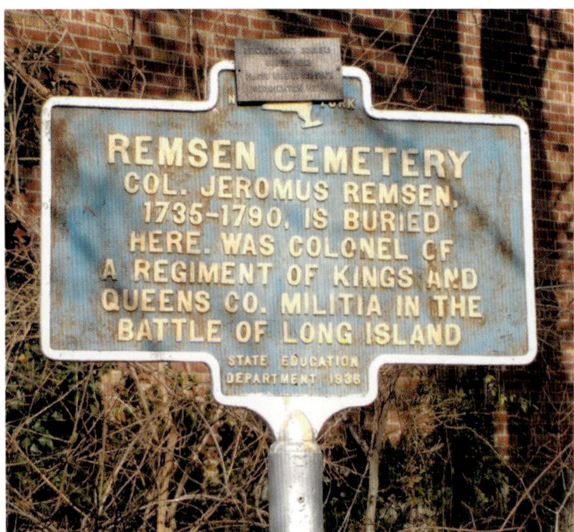

An old historic marker explains the significance of this cemetery.

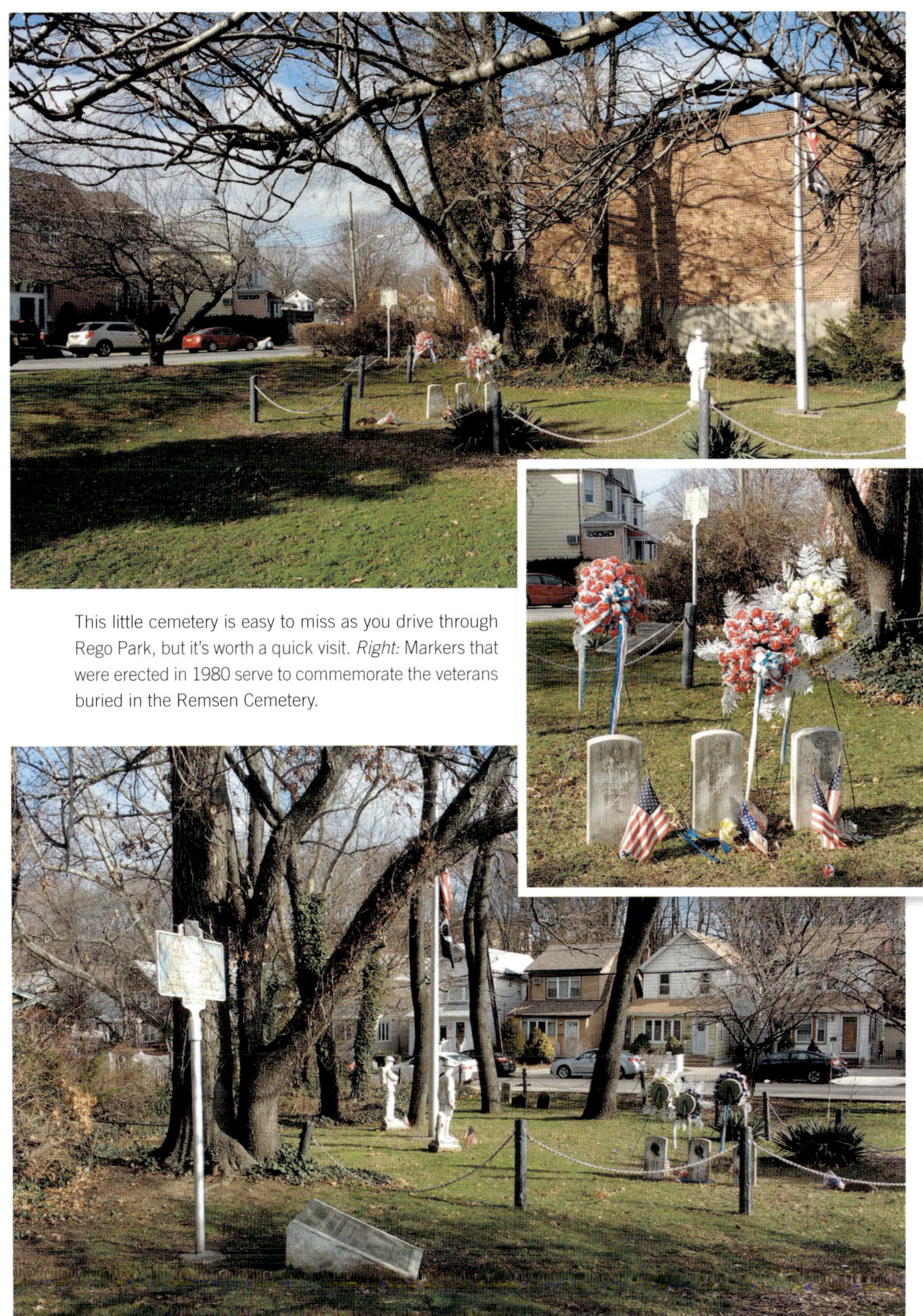

This little cemetery is easy to miss as you drive through Rego Park, but it's worth a quick visit. *Right:* Markers that were erected in 1980 serve to commemorate the veterans buried in the Remsen Cemetery.

Private homes are across the street from this eighteenth-century cemetery that is one of the few vestiges of Revolutionary War-era Queens.

27

Riker Family Cemetery

78-03 19th Road, East Elmhurst, NY 11370

Located in East Elmhurst, this old family burial ground has 132 graves of members of the Riker and Lent families. The cemetery is adjacent to the still-standing Lent-Riker-Smith Homestead, which operates as a museum. The Dutch colonial farmhouse was built in 1654 by Abraham Rycken Van Lent, making it the oldest dwelling in New York City that is still used as such. One of the burials in the cemetery is Catherine Ann Tone, whose husband Wolfe Tone was a leader of the 1848 Irish revolt. It was a Riker who in 1852 wrote the famous (to local historians at any rate) volume called *The Annals of Newtown* (of which what is now East Elmhurst was a part).

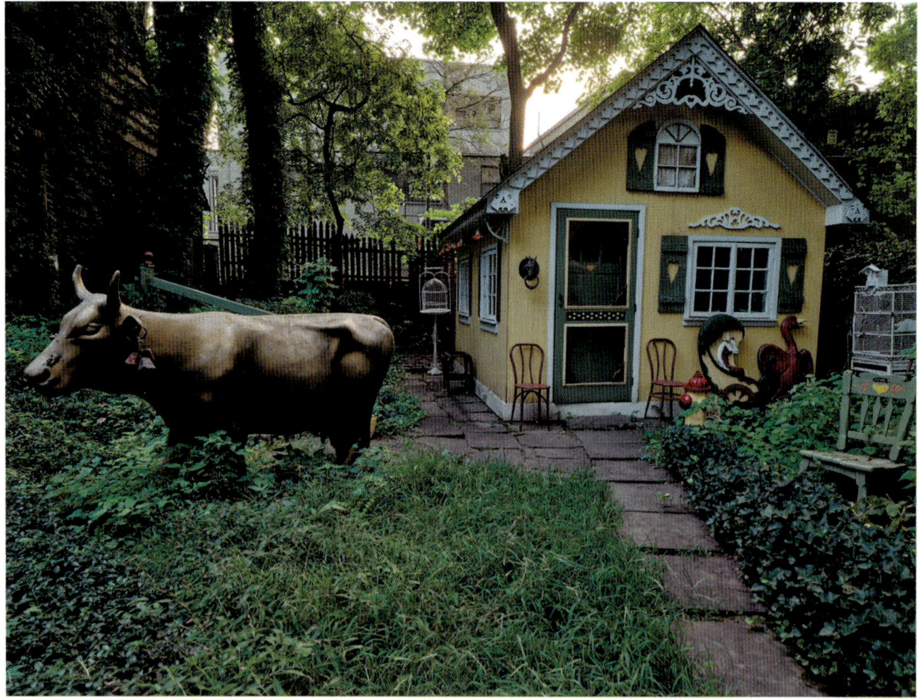

The Lent-Riker-Smith Homestead dates back to the mid-seventeenth century and has a cemetery attached to it.

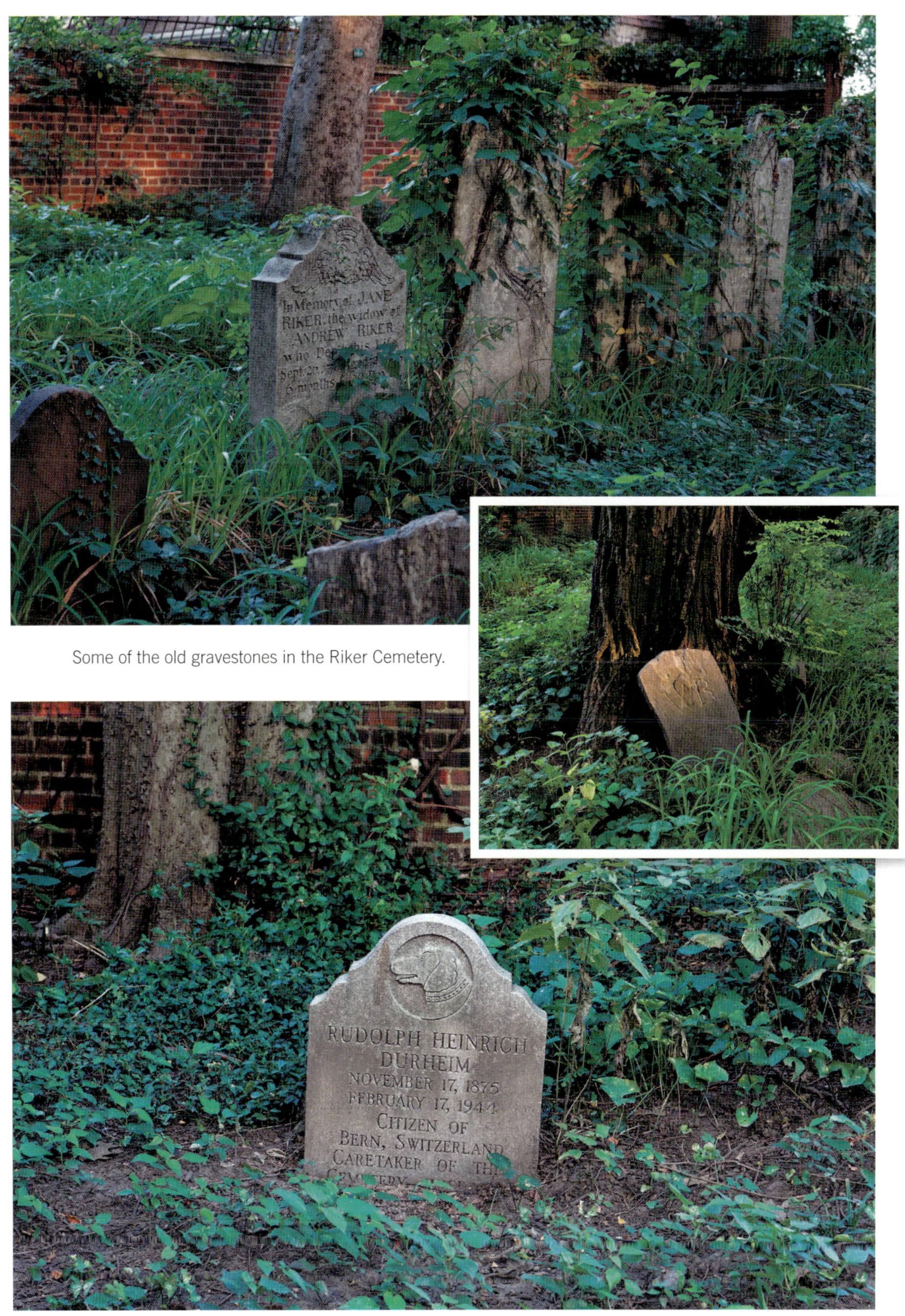

Some of the old gravestones in the Riker Cemetery.

The headstone of Rudolph Durheim, caretaker of the cemetery.

28

St. James Church Cemetery

84-07 Broadway, Elmhurst, NY 11373

Sheltered under the shade of large old trees, the St. James Cemetery on Broadway in Elmhurst is connected to one of the most storied and historic parishes in the history of New York. The original St. James Anglican (later Episcopal) Church was built on the south side of Broadway in 1735 (and is still standing), in the center of the seventeenth-century village of Newtown. The church served the sleepy farming village well, and was used by the British when they occupied Newtown during the Revolution. General Sir William Howe, commander of British forces in America, worshiped at the church. Future King William IV, the monarch before Queen Victoria, worshiped there when he was stationed in Newtown as a teenaged naval ensign. The cemetery across the street from the original church also dates to the eighteenth century and is one of the few remaining churchyards in Queens. A bigger, Gothic-style church was built adjacent to the cemetery in 1848; it burned down in 1975 and was replaced with the current church in 1976. The original eighteenth-century church building received landmark status in 2018. The cemetery is a peaceful enclave in the heart of the thriving multi-ethnic community that Elmhurst has become. Though not open to the public, great views of the cemetery are available from its peripheries either by walking along Corona Avenue or St. James Avenue. The graves include members of many of Newtown's early important families, notably the Moores, of Clement Clarke and Bishop Benjamin Moore fame.

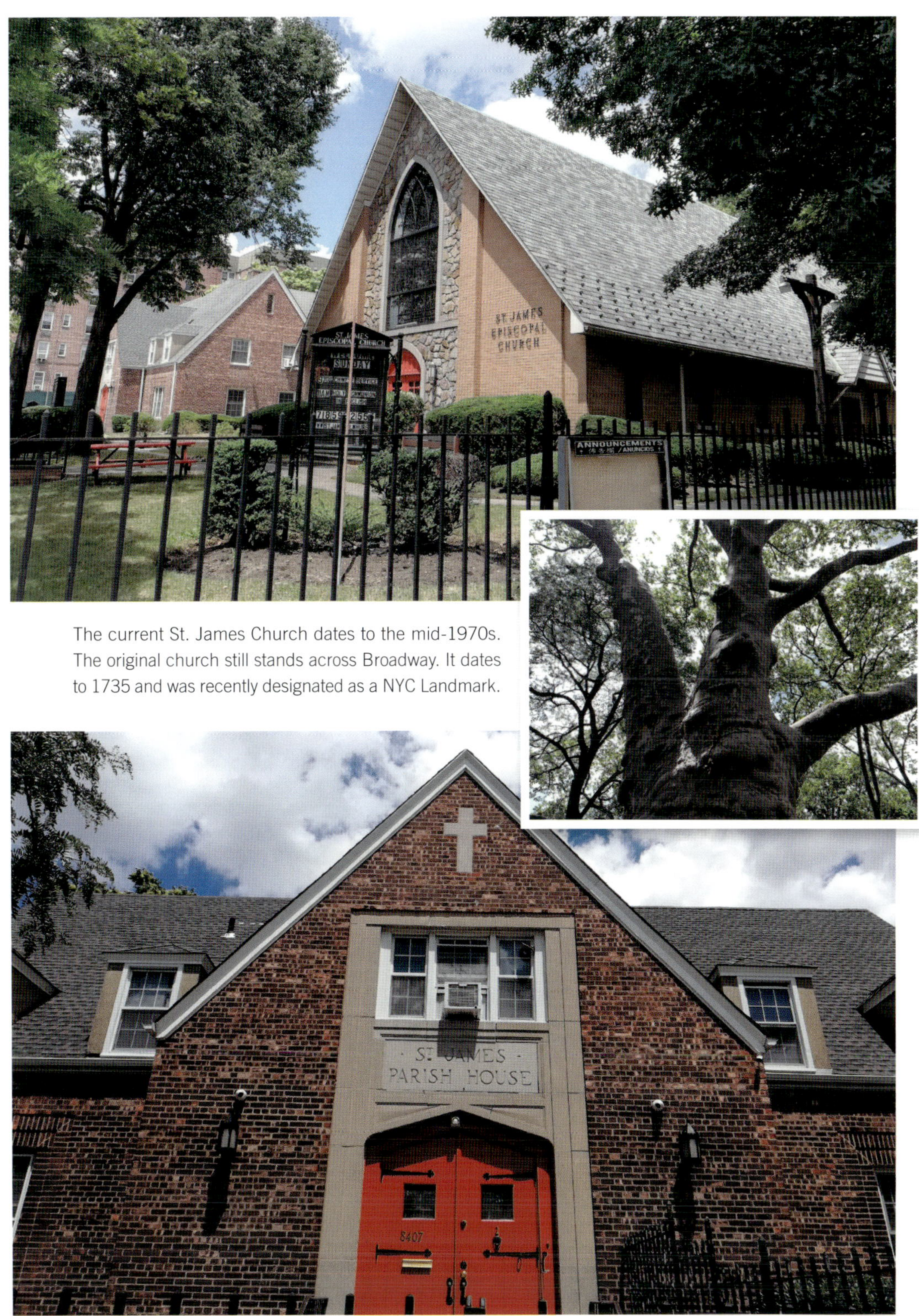

The current St. James Church dates to the mid-1970s. The original church still stands across Broadway. It dates to 1735 and was recently designated as a NYC Landmark.

The St. James Parish House predates the current church, which replaced the 1848 version that burned down in 1975. *Inset:* A gnarled old tree within the St. James Churchyard is a telling sign of the age of the burial ground.

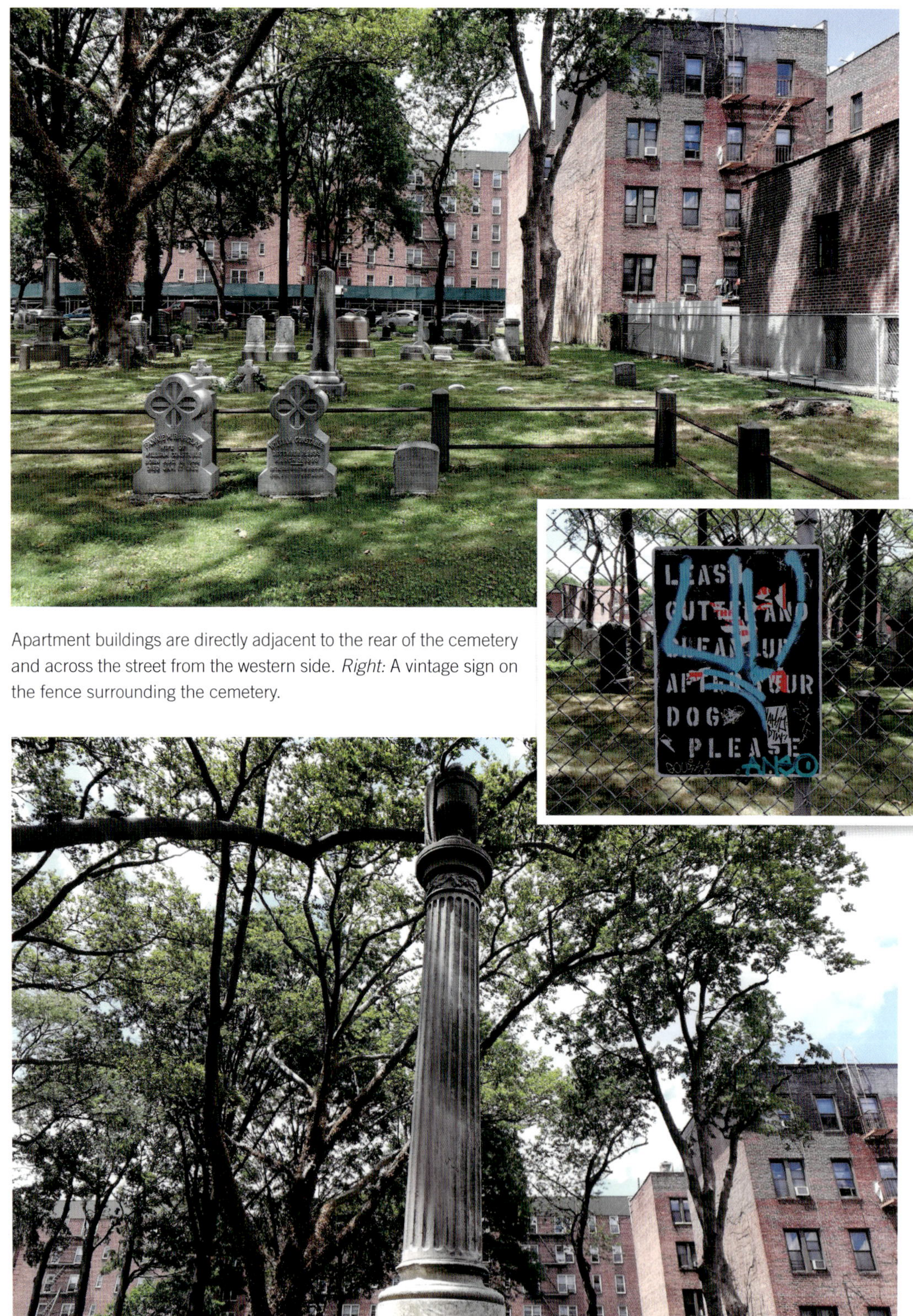

Apartment buildings are directly adjacent to the rear of the cemetery and across the street from the western side. *Right:* A vintage sign on the fence surrounding the cemetery.

One of the taller monuments in the cemetery.

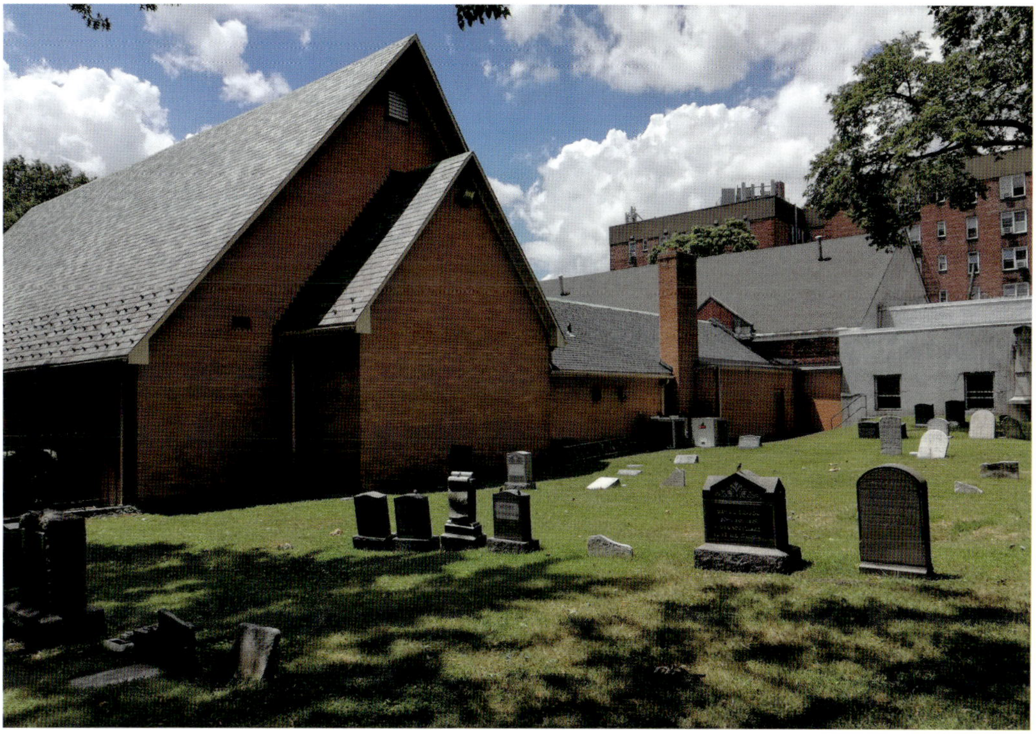

St. James' Churchyard is directly across Corona Avenue from the Dutch Reform Church cemetery.

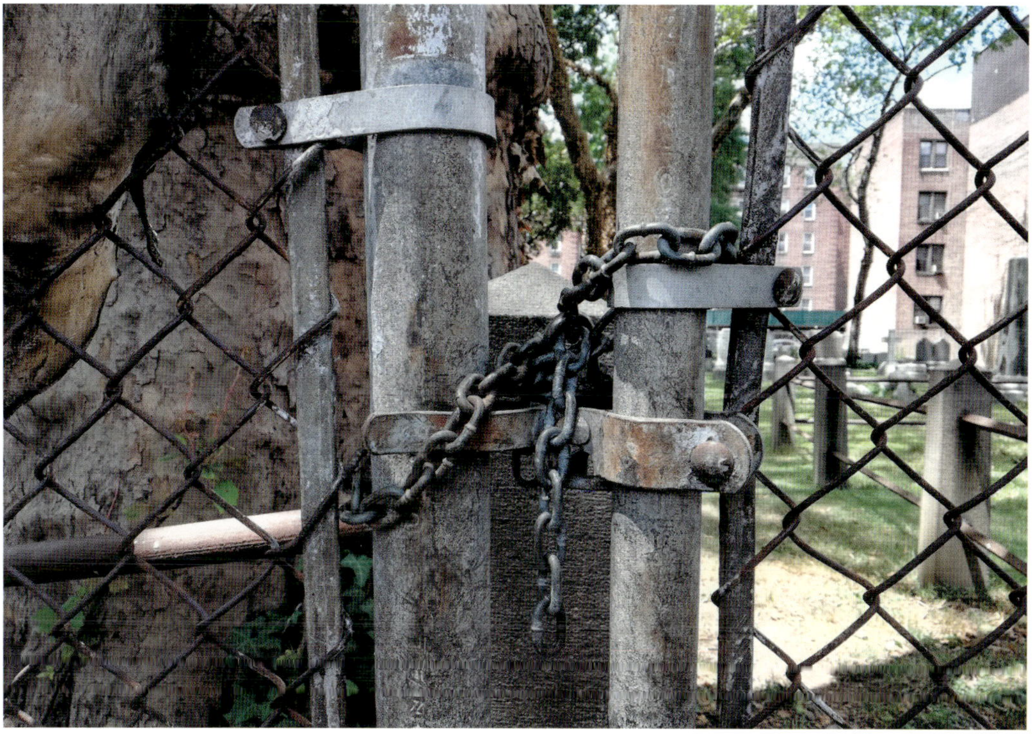

A locked fence means no access for the passerby.

29

St. John Cemetery

80-01 Metropolitan Avenue, Middle Village, NY 11379

Off of Woodhaven Boulevard in Middle Village, just south of Juniper Valley Park, is St. John Cemetery. Metropolitan Avenue cuts through the cemetery just east of the All Faiths Cemetery, with the vast majority of the cemetery on the northern side of Metropolitan. This Catholic cemetery is the main office for the Catholic Cemeteries of the Brooklyn Diocese. The other Catholic cemeteries within the Diocese that are owned by St. John are Mount St. Mary (see page 77) in Flushing, Holy Cross in Brooklyn, and St. Charles in Farmingdale (Suffolk County). Currently at 190 acres in size, St. John was much smaller when consecrated in 1881 on what used to be farmland; like with many Queens cemeteries, additional adjacent parcels of land were purchased and developed over time. There is a special section within St. John for the burial of Diocesan priests. Mass is offered at the cemetery chapel every weekday. New York Governor Mario Cuomo is buried here, as is vice presidential candidate Geraldine Ferraro.

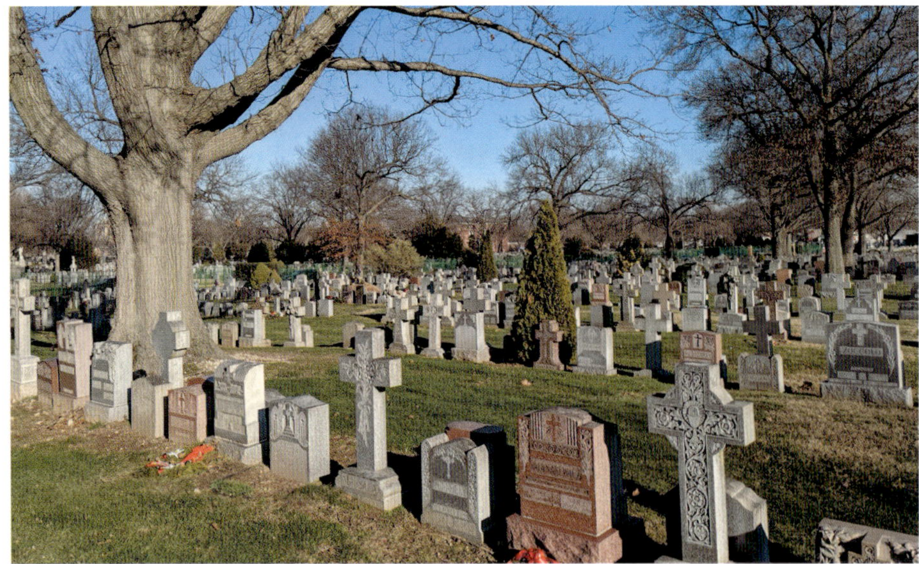

The gravestones on the north side of Metropolitan Avenue are more recent and less grandiose than those in the section across the street.

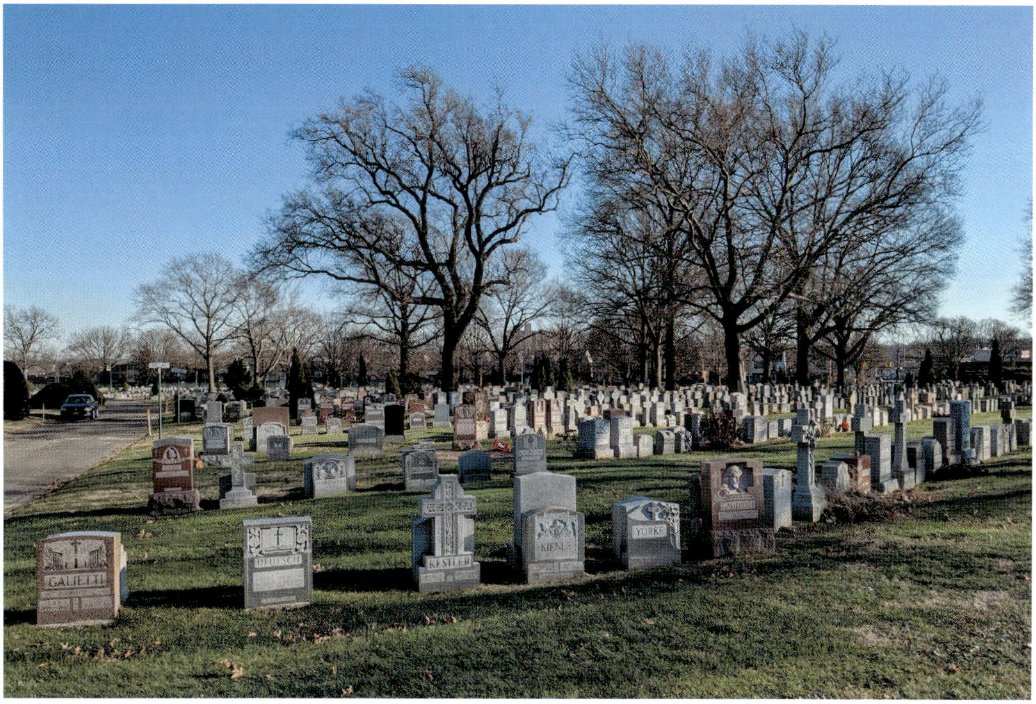

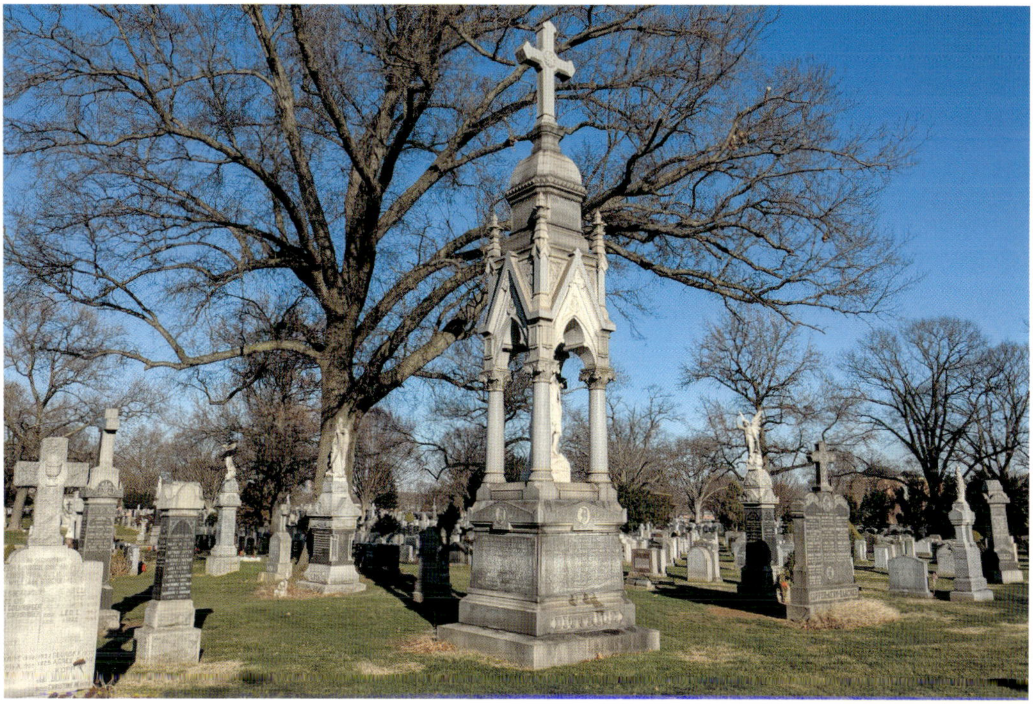

One of the grandest monuments at St. John is right near the entrance and visible from Metropolitan Avenue. It is in memory of Andreas and Katherina Dittrich, who died in 1875 and 1874, respectively, and Mary Hummel, who died in 1898.

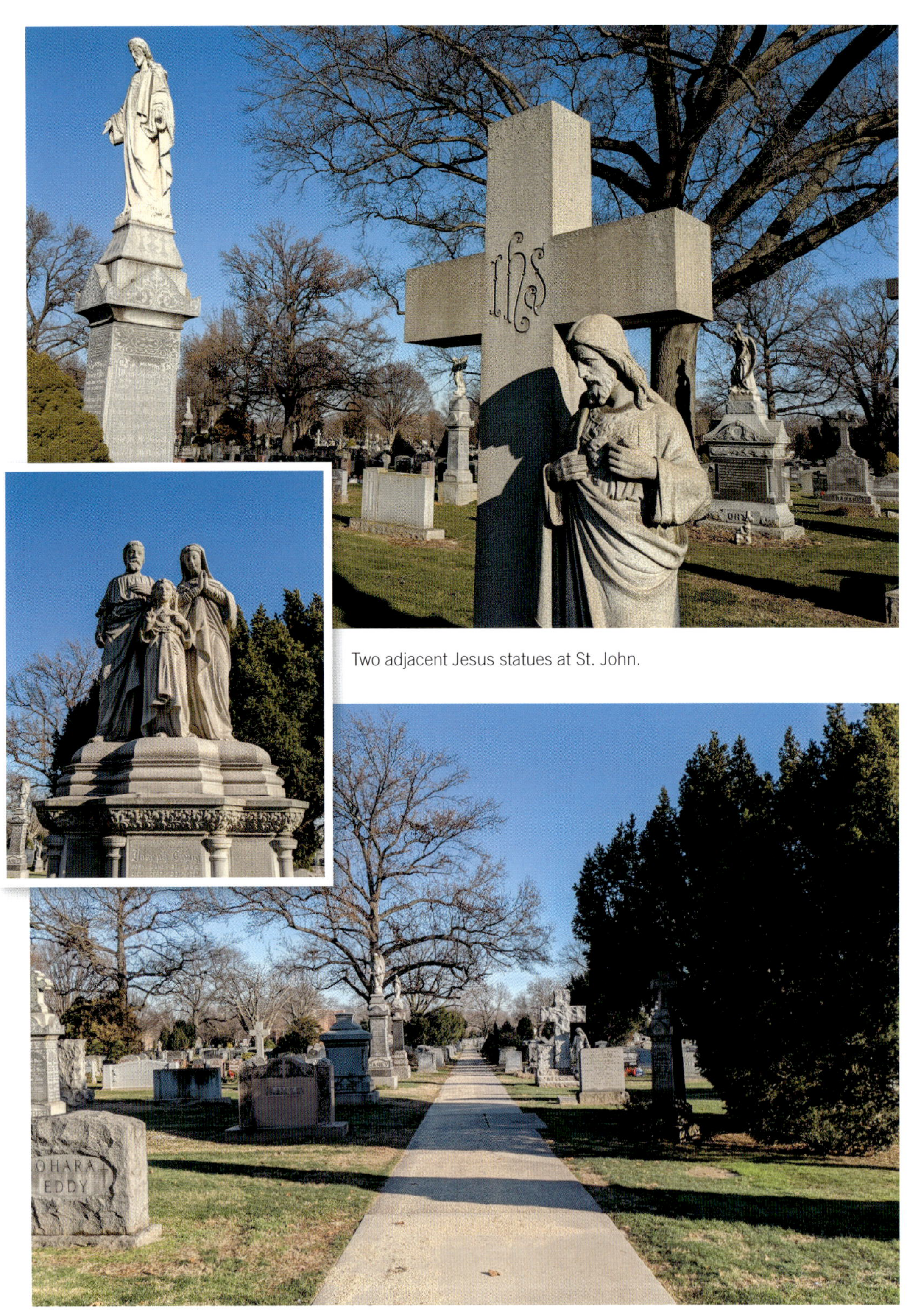

Two adjacent Jesus statues at St. John.

A cement footpath leads deeper into the cemetery. *Inset:* An interesting status showing Jesus as a young child with his parents. It is uncommon to see depictions of Jesus at this age.

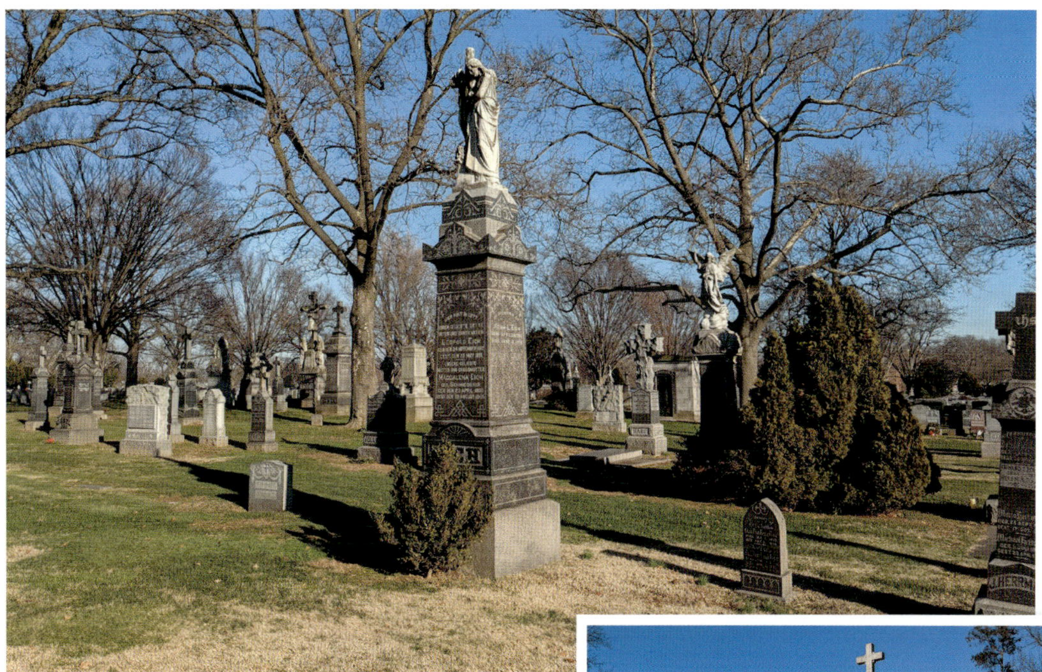

A nineteenth-century monument to members of the Eich family. Many of the German family stones are inscribed in German; these families were immigrants to New York.

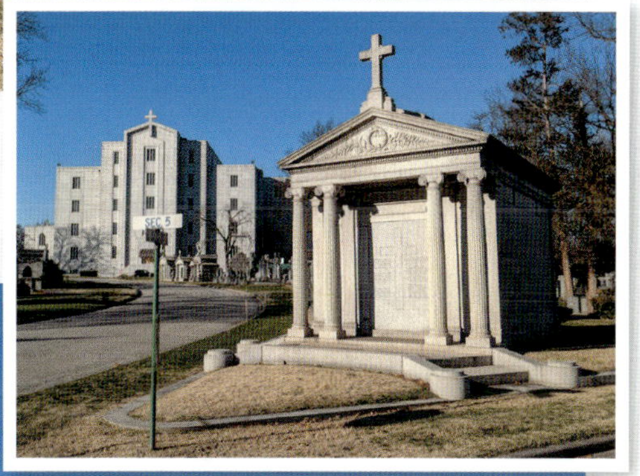

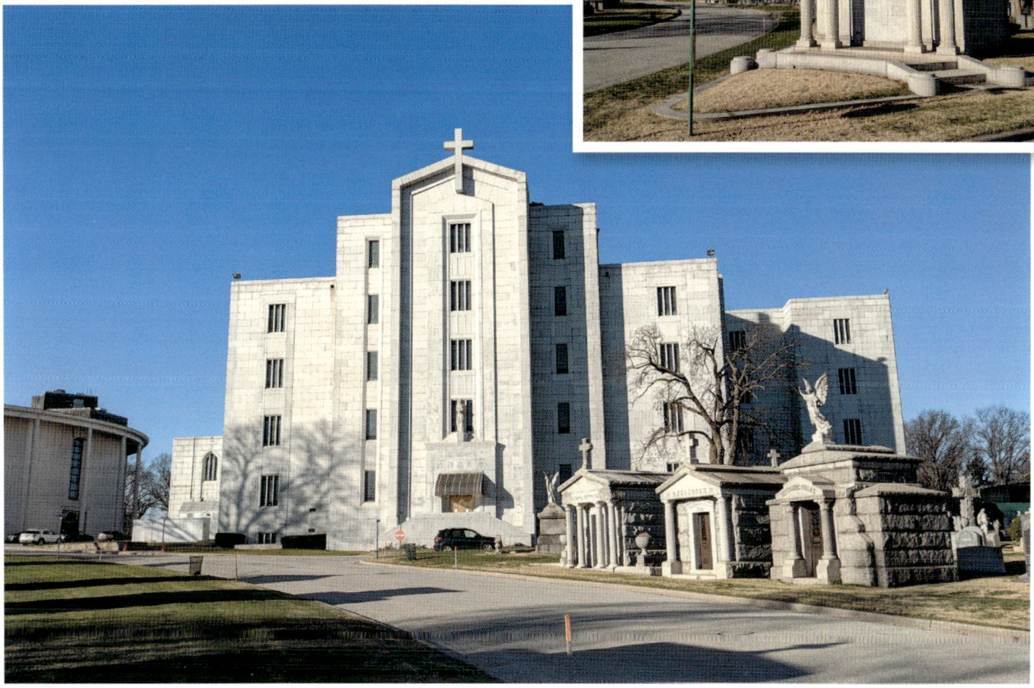

The St. John Cloister Mausoleum building at center, is next to the Resurrection Mausoleum, at left. *Inset:* The Engert family mausoleum. Many of the older stones in the cemetery are of German families.

30

St. Michael's Cemetery

72-02 Astoria Boulevard South, East Elmhurst, NY 11370

This cemetery started out as seven acres and grew over time to its present 88 acres in size. Its geography is unique in that it's located within (and occupies nearly all of) the triangle formed by the Grand Central Parkway and the diverging Brooklyn-Queens Expressway east and westbound roadways. The only other establishments within that triangle are a few industrial buildings. St. Michael's is one of a few Queens cemeteries where I have family members buried. In this case, it's at least eleven relatives on my dad's side, going back to 1903 interment of my great-great grandmother. My great-great grandfather, his brother, and several cousins and in-laws are also buried there. My grandmother's cousin, whose parents and brother are buried at St. Michael's, once told me about getting there from Yorkville in Manhattan long ago: "I wanted to go to Jackson Heights, to St. Michael's Cemetery. At that time, they had the trolleys. I had to take the trolley from First Avenue down to 59th Street, then I had to transfer to one out to Queens, then I had to transfer to get another, I had to pay another 5 cents to [get to] the cemetery." In fact, all of my family members who were buried there lived in Manhattan; its proximity to the city made it attractive, especially in the days before the advent of the automobile. The most famous interment here is probably the ragtime musician Scott Joplin.

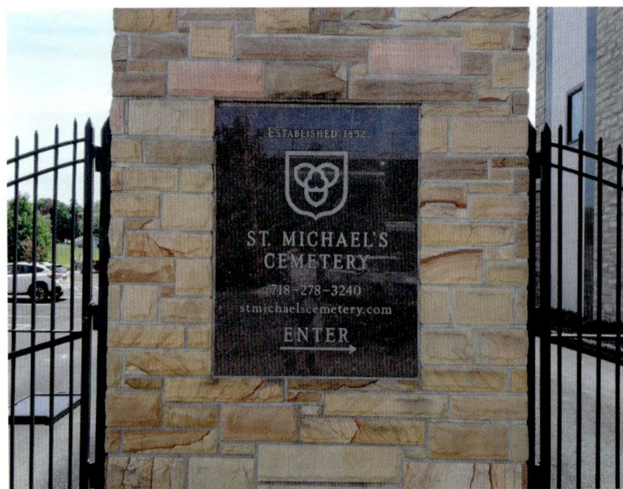

Sign on the main gate at St. Michaels.

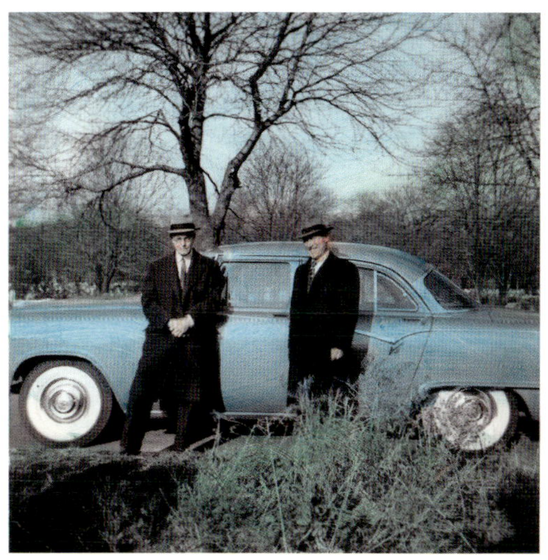

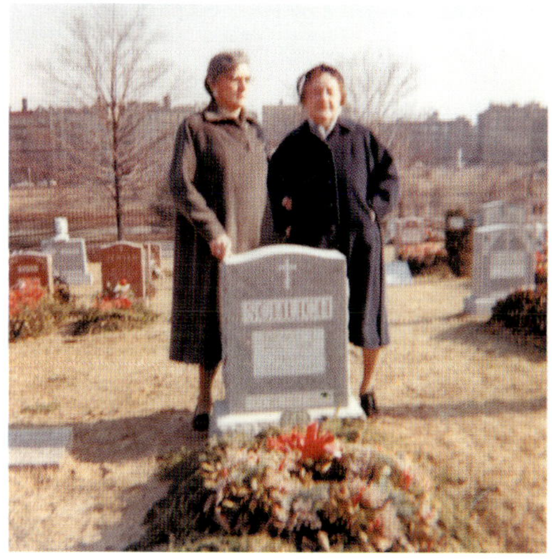

Above left: A colorized photograph from the 1950s shows two men in front of their car at St. Michael's on a trip to visit the graves of their in-laws, members of the author's family.

Above right: A 1963 photo of two members of the author's family visiting the grave of a relative. Note the apartment buildings in the distance.

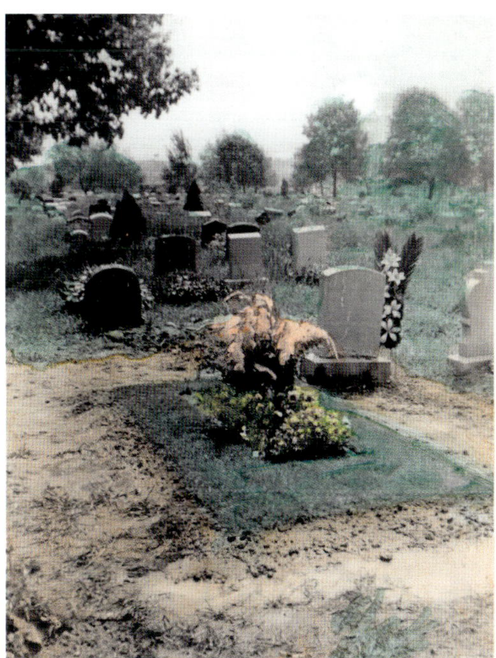

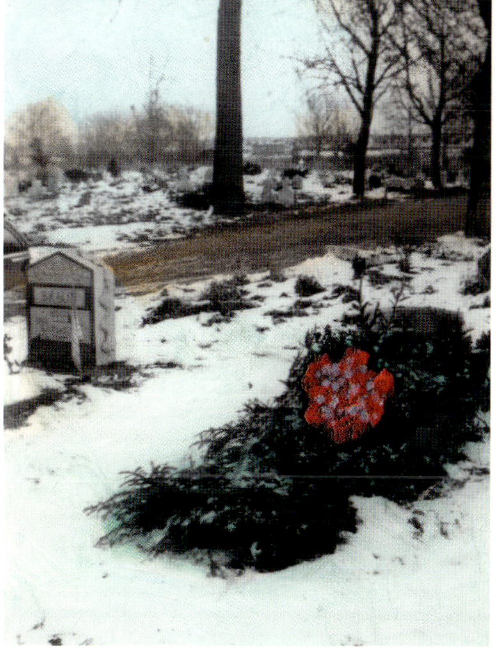

Above left: A 1942 photo shows a recent interment at a St. Michael's plot.

Above right: Christmas Day 1947 at St. Michael's—snow and festive hand-coloring on this photograph.

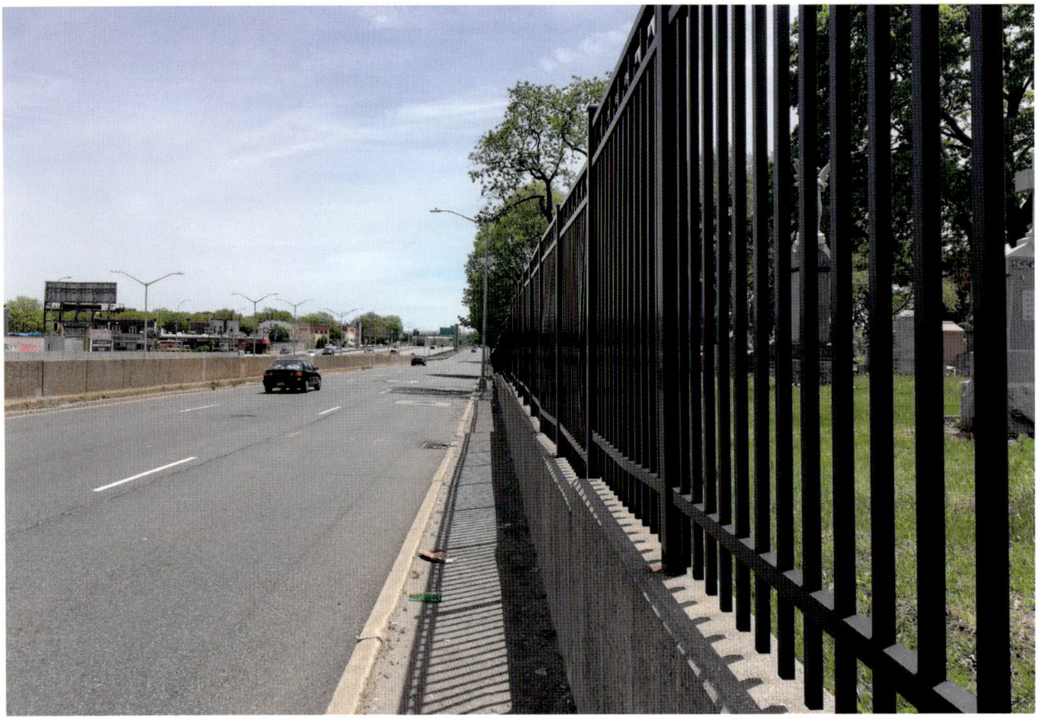

Looking east along the Grand Central Parkway directly adjacent to the northern edge of St. Michael's.

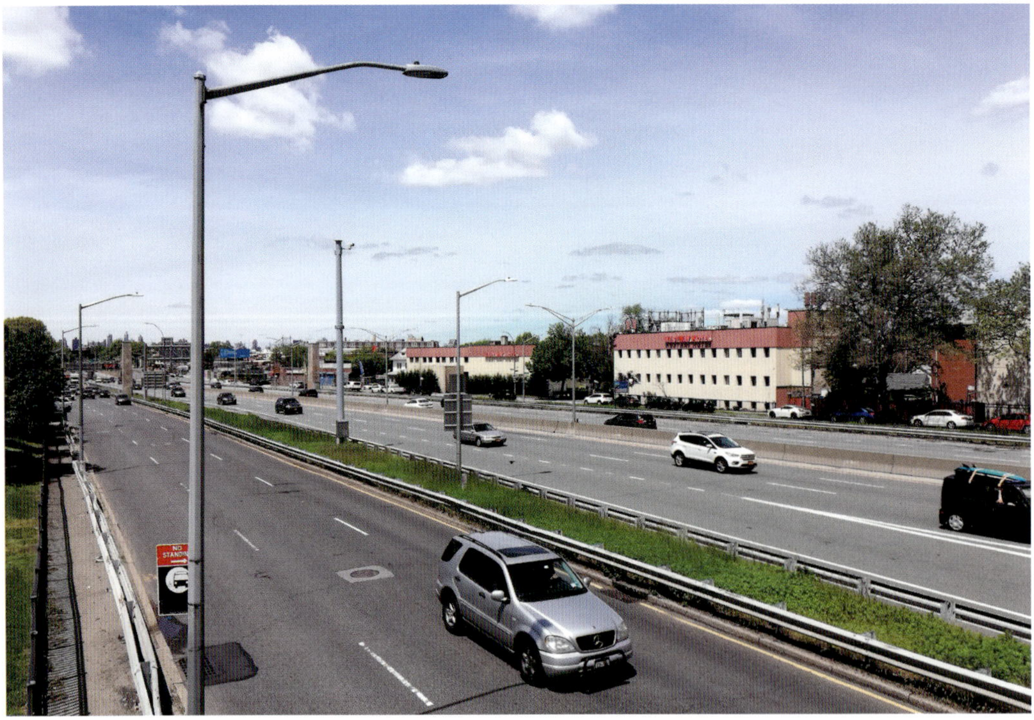

This view looks down on the Grand Central from a pedestrian bridge over the parkway between 73rd and 74th Streets. The cemetery is at far left.

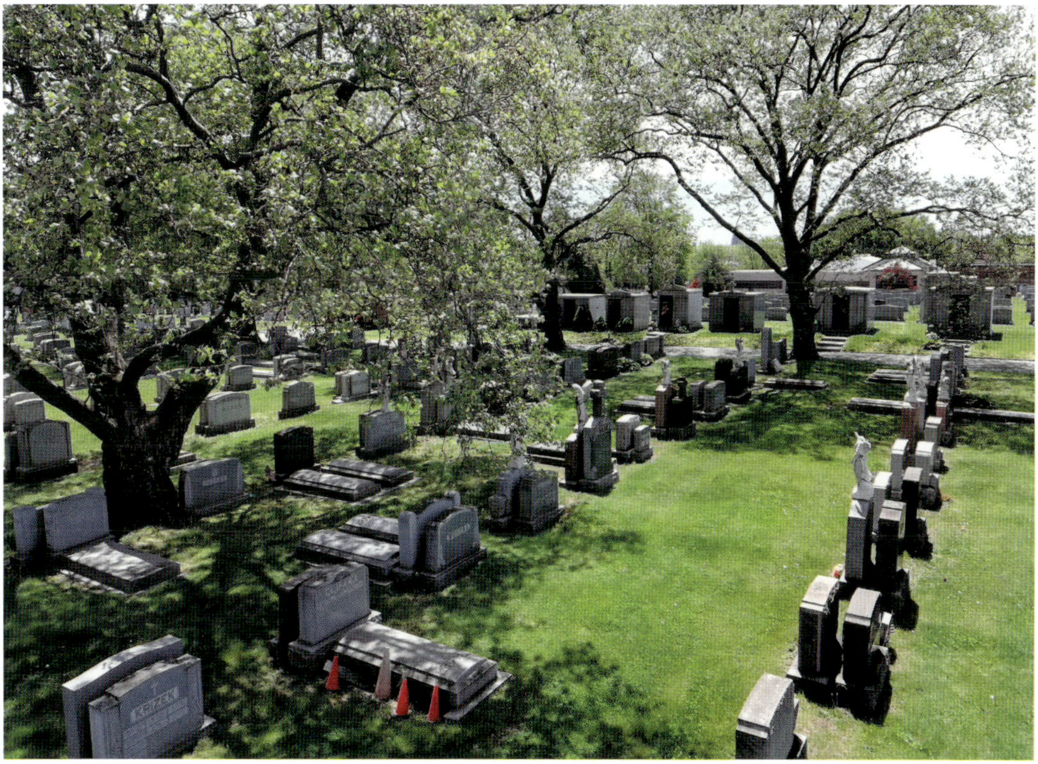

Two views looking down at the northeast corner of the cemetery from the pedestrian bridge.

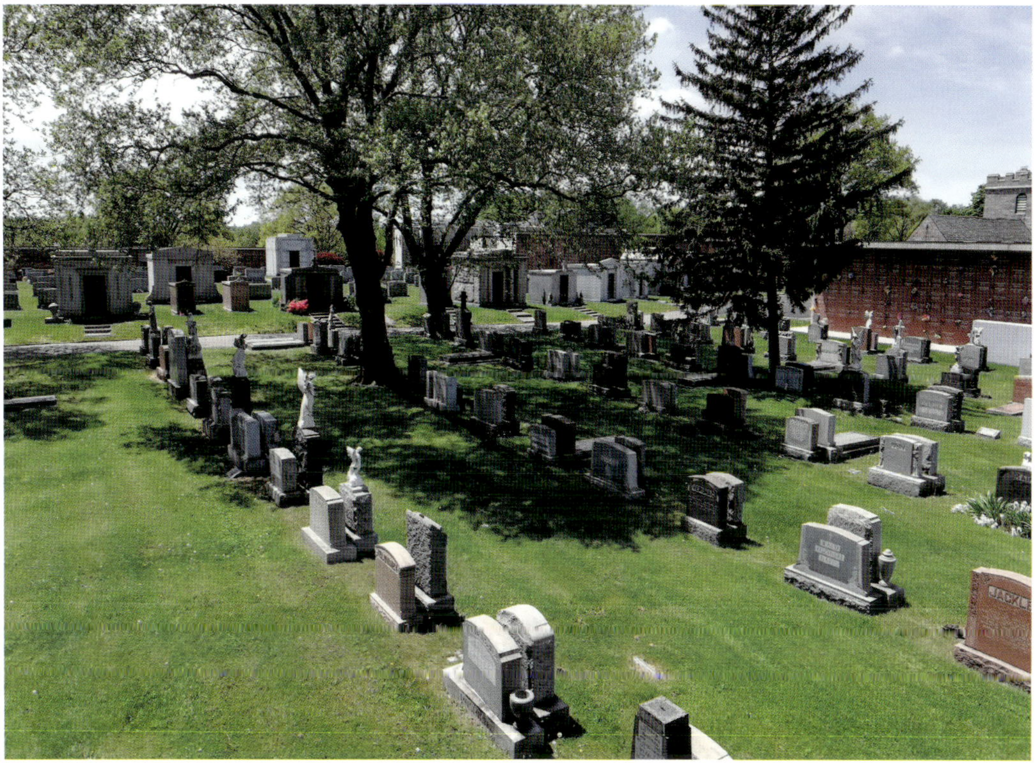

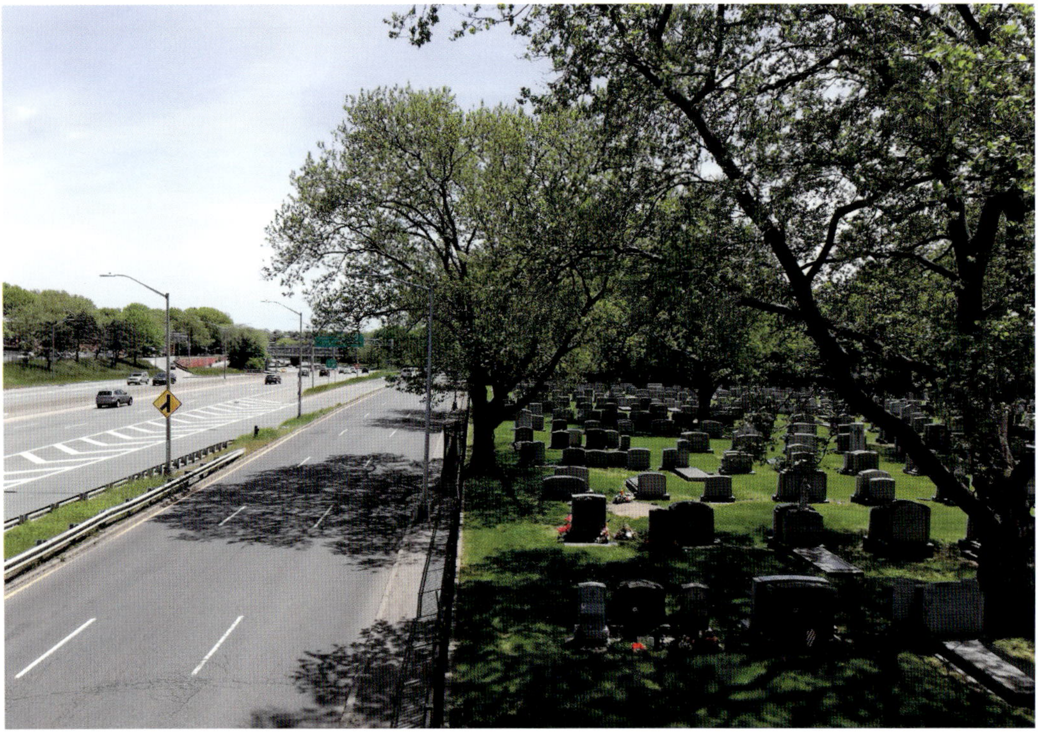

The cemetery's proximity to the Grand Central service road is again visible in this photo taken from the pedestrian bridge.

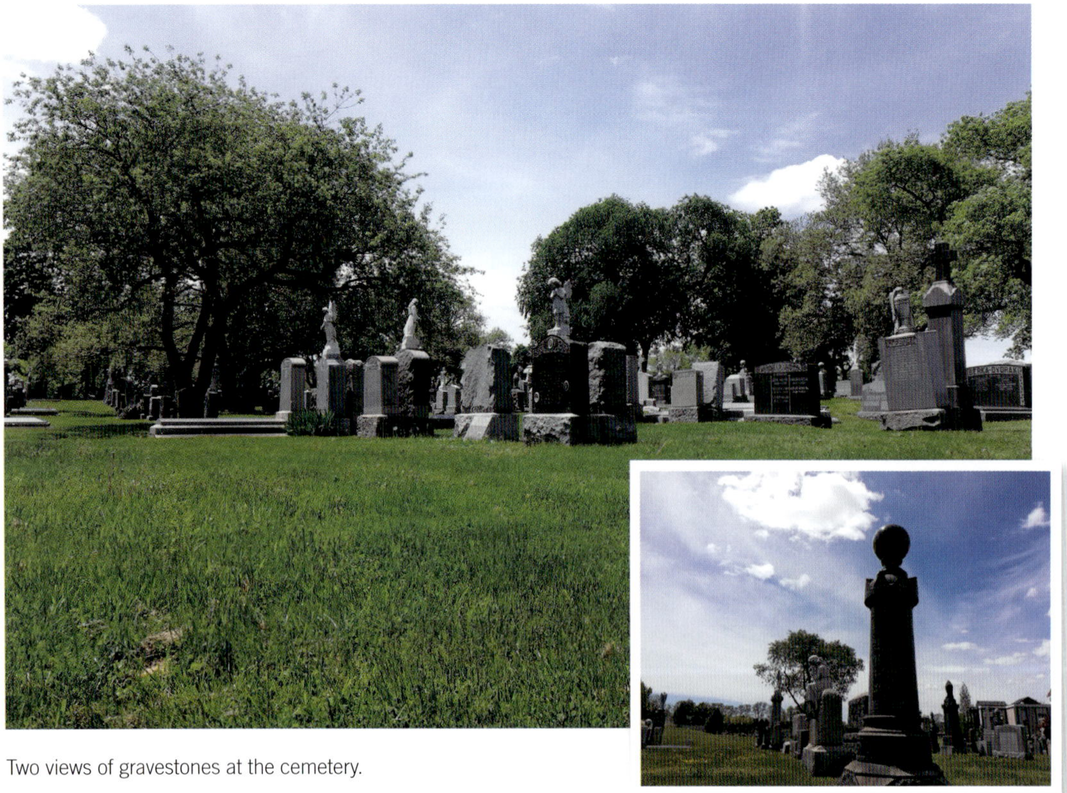

Two views of gravestones at the cemetery.

31

Zion Episcopal Churchyard

243-01 Northern Boulevard, Queens, NY 11362

There simply aren't very many churchyard cemeteries left in Queens. Zion Episcopal Church in Douglaston is one of those few, and it's quite a historic place. Located on a rise along the north side of Northern Boulevard, the property used to be home to the Matinecock tribe of Native Americans. In 1829, the cornerstone was laid for this church, which burned down in 1924 and was replaced with the current building. The churchyard dates to the vintage of the original church building and contains many early nineteenth-century settlers of the local area. The most notable moment in the cemetery occurred in 1931, with the reburial of thirty remains of Matinecock tribe members that had been found during construction for the nearby widening of Northern Boulevard. The original graves were disturbed by the City of New York against the protests of some representatives of the Matinecock tribe.

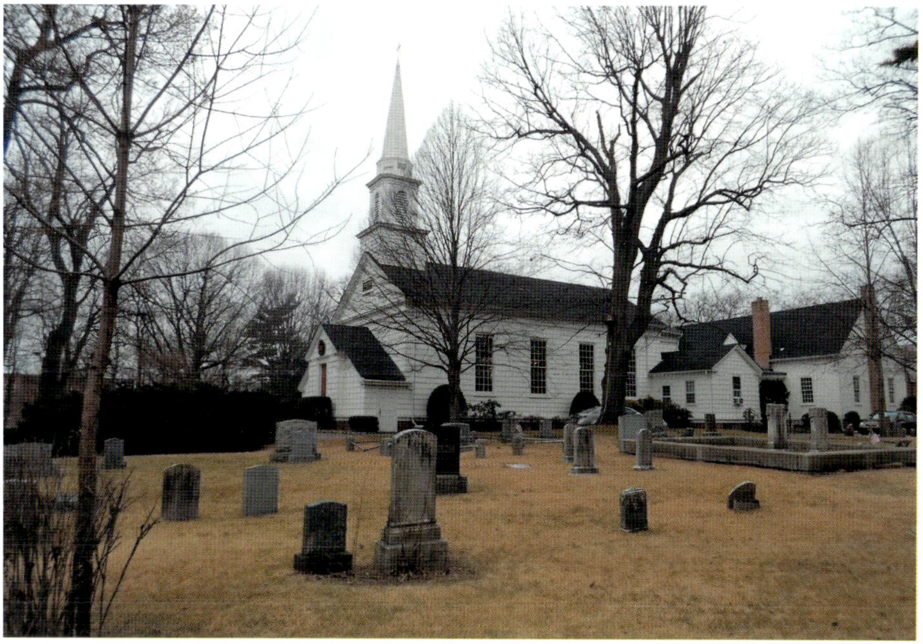

Though dating to the 1920s, the Zion Church has a very nineteenth-century feel to it.

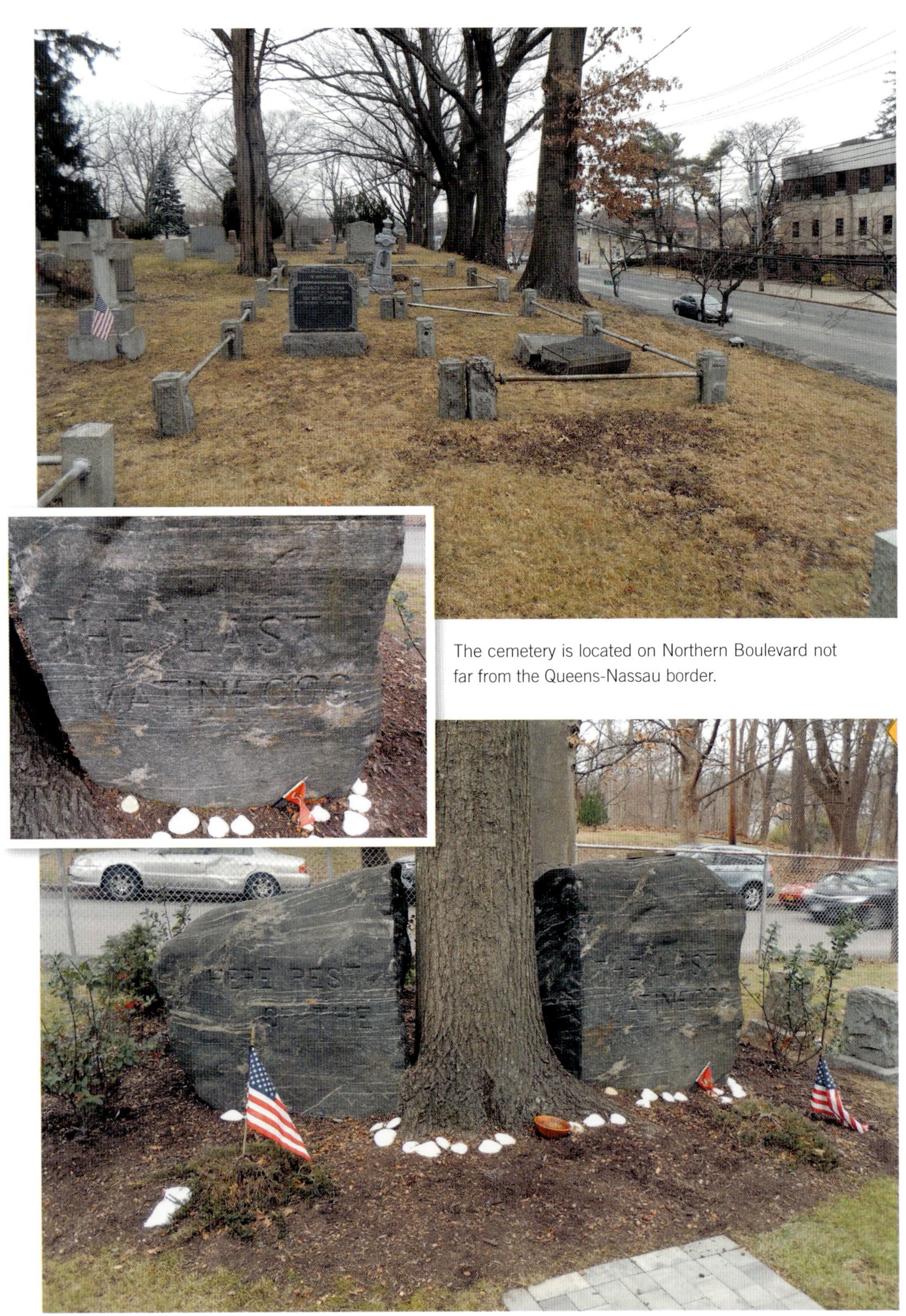

The cemetery is located on Northern Boulevard not far from the Queens-Nassau border.

Two inscribed stones mark the graves of the last of the Matinecock Indians.

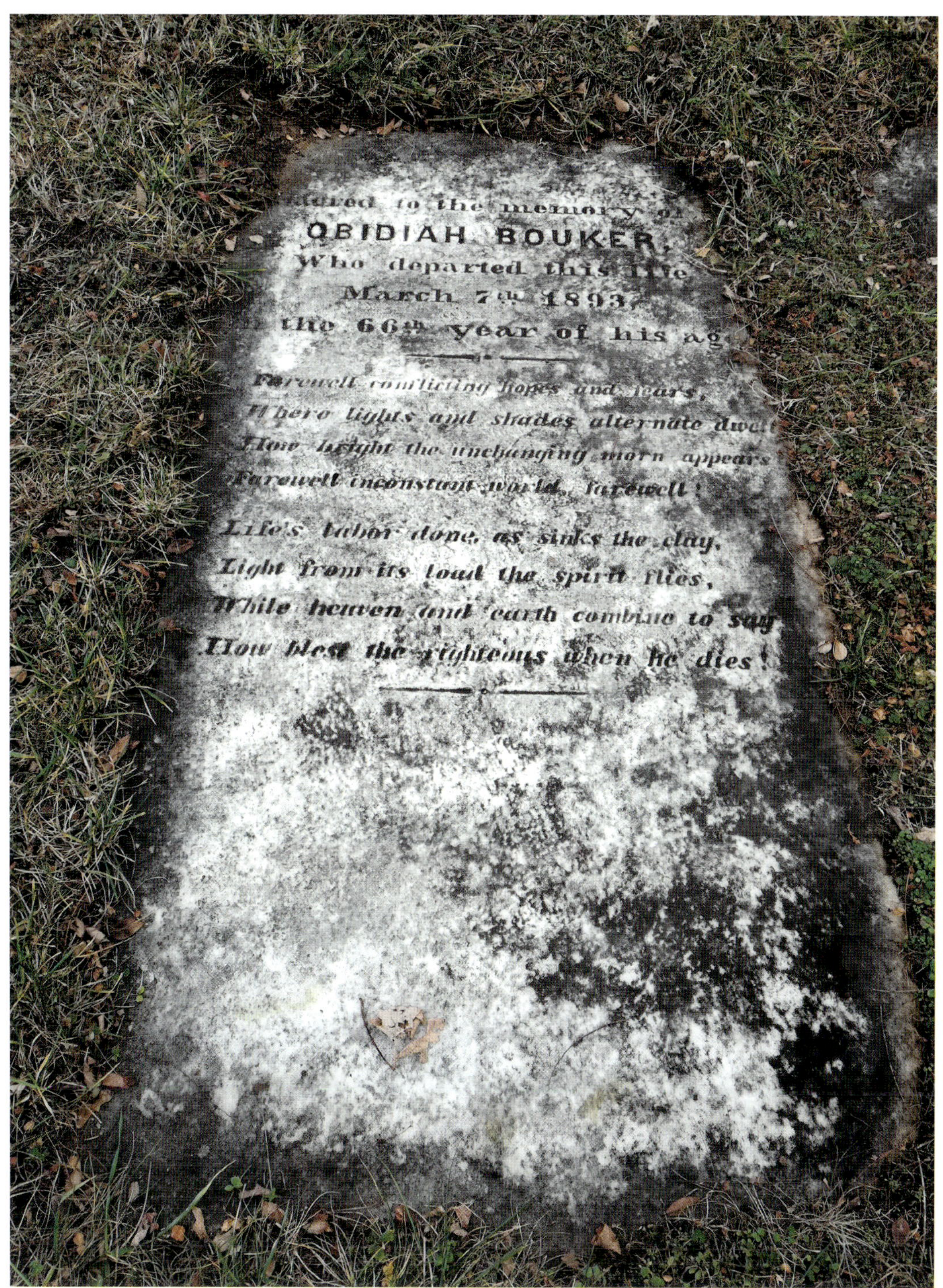

The stone for Obidiah Bouker includes a two-stanza poem.

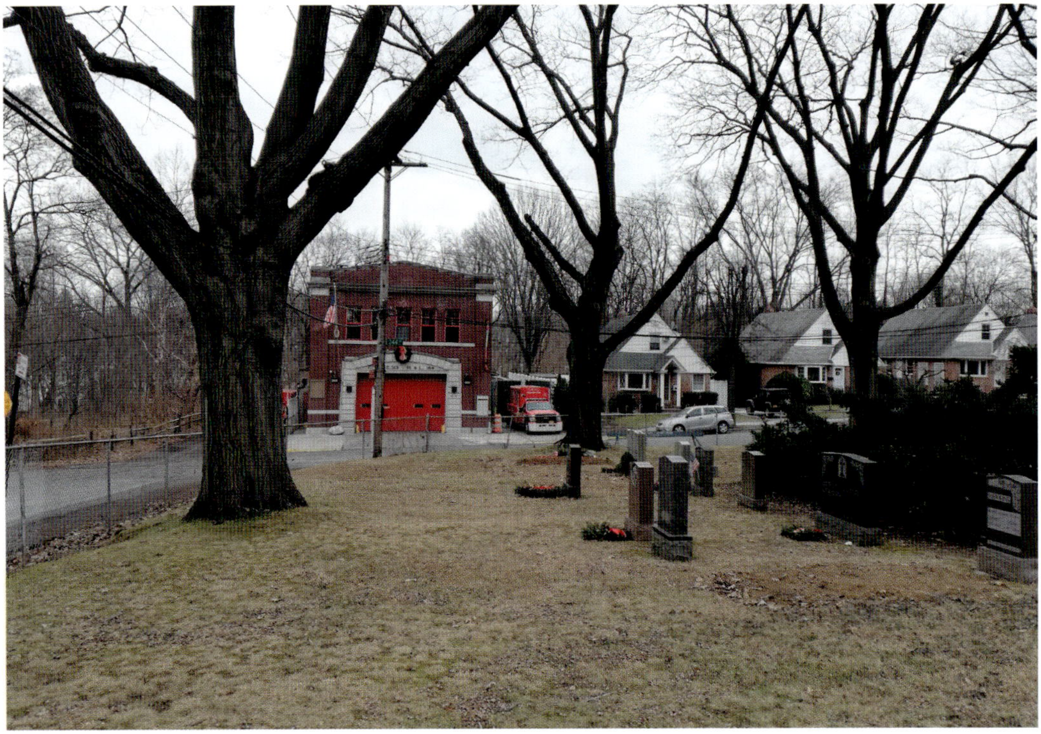

FDNY Engine 313/Ladder 164 is located across from the cemetery, at Church and 244th Streets.

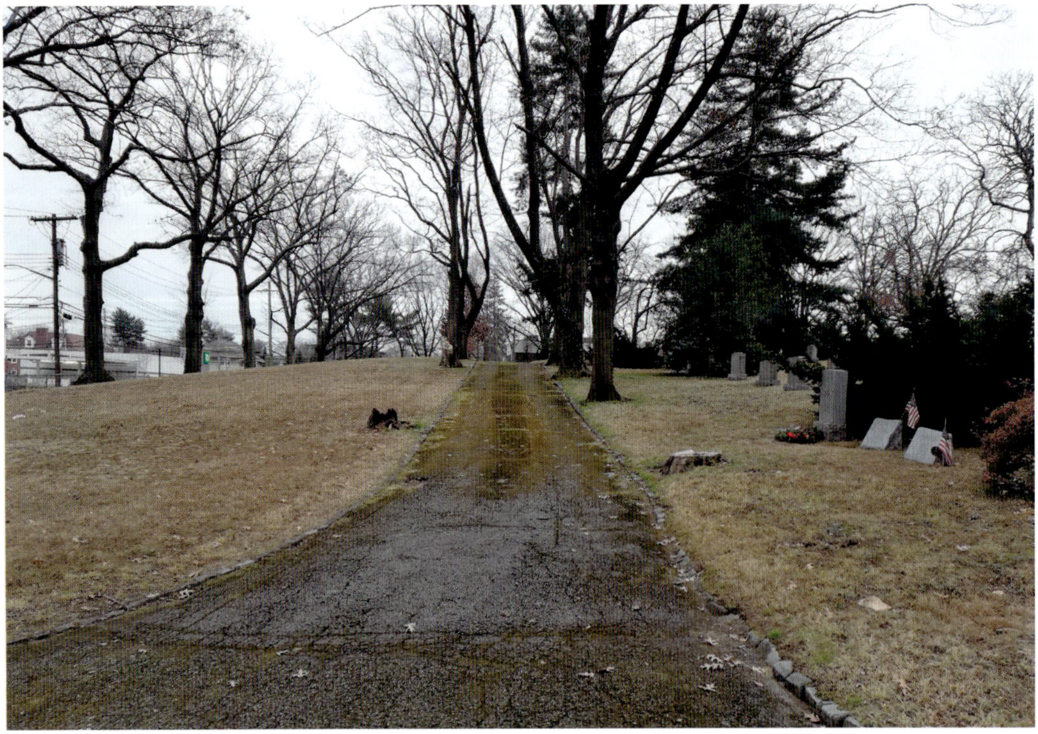

A footpath on a slight rise within the cemetery.

Appendix

Cemetery Businesses

With all the cemeteries in Queens, it's only natural that related businesses would also be commonplace, especially in areas with high concentrations of cemeteries. Monument stores, for example, sprung up in various locations; as of 2020 there are four monument establishments adjacent to Calvary Cemetery, for example. Funeral homes, of course, are plentiful throughout Queens, and florists are also popular in areas near cemeteries. Certain restaurants near cemeteries are popular places for a post-funeral meal.

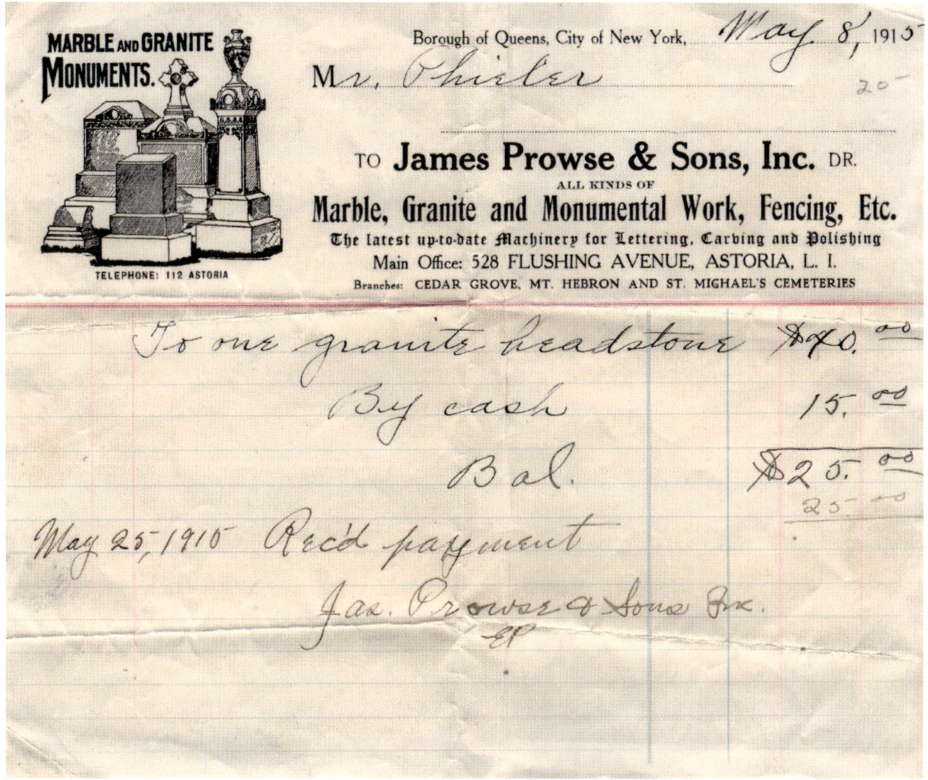

MARBLE AND GRANITE MONUMENTS.

TELEPHONE: 112 ASTORIA

Borough of Queens, City of New York, May 8, 1915

Mr. Phieler

20

TO **James Prowse & Sons, Inc.** DR.

ALL KINDS OF

Marble, Granite and Monumental Work, Fencing, Etc.

The latest up-to-date Machinery for Lettering, Carving and Polishing

Main Office: 528 FLUSHING AVENUE, ASTORIA, L. I.

Branches: CEDAR GROVE, MT. HEBRON AND ST. MICHAEL'S CEMETERIES

To one granite headstone	$40.00
By cash	15.00
Bal.	$25.00
	25.00

May 25, 1915 Rec'd payment

Jas. Prowse & Sons Inc.

EP

In 1915, a granite headstone from the James Prowse & Sons company in Astoria, cost forty dollars.

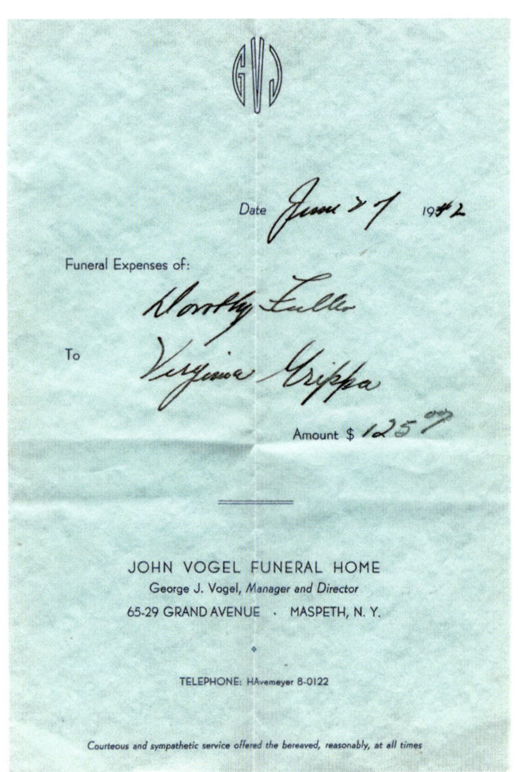

GVJ

Date *June 27* *1942*

Funeral Expenses of:

Dorothy Fuller

To *Virginia Grippa*

Amount $ *125.00*

JOHN VOGEL FUNERAL HOME

George J. Vogel, *Manager and Director*

65-29 GRAND AVENUE · MASPETH, N. Y.

TELEPHONE: HAvemeyer 8-0122

Courteous and sympathetic service offered the bereaved, reasonably, at all times

A receipt from the now defunct John Vogel Funeral Home in Maspeth, dated 1942.

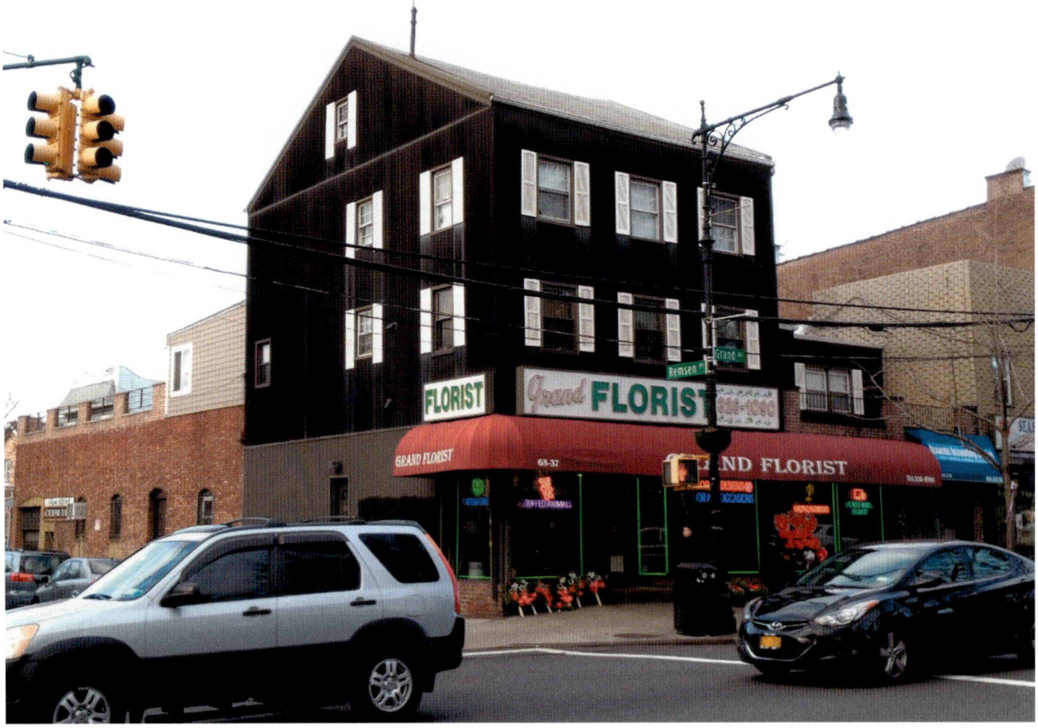

A florist shop directly across the street from Mount Olivet Cemetery

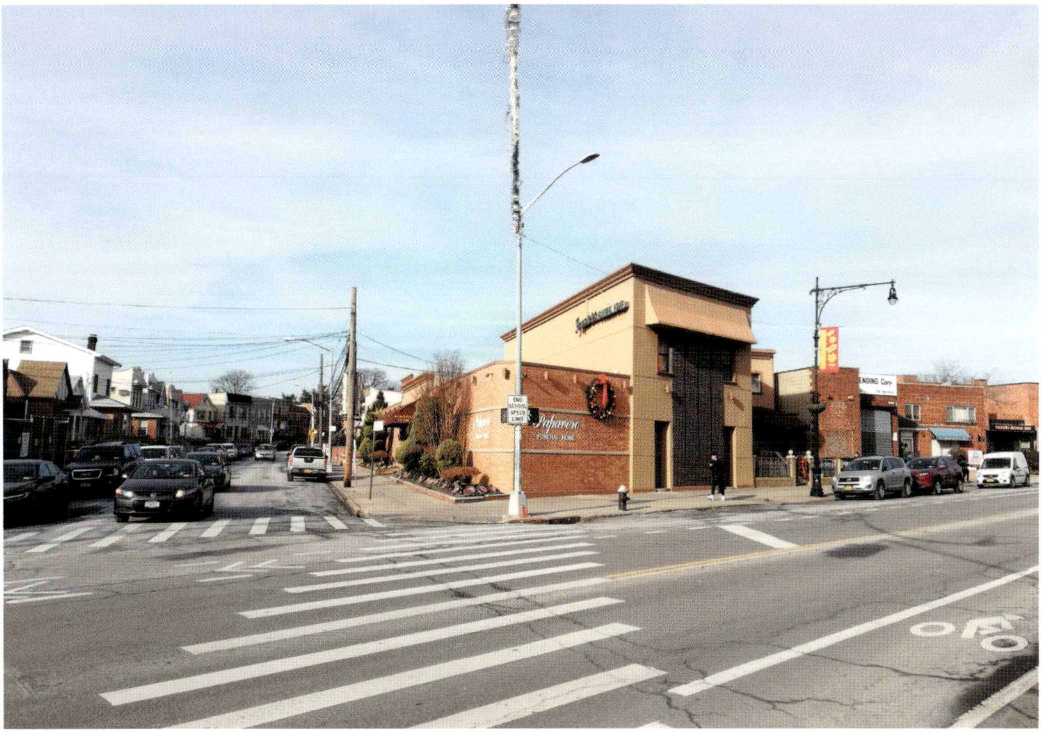

The Papavero Funeral Home on Grand Avenue in Maspeth is located close to several cemeteries.

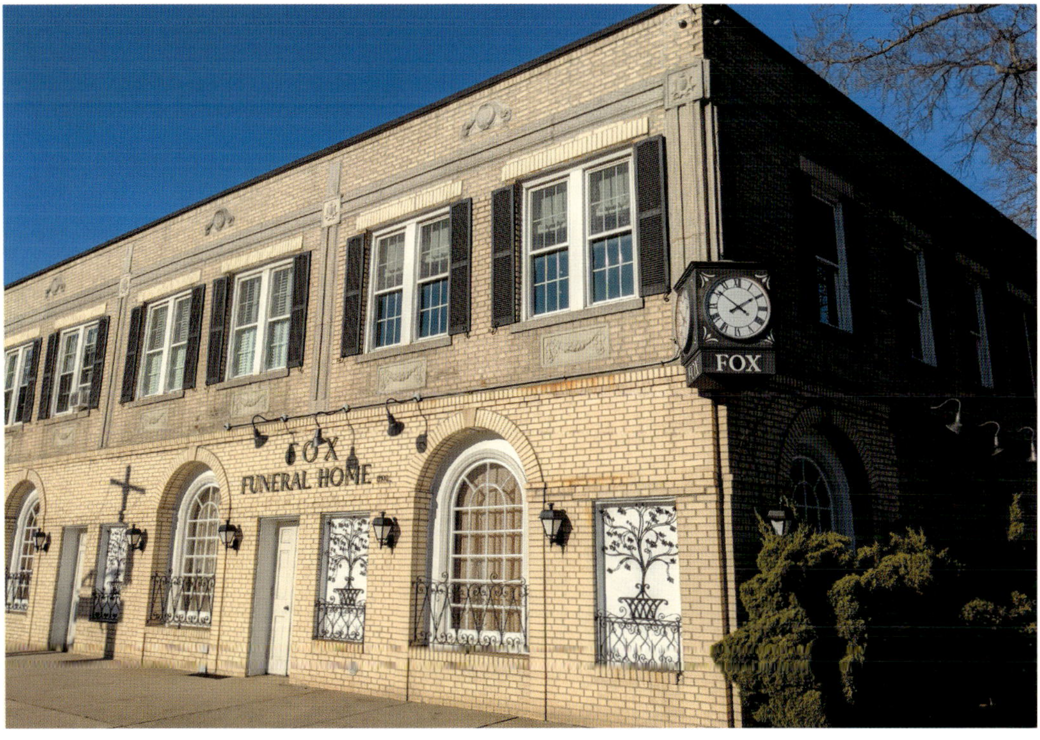

The Fox Funeral Home on Metropolitan Avenue and Ascan Avenue in Forest Hills is housed in an attractive old building.

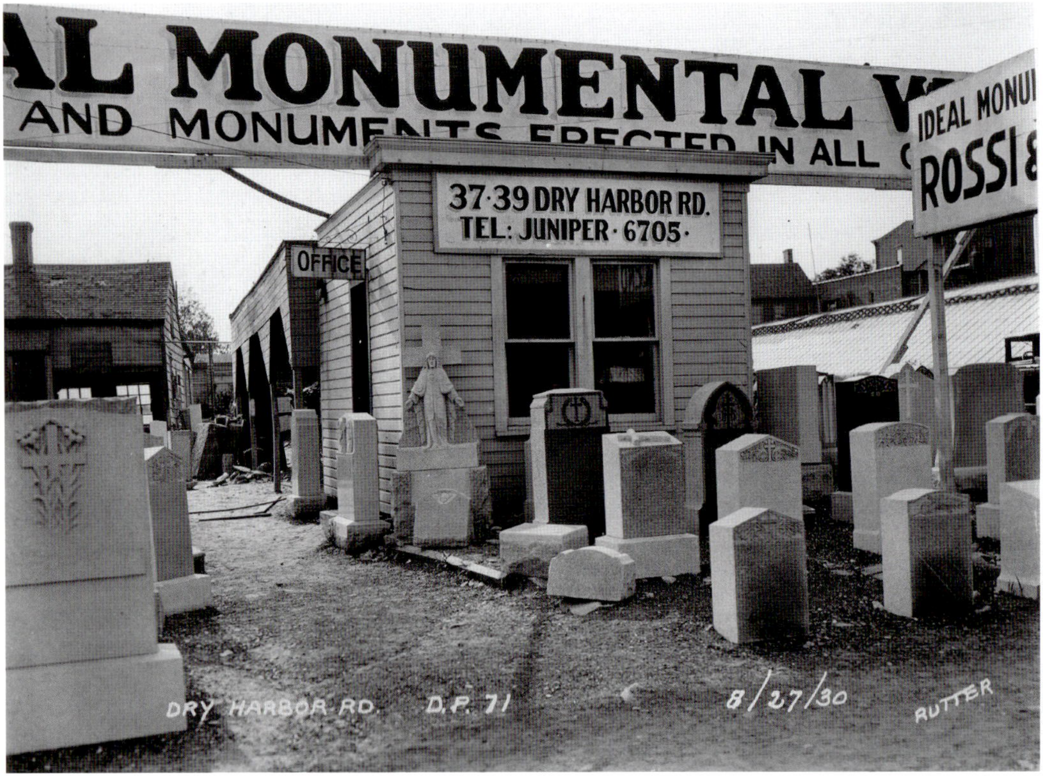

A 1930 photograph of a monument establishment in Middle Village.

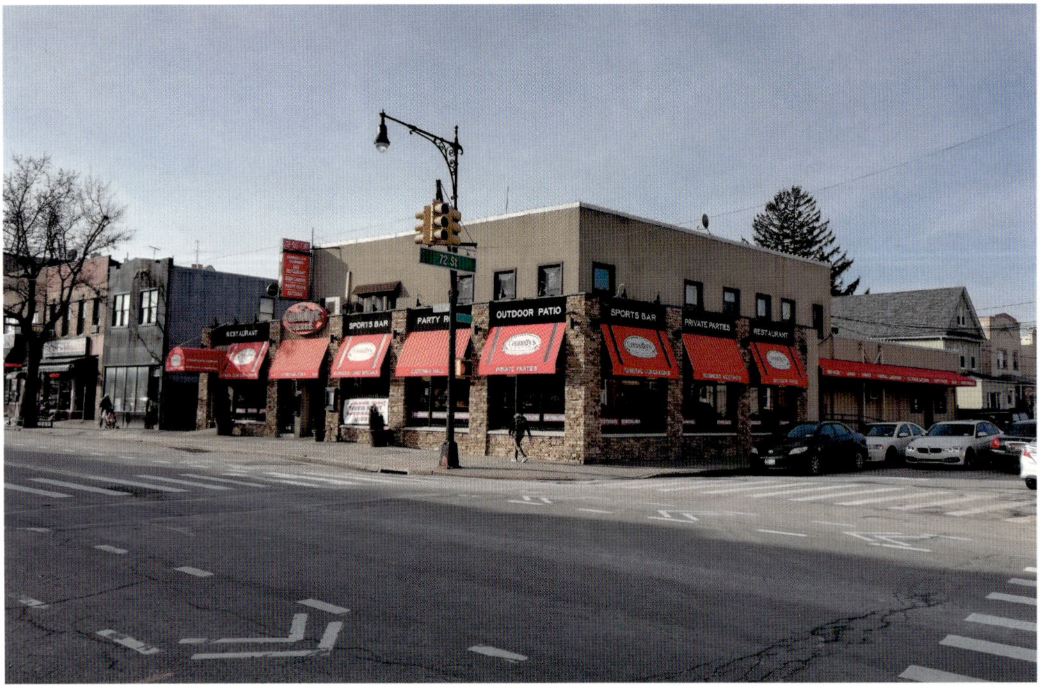

The awning of Connolly's Restaurant on Grand Avenue in Maspeth says "Funeral Luncheons."